THE
SILENT TRAVELLER
IN PARIS

Perpetual Sunday Crowds in the Place de la République

THE
SILENT TRAVELLER
IN PARIS

記畫黎巴

Written and illustrated by
CHIANG YEE

With a foreword by
SIR WILLIAM HAYTER

W. W. NORTON & CO. INC.
NEW YORK

Library of Congress Catalog Card Number 56-10852

PRINTED IN GREAT BRITAIN

To

Van Wyck & Gladys Brooks

and

also to

Alan & Marjorie White

Foreword

by

SIR WILLIAM HAYTER, K.C.M.G.

H.M. Minister, Paris, 1949-53

THE charm of Chiang Yee's books lies chiefly in seeing familiar, or generally familiar, objects from an unfamiliar angle. Lines normally thought of as straight are suddenly seen to curve up at the ends, and everyday objects or episodes provoke an elegant Chinese quatrain. Moreover we not only see things differently; we see different things. In a familiar landscape the features that used to dominate are concealed in a strange mist, while hitherto unnoticed objects assume an unwonted prominence.

Paris is certainly an admirable theme for writing of this kind, for behind a front that is typically classic and European she hides a diversity as rich as that of Peking itself. When I met Chiang Yee in Paris I wondered a little if he was going to be able to penetrate behind her stately façade, below her glittering surface. His silence is as deceptive as it is notorious, and I need not have worried, as this book shows. The familiar miracle has worked. Young men dress as chimpanzees, a gate near the Pont Neuf becomes a porcelain vase, and falling snow thinly veils the view from the towers of Notre Dame. All this is undoubtedly Paris, but there are hints too of mysterious affinities with more exotic realms. Those who thought they knew Paris will find they have missed much, and even the most famous landmarks of the French capital will never seem quite the same to them again. But they will find that the pleasure they have always taken in Paris is enhanced, not diminished, by this charming and unusual book.

Contents

Plates

Three Sights of Paris

EARLY in 1933 I made a decision to see people and things
outside China. My trip to England was fixed for May in that
year. Before I left Shanghai I was asked to accompany one of
my cousins' young sons, who wanted to study law in Paris. We
travelled on a French liner, the *Lebrun*. Neither of us knew
French or, except for a few words, English. We embarked at
Kiangwan and bravely endured the long, rough voyage,
talking only to each other, for thirty-three days. The sea air
was bracing, so different from the inland air of the Asian
continent to which we were accustomed from birth. The flying
fish of the Indian Ocean kept us amused from time to time,
though we were not always quick enough to see them. A new
leaf of our life had been turned and nothing dimmed our
anticipations. At last Marseille came into sight in a dense
morning mist, and soon afterward we were thrown on to a
train for Paris like pieces of cargo. We arrived at dusk. A friend
came to meet my companion and found rooms for us in a small
hotel. He also handed me a telegram from another friend in
London, who urged me to cross as soon as possible. As everything seemed to be well arranged for the young man's stay, and
as I thought I should enjoy Paris better if I paid her a visit after
I had settled down in London, I decided to cross the Channel
early next morning.

I had heard and read much about Paris in Chinese translations and I felt I was being rude in leaving such a world-
renowned city so quickly. Standing on the open deck of the
ferry boat and trying to visualise the evening glimpse I had
had of Paris, I composed the following lines:

> Surely she outvies western Europe in luxury!
> Her lofty premises and tall buildings mystify my gaze.
> I have come ten thousand *li* and stayed but one night;
> The wind on my face reproaches me for being unjust to Paris!

Li is a Chinese measure for distance, about three *li* making
one mile.

I did not manage to return to Paris until July, 1935, and then the trip was not made on my own initiative. My cousin had urged me to find out what his son had been doing in Paris for the past two years. The young man had never been short of money from home, yet he had not managed to get a place in a Law School. My proposal to him that he should come to England to study met with flat refusal. Though I spent a week in Paris on this mission, most of the time was occupied in talking to the young man. Bad company, I found, was the hindrance and I had to warn him that he might have to return home if he did not pull himself together in the next few months. Eventually he went back to China in the Spring of 1936 as a 'foreign-educated scholar'! But his bluff did not carry him very far towards a job.

However, during odd moments in my mission I managed to

自 宿 里 眼 閣 冠 繁
貞 臨 來 迷 雲 歐 筆
巴 風 成 三 房 西 真
黎 武 一 萬 到 霧 許

see the street dancing around the Place de la Bastille on the eve of July 14th; for I happened to be there at the festival. I also took walks along the quays of the Seine and along the Champs Elysées. In a light-hearted mood after a walk in the Avenue one evening, I wrote a verse which may be roughly translated as follows:

Laughing chatter follows the wind to chase my heart
Down the 'Wide-long-street' where the bright lamps shine like day.
For the first time I recognise the face of Paris;
Friends ask casually if I will bury myself beneath the pomegranate
    skirt.

I interpret the Champs Elysées in Chinese as 'Kuang-ch'ang-chieh' or 'Wide-long-street'. The last line of the verse probably requires an explanation. The pomegranate skirt is a kind of skirt with designs of pomegranate blossoms on it, or one in

The Secondhand Book Sellers on the Quays of the Seine

scarlet silk hanging from the woman's waist like a drooping pomegranate flower. Centuries ago it was a fashionable skirt for Chinese women, attracting the attention of men. Thus 'chasing the pomegranate skirt' became a common poetic expression in Chinese. One noted poet once wrote the lines:

> Even if I die beneath the peonies,
> To become a ghost is still romantic.

Peonies symbolise wealthy, beautiful girls; I use 'the pomegranate skirt' instead.

In the middle of August, 1939, I went to see the Prado Exhibition in Geneva and planned to stay in Paris for a time before returning to England. Unfortunately, the hysterical voices of war were in the air; many visitors were rushing home from Geneva. After paying two visits to the Exhibition, I took

榴 面 衲 長 燈 逐 笑
裙 漫 識 街 如 裁 語
下 說 巴 而 畫 懷 隨
埋 石 黎 今 廣 明 風

the advice I was given to return to London immediately. Paris did not even manage to keep me for one night.

Directly after the end of the Second World War I went to New York for six months, and was called back from there by friends in London who wanted me to do some office work in an international organisation in Paris. I left China just because I had had too much indoor office work, and it seemed futile to undertake more of it in Europe. After a long talk, my reasons were accepted. My one regret was that I lost the chance of getting to know Paris well. But in May, 1947, I was asked to attend a Unesco Conference of Arts and Letters in Paris for a fortnight. Most of the mornings and afternoons were spent in meetings, and perhaps I was over-conscientious in my attendance and in pondering the discussions in the evenings, for I still saw little of the city. Another difficulty

was that I was always in company. I was motored to see the
roses at Bagatelle, to have a cup of coffee by the cascade in the
Bois de Boulogne, and to see some places outside Paris. Of
'silent travelling' all I found time for was some strolling along
the quays. The following is a translation of a little poem I
wrote then:

> I did not make this journey in search of spring,
> Yet spring is at its height and full of wonders.
> Alone I stand by the shore of the Seine;
> Vaguely, I try again and again to identify old Paris!

認 正 賽 象 値 尋 此
舊 依 岩 奇 春 春 行
巴 稀 河 裁 深 至 不
黎 重 畔 自 物 部 為

My impression of the city was still very vague. Time after
time I tried to arrange other trips, but was always put off by
one thing or another. Life is full of entanglements and interruptions. In December, 1951, I was at last able to set out for
Paris for a long stay. Before leaving Oxford, I jotted down the
following lines in the form of a Chinese poem:

> London, where I have lived long, is like my home;
> The wind and light of New York are not yet forgotten.
> My three visits to Paris have passed as if in a dream;
> This time I go there to wander at leisure.

去 遍 巴 未 約 似 倫
慢 者 黎 忘 風 吾 敦
橋 番 如 三 光 鄉 久
徉 前 夢 顧 尚 紐 住

II

French with Tears

PARIS was in a temper when I began to learn French. I am not by nature as patient and tolerant as Chinese people are reputed to be; but when my own stupidity and age put insuperable obstacles in the way of learning a new language, I had to submit to temper, whether reasonable or otherwise. Tears do not rise to my eyes now as quickly as when I was a youngster, yet they almost did so on many an occasion in the French class. I felt irritated at being such a poor pupil. On the other hand, the unexpected presence of tears in my eyes cheered me up, for it made me realise that, though middle-aged, I am not hardened.

I ought to have tried to learn some French during my eighteen years' stay in England; but the English language itself caused me enough headaches. I was resolved now to learn enough French to enable me to enjoy my travels round Paris to the full. I chose to arrive in December, instead of in the Spring, so that I should have some time for study before the better weather for wandering came. And in any case I like to see places in their wintry, unmasked aspect.

The Chinese friend who met me on my arrival and who promised to find me a French teacher kept me waiting for two weeks, and in the end did not fulfil his promise. In order not to waste any more time, I joined a class in a language school.

At the first lesson I sat with eighteen others in grave and attentive mood. None of us uttered a sound during the whole hour. We were all beginners in French, though not all of us had arrived in Paris at the same time. Most were either to become students at the Sorbonne eventually or intended to reside in Paris for a good while. It was indeed an international assembly, for it consisted of an Indian, two Iraquis, three Turks, a Spaniard, a Dane, a Hungarian, three Britishers, a Chinese (myself) and five Americans. France was represented by our professor. Later a young Italian of fifteen joined us, with two

Brazilians, a Persian, a husband and wife from Africa, and some more Americans. By the end of the first month we numbered thirty.

Our professor was a charming *Parisienne*, full of teaching experience, as indicated by two or three thin lines on her forehead. They were invisible when her face wore its charming smile, but became noticeable if she knitted her brows over our dullness. She always wore a plain suit, sometimes red, but more often black, and a short heavy fur coat, for January in Paris is very cold. After responding to our greetings and taking off her hat and coat, she would step to the radiator and make a remark at which we would all laugh. We did not understand her French, but the mime with which she accompanied her words conveyed perfectly clearly that the radiator suggested warmth, even if it didn't radiate it. "There are radiators in every school in Paris," she would say in English, "but very few of them work." Her friendliness and her knowledge of English eased my mind considerably.

I was soon to be disillusioned. After that one English sentence we heard nothing but French throughout the whole hour. We listened to and copied words from the blackboard, but we had no time to look them up in a dictionary. French words came out of our teacher's mouth like bubbles rising on boiling water and their sound vanished from our ears as quickly as the bubbles burst. Real difficulty descended on us when someone was asked unexpectedly to answer a question in French. The victim would rise to his or her feet to show willingness to answer, but would only stare at the blackboard or the professor with a vacant air, not having understood the question. A timid plea, made in the native tongue of the victim, for further explanation of the question would bring a stamp of the foot and a torrent of French which we interpreted as meaning that native tongues were strictly forbidden. When at last a bell rang, I experienced the same joyful relief as I did some thirty-five years ago at the sound of the school bell.

Some pupils who joined the class late did not know what we had been through. A Brazilian lady with tomato-red cheeks, when she found herself standing and unable to answer the question, suddenly burst into a strange trumpet tune in Portuguese, which drew forth a counterblast in French. While this was going on, an American lady, who was not aware of the tension, idly enquired in American-English what was the French for fur-lined boots, picking up her own pair and holding them high as she spoke. Absolute silence prevailed in the room for a moment. Then the solo instrument in our concerto played its French tune again. Our professor was quite right to say that she was not teaching boys and girls and that we should do much more to help ourselves. We were with her to learn French and must speak French only. These words were spoken in English, and that was that. Her usual charm was veiled for the moment; her good humour had left her that morning. Nevertheless, I admired her seriousness and her eagerness to teach us.

She had, I thought, a good method of dealing with a class. First she would write a number of simple words on the blackboard, explaining them in French as she wrote. Then she would hang pictures on the wall and point out objects on them, giving each its name in French and a few words to make simple sentences, and finally weaving the sentences into a story. I have already spoken of my joy at the sound of the school bell: now I imagined myself in the kindergarten, and half expected to be put into bed for an afternoon nap!

After a number of lessons some of us were called to the platform. At first we were only asked to check the words on the board. Even this I dreaded terribly. The trouble was that, after days of listening to them, I seldom knew the meanings of the words. Verbs and adjectives kept changing and making themselves unrecognizable. The articles *le* and *la* jumped about like a pair of toy monkeys on a London pavement. Should anyone of us hesitate while on the platform, the foot began to stamp and our instructress would exclaim, "*Alors . . . alors . . .*" Then she would say a few words. But none of us knew whether they meant that the victim on the platform was to come down or remain there, until he or she felt a push on the back. I was twice called up, and twice wished I had been born in the southern provinces of China, where people do not as a rule grow tall and broad!

Once two of us in succession became shop-window dummies. The first was our Hungarian. We had already learned, from the original roll-call, that she had married an English gentleman and was in business with her husband in Paris. She was always beautifully dressed, seldom twice in the same outfit. That morning an orange feather in her hat and a brilliant

orange silk scarf matched the flashing rays of her big gold ear-
rings, gold necklace and gold watch, and set off her deep purple
suit. She stood on the platform facing us good-naturedly and
gave us an occasional smile. But our faces quickly grew solemn
when the professor began to point to the various items of her
attire. *Le chapeau . . . l'echarpe, la blouse, la redingote*, etc., each
had its turn. Soon they were all confused in my mind and I
wished I had made notes of those names when I gazed at the
shop-windows along the north side of the Avenue des Champs
Elysées. Presently we were labelling the parts of the Hungarian
lady herself— *la tête, les cheveux, le visage, la bouche, la main*, etc.,
gazing at our classmate as if we had all suddenly turned into
art students, or were a group of medical students in a hospital,
sitting before a patient, who was in fact one of themselves,
while doctors and nurses discussed 'the arms,' 'the legs', seemingly treating the patient like a carcase of meat.

Before I could sort out my thoughts, my name was called.
The professor had noticed that the American boys were in
miscellaneous garb and that the other males in the class,
especially the Turks, were also dressed unconventionally, but
I happened to be wearing a complete lounge suit, for I had

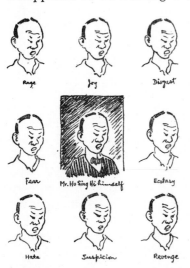

a luncheon engagement. I
gasped and wished I had refused that invitation to lunch.
Reluctantly I went up to the
platform and stood there as
amiably as possible, knowing
what lay ahead. I had never
expected to become a dummy
in the hands of a lady window-
dresser. I was thankful to have
been born a Chinese. In an
old number of *Punch* I once
saw a cartoon consisting of
nine identical faces with the
nine different captions: (1)
rage, (2) joy, (3) disgust,
(4) fear, (5) ecstasy, (6) hate,
(7) suspicion, (8) revenge and (9) Ho Sing Hi himself. These faces
belonged to one of my countrymen, for his eyes slanted slightly
upwards above his high cheek-bones. I could have been he

as I stood on that platform, though in fact my eyes slant slightly downwards and my cheek-bones are not noticeable. As I did not show my agony, the whole class supposed me to be smiling. When I returned to my seat, the air was filled with good humour and merriment as if I had played my part as a comedian quite well. The experience made me realise how difficult is the job of an artist's model or a mannequin, for they are seldom Chinese!

The blackboard was always full of words, sentences and simple stories in French for us to copy, while our ears were straining to hear what we could make out of what was being said. I thought that many of my classmates must have grasped more than I, but when I asked questions of my neighbours I found them just as ignorant.

My knowledge of English helped me to copy quite quickly, but my English accent hindered me in many ways; not knowing anything about Latin grammar, what I knew of English grammar made me stare at the constant change in French verbs, regular and particulary irregular, not to mention the agreement of adjectives and genders of nouns. My mind was completely confused.

Within a couple of weeks the members of the class were friends, to the extent at least of being able to exchange a few words. Each time we met, there would be a hearty *"Bon jour, monsieur,"* or *"Bon jour, madame,"* accompanied by a smile broad enough to signify that we had known one another for years. Nothing would follow the greetings. In any case, there was little time for us to talk in the class.

As we had not all been born on the same square of land on this earth, our native tongues interfered in their various ways with our pronunciation of this new language which we were learning. Although I have been speaking English for a good many years, listeners can easily detect my Chinese accent. An Indian, though he may have been brought up in an English family and have had an exclusively English education, will retain his distinctively Indian intonation. The Indian lady in our class had great difficulty in pronouncing a certain sound correctly, no matter how many times the professor made her repeat it. She was very brave and went on practising unperturbed by the stamping of the professor's foot. Our youngest member, a Persian lady, showed her courage in a different way, for she just would not open her mouth to pronounce a single syllable!

Certain Chinese from the southern provinces of China have difficulty, owing to their local dialects, in pronouncing the English letter *R* correctly. Generally they make it sound to English ears like an *L*. It is common in English-speaking countries to mock this difficulty. Thus, 'fried rice' becomes 'flied lice'. I have no such difficulty with *R*, for I was born in central China, but I do have difficulty with *N* and *L* because of my peculiar nose. I had thought my nose, which has no other advantages, might help me with the frequent French nasal sounds. Quite the contrary. The letters *N* and *L* appear in French phrases far too often. For instance: *ne sortez pas avant que la pluie n'ait cessé* (Do not go out before it has ceased raining) I could never get the *N*s and *L* right, and this played havoc with my efforts at conversation.

The hardest task for us all was dictation. To be able to write correctly what the professor dictated demanded thorough knowledge of the meaning of each word, its spelling and pronunciation. Dictation revealed our insecure grasp of French verbs. *Il préfère* and *ils préferent* sound identical. None of us beginners could tell which to choose. "Liaison" puzzled me even more. The word *Enfant* did not retain the same intonation in *les enfants*, and we searched our memories in vain for this new word. Every dictation brought us confusion and our eyelids often burned with unshed tears, but we continued to struggle valiantly.

After dictation came translation, for which most of us had to employ English. Once the African gentleman was called upon to translate the phrase, *Il a dix ans*, and said unhesitatingly: "He has ten eggs." We could not help bursting into laughter. A few of us guessed that the word 'egg' in his native language must sound like *an* in French.

We had moments of diversion from our struggle; indeed, the class was seldom dull. An American lady, having dined with a French family one evening, wanted to know next day what a certain French dish consisted of. She asked very casually. But our professor's seriousness about anything coming her way made her develop her answer into a lecture. After mentioning the ingredients in the dish, she deplored the habit of American and English housewives of reading their cookery book and measuring the foodstuffs with scales and tablespoons or cylinders before they began to cook. She declared that that was not cooking at all. *"Il y a deux cuisines,"* she declared: *"la cuisine française et la cuisine chinoise."* The Spanish lady sitting just in front of me turned and gave me a nod. I felt a little flattered. No sooner had I acknowledged her courtesy than I heard one of our Turkish classmates disagree with what had just been said. The professor silenced him easily. But when she began to praise French coffee-making he returned to the attack, saying that Turkish coffee was the best in the world. I could not judge of this, but I enjoyed his warm partisanship. Many exchanges of the kind occurred in the class, on such subjects as Indian tea, Hungarian goulash, American nylon boots, and Brazil monkey-nuts. The professor herself sometimes forgot the unwritten rule that no language but French must be spoken, until finding herself on the losing side of the argument she would stamp sharply to call herself to order. She did not mind us laughing then.

We never knew what next she might have up her sleeve for us. *'Monsieur Duval est un facteur'* led to our having to state what profession we were following. Some were evasive: *"Je suis étudiant"* or *"Je suis étudiante"*; others, including myself, said something near the truth, which resulted in more questions and often ended in a busy search for words in the dictionary. *"Lili est âgée de huit ans"* resulted in the men students having to announce their ages. The Iraqui boy with his thick black beard made our professor gasp by stating that he was only nineteen. Nor did she believe me when I said, "I have forty-eight eggs." She immediately replied: *"Vous êtes beaucoup plus jeune!"* All turned to look at me and smiled. I at once realised that I was the oldest member in the class. I seemed to have acted my part not too badly in the international version of *French with Tears.*

III

Did I Meet a Poet-Policeman?

It is always best to stand well with the police on arriving in a new country. The wisdom of this principle has been imprinted in my mind for some time now.

The London policeman has won my admiration for his dignified and deliberate gait. He walks as if he would not harm an ant on the road. The New York policeman reveals his alert efficiency through his eyes, which follow one wherever one strolls about. But I have come to *shake hands* with a Paris policeman, and a poet-policeman at that!

I would not have dared to do this had I not noticed that Paris policemen like to shake hands. I often think that a uniform takes away the human look of the man who wears it; but the Paris policeman retains humanity of appearance despite his uniform, especially when he walks about. He walks carefreely; he is not tall enough to have, like the London policemen, the air of always looking over everyone's head: nor does he move fast and dodge here and there like the New York policeman, as if following up some trail. He will shake hands with people, friends no doubt, even on point duty.

One morning I was trying to locate a place in the Fifth Arrondissement, and after three people of whom I enquired had proved unable to help me, I decided to ask the policeman at the intersection of the rue Censier and the rue Geoffroy St Hilaire. Before I left the pavement to go over to him, I saw the stooping figure of an elderly gentleman approach him from the other side. I paused to let this gentleman finish his enquiry, for I was not in a hurry. The policeman raised his white baton in his left hand to direct the traffic, which was not heavy at that moment. The elderly gentleman walked close up to him, but did not seem to make any enquiry. Instead, he shook the policeman's free hand while the other was still directing the traffic. They exchanged a few words and smiled at each other. I overheard the policeman say *"Merci"* when the elderly fellow moved away. The policeman then undid a paper and put a sweet into his mouth, the gift of his friend. I was happy to see a Paris policeman on duty behaving so naturally. A moment later he gave me my directions.

On another day, after lunch, I had an appointment near the Place de l'Opera. I arrived half an hour early, so I went for a stroll along the avenue towards the Grand Opera House. Standing by the entrance of the Opéra Metro and meditating on the sea of traffic, I heard a loud whistle sound again and again. I turned to watch the policeman who was directing the traffic from the top of a tall steel structure. Then another policeman began to climb up the structure as if to relieve the one on top. But instead of climbing to the top he stopped about two-thirds of the way up. The policeman on top, still busy with the whistle in his mouth and the baton in his left hand, bent down and stretched out his right hand to shake the hand of the newcomer, who then climbed down again. I felt a little puzzled at this friendly gesture at such a busy moment. When I related the scene to a French friend, I was told that they must have been *copain*.

How I myself came to shake hands with a Paris policeman, and a poet-policeman too, is connected with my repeatedly frustrated endeavour to see the Musée Balzac at No. 47 rue Raynouard.

I went there first with a friend one afternoon, but the door was shut. There was no notice to say at what hours the museum was open. My friend made an enquiry at a house opposite. An old lady who was sitting near the window, sewing, looked at us over the top of her glasses and said that the museum had been closed for repairs for the past ten months and that it might take another year to put it in order.

I wrote to tell Francine—she it was who had urged me to visit the place—of my lack of success, and she replied that she would take me there herself. We met on a Saturday afternoon outside the Palais de Chaillot at the Place du Trocadéro. My first remark was that the Musée Balzac must be very large if it was taking nearly two years to repair. She laughed and said it was not at all big. But first she wanted to show me something inside the Musée de l'Homme. We entered this building and went straight through to the library. After a word with the librarian, Francine obtained a key and took me up a number of staircases behind the general office. We emerged on the roof of the Palais. A thin layer of snow took our footprints clearly as we walked along the parapet. It was late February and Paris was still cold. Soon we were standing behind the huge sculptured group of a man and woman facing the Eiffel Tower, the upper half of which was hidden by low clouds. My companion was busy pointing out the Jardins du Trocadéro and the aquarium down below, but my eyes were more attracted by the topless Eiffel Tower. This famous landmark seemed suddenly to have become an ultra-modern sculpture of a massive, headless man with his gigantic legs planted wide apart—maybe a twentieth-century version of a statue of St Denis! As I gazed hard into the clouds, which were moving very fast, the faint lines of the upper part of the tower became visible for a moment, only to vanish again. My mind suddenly

leapt from the twentieth century back to the third century
B.C., when the First Emperor of the Chinese Ch'in Dynasty tried
to construct a T'ien-t'i or Ladder-to-Heaven. I was facing a
T'ien-t'i at that moment.

Francine suggested that we go down, and in a minute we
were passing between the show-cases of the Musée de l'Homme.
I was not given time to linger, but I caught glimpses of exhibits
depicting the evolution of man. My companion explained that,
a year ago, she had been studying anthropology and often
came here to read in the library. "It is an interesting museum,"
she said, "and the racial variety of the exhibits inevitably makes
one internationally-minded." I agreed that that would be so,
but remarked that this museum seemed also to reveal the
oddities of mankind as a species; and I could not help suggesting,
with our visit to the Musée Balzac in mind, that *La Comédie
Humaine*, the general title of Balzac's chief series of novels,
would make quite a good alternative name for the Musée de
l'Homme.

Down the steps by the side of the Musée de l'Homme we
walked, in the direction of the Place de Varsovie, but turned
left before we reached it and so found ourselves standing far
below the Passy Metro station. Francine knows this part very
well, and was soon taking me along the rue des Eaux, a short,
low-lying road with a number of low houses surrounded by
many tall buildings. It was like a hidden land of miniature
houses unknown to the outside world. In a narrow gap between
the tall walls of two impressive houses she showed me some
hundreds of stone steps leading to the main road above—a
hillside until the seventeenth century. "Just think," said
Francine. "All this neighbourhood was full of water two
hundred years ago." This was the centre of old Passy, a place
with a great reputation for the mineral springs in its hillsides.
It was discovered in the fifteenth century that the water of
these springs contained sulphur and iron, and by degrees
people came to 'take the cure' at Passy. Soon Passy became
fashionable, and wealthy people began to build houses with
flower gardens there. Assembly rooms, gaming tables and a
theatre followed. It is said that one restaurant, famed for its
excellent cooking, gave a free meal to any medical man! I
suppose its owner felt impelled to express his gratitude for the
constant flow of patients to Passy.

We climbed the steps. I said that they reminded me of Edinburgh, which my companion knows, and she agreed, adding that the steps in Edinburgh are not so steep. Eventually we reached the top and were on the main road, the rue Raynouard, our objective. On our way to No. 47, the Balzac house, I learned that Benjamin Franklin used to stay in old Passy and actually put up his first lightning-conductor in this very road. He liked drinking the *eau rouge* or red water of the spring of Passy.

The door of No. 47 was still locked. This distressed my companion considerably. She then thought of the back entrance to the Balzac house, through which the great novelist used to run away from his creditors. So we went on a few yards and turned left down some stone steps into the rue Berton. Part of the rue Berton runs parallel to the rue Raynouard, so we had to identify No. 47 from the back. On seeing a big wooden gate on our left and apparently recognising it, Francine gave it a push. It did not budge. My effort with my shoulder only made it squeak feebly. We both felt despondent. A childish whim made me peep through a hole in the wooden gate. A part of the description in Balzac's short story, 'The Mysterious Mansion', seemed to me to fit his own dwelling:

Should your curiosity lead you to glance at this house from that point of the road, you would perceive a great door which the children of the place have riddled with holes. I afterward heard that this door had been closed for the last ten years. Through the holes broken by the boys you would have observed the perfect harmony that existed between the facades of both garden and courtyard. In both the same disorder prevails. Turfs of weed encircle the paving-stones. Enormous cracks furrow the wall, round whose blackened crests twine the thousand garlands of the pellitory. . . .

As there was no way of entering the house, I raised my right hand to wave it farewell before we moved on. Presently the rue Berton narrowed to a winding cobbled footpath, with a mossy, irregular brick wall on either side overhung by trees—a country lane in the heart of modern Paris. Our steps echoed in this narrow lane as we walked on, talking of Balzac. I learned that the room used by Balzac was very small and sparsely furnished. Francine had been in it.

In his own living quarters at No. 47 rue Raynouard and his suburban villa at Les Jardies he had hardly any furniture worth mentioning. Yet he was known in his social life as extravagant, showy, even vulgar: he ate enormously, often decked his fat figure in silks and satins, and at one time kept a carriage and horses. His walking stick, studded with turquoises, was famous. He moved his living quarters often, and whenever he could he filled his rooms with costly furniture, antiques, pictures, objets d'art of all sorts, gorgeous hangings, carpets and so forth. He must have been a connoisseur, for he displays great knowledge of these things in his novels—Old Pons in *Le Cousin Pons*, for example. This was one of the reasons why he was never able to balance his finances and was always in debt. During the last twenty strenuous years of his creative life he was almost weekly involved in settling old debts by contracting new ones. In fact he had to be on the move all the time and to change his lodgings constantly to keep his creditors off his track. He seldom worked in the daytime. But when night came he would start working feverishly and continue till daybreak, drinking cup after cup of black coffee. His eight years at No. 47 rue Raynouard was a record stay for him. I remarked that he must have found this house with its two entrances ideal, especially as it takes some time to get round from the front entrance to the back one. When he heard his creditors at the front ringing the bell and exchanging words with his rather deaf old servant, Balzac had time to slip out by the back way and vanish along the rue Berton. Francine smiled and nodded. "What's more," she said, "by and by, when the creditors caught up with his little trick, and took to waiting for him at the back entrance as well, Balzac arranged with the occupant of an adjoining house to allow him to escape through a secret passage which led to the beginning of the 'lane' part of the rue Berton!" We both laughed. We had forgotten our disappointment. As French law does not permit creditors to bother their clients at night, Balzac could then work in peace.

The countrified look of the rue Berton had intrigued me so much that I determined to walk there again one night under the moon. The lively scene at night along the boulevards, with their pavement cafés, was always exhilarating, but quickly familiar. To stroll in a quieter quarter, half country and half city, under the moon, would provide a change and ease the tension of city life that had gripped me. On March 23rd the moon promised to be just right. I left the Metro at la Muette and, walking across the Place de Passy into the rue de l'Annonciation,

I reached the beginning of the rue Berton where it forks from the rue Raynouard. On my right in this part of the road was a row of tall houses, seemingly new, but on the left a line of iron railings along the rue Raynouard, which is higher than the road I was walking on. The moon was almost full and shone brilliantly overhead, but her rays became yellowish and even reddish as they met those from the street lamps. Slowly I walked and gradually the scene changed. A number of tall houses appeared on my left, among them Balzac's. This row of houses hid the street lights, so that the moonlight all round me seemed whiter, even bluish. Clear shadows of the interlacing branches of the few tall trees overhanging the high wall that faced the back entrance of Balzac's house fell on the wall. I could even detect the first young leaves on a few of them. The night air was unusually still. I began to feel rather chilly. But the following poem by Han Kuan of T'ang Dynasty (A.D. 618-905) entered my mind to give me warmth:

The moon rises beyond the edge of the Eastern horizon;
The heavenly clouds have rolled away to leave the evening cool.
It is a joy to see this clear, pure scene
Which reflects my simple open heart.
My ears and eyes are at peace from uproar,
My soul becomes carefree, while my understanding of truth deepens.
I pursue my desire to gain happiness;
Therefore I recite these lines continuously.

寓乘神耳象愛天月
言興超目吾見雲生
因得道靜靈澄收東
永至性無白清夕罘
吟樂深譁心景陰外

閣寬春宵
覽月

A lamp-post, which stood by the wall of a house on my left just at the point where the rue Berton turns into a narrow country lane, loomed up. Its lamp threw its rays inside the lane, where the moonlight could not reach because of the high walls on both sides. But the lamp rays were short and beyond them the lane became darker and darker. The far end was veiled in

mystery. Between content and longing, I moved on, with a
little chilly feeling now and then. Suddenly a faint noise stole
towards me from far away. I wondered if it was another Paris
visitor filled like me with a fancy for solitude, or perhaps someone returning home that way? It did not surprise me, but later
I became a little disturbed when the noise grew fainter and
then ceased altogether. A whimsical thought sprang up in my
mind. Maybe Balzac was on his way home to begin writing
again, but had turned away when he heard my footsteps, lest
I be one of his creditors! I never turn back in my travels, so I
moved on. The noise returned and sounded louder than the
first time. Again it receded. A third time this happened. Gradually my eyes could see a feeble light and I realised that I was
not far from the other end of the lane. At last the rays from the

lamp on the next lamp-post grew strong enough to reveal the
shadow of the person walking towards me. It was no less a
figure than a Paris policeman in his black coat!

Fancy meeting a policeman in that deserted quarter at night!
What would he say to me when he noticed my unfamiliar
face? My steps became hesitant, for I was in a real dilemma. It
would do me no good if I began to run. I had no alternative
but to continue my walk. Strangely enough, the policeman
turned back to walk in the same direction as I, as if I was
pursuing him. When I came out of the lane into the Avenue
de Lamballe he turned and caught my eye before he walked
back into the lane again. He had a piece of paper in his right
hand and looked down at it now and again. He seemed to be
reciting something to the moon. This roused a sympathetic
curiosity within me. I did not want to hurry away. I took out

my little book and stood at the corner to make a sketch with the help of the lamplight. The other end of the lane was now dark and distant. The back of the policeman was visible. He did not walk far, but soon turned back again. I could see him more clearly now. He was young, and had a kind, gentle, round face. His lips were moving. He gave me a smile when he came out, then he took up his stand near some modern office buildings on the other side of the road.

I went on with my sketch. At the same time I could hear the young policeman murmuring behind me. I longed to speak to him, but my lack of French prevented me. Before I moved away, *"Bon soir"* slipped out of my mouth involuntarily. An echoing *"Bon soir"* answered me. Impulsively, I stepped forward to shake hands and he responded willingly.

"La lune, c'est belle!" I said, pointing with my hand to the moon.

"Oh, Oui!" was the answer.

He *must* have been a poet-policeman. Another player in *La Comédie Humaine!*

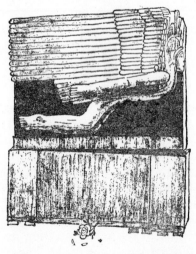

A fallen rose by the side of the tomb of
Oscar Wilde, carved by Jacob Epstein,
in the cemetery of Pére Lachaise

Rue Berton at Night

IV

What It takes to be Gay

THAT unacknowledged pavement artist, the Clerk of the Weather, was painting a street scene with the intense white pigment of snow. The low, shadowy ceiling of the sky increased the normal darkness of a January evening. Light seemed to come upward from the ground, rather than downward from the yellowish street lamps; and the city took on the quality of a lunar landscape from which, however, all life had not yet departed, though it was rapidly moving indoors.

I felt no cold myself. The beauty of the scene, and the gratitude I felt towards my kind hostess, Madame Odette Arnaud, who was giving a dinner party in my honour, warmed my heart; and when the heart is warm the body is seldom cold. I walked to the party regardless of the snow, and even exhilarated by it.

Madame Arnaud is a literary agent with whom I had corresponded long before I contemplated visiting Paris for any length of time. Immediately on my arrival she said she wished to give a party in order to introduce me to some friends of hers. Today was the chosen occasion.

My fellow guests were a French Countess; Miss Sterling, an English writer who lives in Paris; and two Frenchmen, the younger of whom was not more than twenty-one. Dinner began about half-past eight. A choice of wines was offered me, and delicious food. After a savoury came the main dish, boned chicken garnished with juicy mushrooms and other vegetables in a manner not very different from the Chinese dish, *hung-shao-tze-chi*. I felt handicapped by my inability to talk about food and wine. But two glasses of wine reddened my cheeks and lifted the corners of my mouth, and—well, I did not *feel* dull! As I finished my third glass, Madame Arnaud rose. The elder Frenchman, an architect, merrily asked me what I had found interesting in Paris in my first few weeks. I was obliged to reply, "*Les cafés et les boulevards*," these being the only words

I could pronounce at all adequately. The jolly questioner made a grimace, shrugged his shoulders and went away to talk to the younger man, pointing at me now and then.

Presently Madame Arnaud packed us into her little car (except for the Countess, who did not fancy the cold), took the wheel and off we went past the Parc Monceau and along the Boulevard Malesherbes and the rue Royale. As we drove across the Place de la Concorde I was exhilarated again by the vast white carpet spread over the empty square. Personally I should have liked to get out and have a look from the Pont de la Concorde, but the majority of the party plainly preferred the warmth inside the car. We moved on, slowly, along the Quai des Tuileries and the Quai du Louvre with their tall plane and elm trees on one side and the garden and high walls of the Musée du Louvre on the other. The car wheels hissed in the fresh snow, but otherwise all sound was muffled. No shop lights, no neon signs outshone the dim, regular street-lamps. I fancied I could hear the soft whisper of the snowflakes on the branches and trunks of the trees and the water of the Seine. None of us said a word.

I guessed that by this time we must be moving along the long straight rue de Rivoli. Then we seemed to be bearing to the right and making a big circle at rather high speed. I learnt that we had arrived at the Place de la Bastille. After that our quick turns through one narrow road after another made me feel dizzy. Eventually we got out of the car in front of a shop-like building with a bright neon sign and its windows boarded up. There the car was parked, though there was no room for another car to park at the same point on the opposite side, if pedestrians were to be allowed to pass. It was now raining. Madame Arnaud and one of her friends peeped into a few cabarets, chose one, and we all pushed our way in, cleaving the smoke-laden air like ships in a fog. As we did so a roar of laughter seemed momentarily to have some connection with us! Singing and dancing to loud music from the radio were in full swing, with occasional shouting and whistling. People sitting at rows of long tables tossed their heads and swung their bodies this way and that, joining in the choruses with the singers, who were dressed in black silk with scarlet scarves and belts. I know nothing of Western music and dancing, and I had no notion whether the show was typically French; to me it seemed similar to shows I had seen in the United States.

When the singing and dancing ended with a burst of loud applause, the sound of clinking glasses followed. We had not found seats. I was standing close to the narrow gangway left for the waitress. A large party of guests now rose and squeezed their way out. They were members of a conducted night-tour of Paris. One of the waitresses (who, like the singers, were dressed in black silk with scarlet scarves) led us to the vacated seats, where glasses of red wine were placed before us. A rather stout woman in her late fifties, dressed in the same costume as the waitresses, seemed to be the manageress. With a bundle of papers in her hand, she watched carefully while the tourists left and we seated ourselves. Many seats and tables were now empty, though round the counter the crowd was as tightly packed as when we entered. After waiting a while to see if any more people came, the stout woman moved into the centre to make an announcement. The music started and four women in black and scarlet began to dance. One of them suddenly appeared in front of me and stooped to ask if I would care to dance. I gulped, shook my head, and smiled wanly. She moved on to the younger of the Frenchmen in our party, who astonished me by saying that he could not dance; I had imagined that all young Frenchmen could dance. It occurred to me that perhaps this was the right way to express polite refusal. The architect led Miss Sterling on to the floor. Two men now appeared in the centre and each partnered a woman in black. The other two scarlet-scarved women danced together. The music was not unusual to my ears, nor the dance to my eyes. I was only sorry that I could not offer to partner my hostess.

Next the stout woman sang a French folk-song, in which all in the room joined, except me. I was sitting on the flank of our party, by the side of Madame Arnaud, and one of the women in black, evidently thinking that I needed encouragement, came and put my arm through hers and my other arm through my hostess's, and we all began to sway from side to side as the conducted-tour party had been doing when we first entered. The red wine had made my face flame anyway, and I now had the sensation that I was in the tropics.

Immediately the singing stopped the next act started. A small man with a navy-blue beret on the side of his head, wearing a sleeveless singlet to display his biceps and bathing trunks to display his thighs, strutted to the centre of the room followed by a young woman in a short black skirt which exposed her whole leg from time to time. The pair strode rhythmically about as if sharing one pair of legs between them. The small man's eyes rolled and flashed, shooting fierce glances at the woman's legs, but the sight appeared to cause him no particular satisfaction, for he grasped her more wildly, half wrestled with her and stamped his foot on the floor. Finally he joined his outstretched hands and whirled the girl round and round horizontally till she was nothing but a flashing circle of legs. Suddenly he dropped her on the floor with a thud, a finale which she appeared to appreciate, for she bounded up and stood bowing and smiling before us. This might have been what is known as an Apache dance; I would not know. Few applauded; the audience seemed for the most part to share my feeling of bewilderment.

Now the tallest of the four women on the cabaret 'staff' rushed out. She had changed her black dress and scarlet scarf for a flowing white skirt with a dark red satin blouse widely belted at the waist and tightly laced from the neck down with white cords. When she stretched out her arms to lift the corners of her skirt, she appeared scarcely to have a body at all. Her neck, too, was elongated by the tight waist, and her head appeared at least half the size of her body. Her face was painted white, with a big spot of red on each cheek; this made her eyes virtually disappear, and intensified rather than concealed her wrinkles. Her grey hair was tucked inside a cap from which projected three not-so-white ostrich feathers, which added a couple of feet to her height. She dwarfed everybody. I do not know if her costume signified anything in particular. She danced very fast. Her long, outstretched arms and extended skirt made her resemble an enormous butterfly fluttering round the room in frantic search for the window. She came so near to us at times that her movements fanned my face agreeably. But I could not imagine what my grandparents would have thought of such a performance. . . .

A tap on my shoulder from my hostess roused me. The room was emptying, and we left too. There was more snow on the ground and more water in the puddles; we had to pick our way. Madame Arnaud explained that the place we had just left was one of the Bal Musettes or popular dance-halls, a typical example of lower-middle-class night life in Paris. She had felt that I ought to see it, and not confine myself to the famous night-clubs along the Avenue des Champs Elysées and elsewhere. Before the Second World War, she continued, the narrow road where we stood would have been filled with people; often it was impossible to get into a Bal Musette after ten or eleven o'clock. But post-war conditions had brought about a decline in their popularity.

When we had settled ourselves into the car again Madame Arnaud asked the architect where we should go next. An exchange of suggestions took place between them in French, and we set off. It was not until we stopped and got out that I realised we were to the north-east of the Panthéon, not far from where I was staying. We entered an establishment called 'La Montagne'. The house was full, the orchestra was playing, and there was dancing. The lights were dimmed and a pall of smoke made them look even dimmer; I could hardly see my friends' faces. The architect danced with Miss Sterling; the other three of us just sat gazing round.

Suddenly the room was plunged into pitch darkness. Then a shaft of violet light transfixed the band in its balcony, while another hit the floor. The effect on the dancers was bizarre:

the heads and hands of the circling crowd lost their flesh tints and took on a deathly greenish tinge; here and there teeth or the whites of eyes caught the gleam, making the heads in which they were set like polished skulls. It was as if a ghostly mass was writhing slowly in hell. What gaiety! When the ordinary lights went up again, I had to keep my eyes shut for some seconds before I could look at anything.

Another dancing item was followed by two women, one a gipsy-like creature with large gold hoop earrings, the other in a greasy pink satin dress, moving slowly among the audience

singing French folk-songs. While Madame Arnaud was interpreting and explaining these to me, the architect chipped in to
say that all the good old French folk-songs and folk-dances had
been replaced by American jazz. He and Miss Sterling had
just danced to jazz music, and the band was still playing jazz.
Jazz was everywhere in Paris. I wanted to ask for an example
of a typical French folk-song and folk-dance and also why
Gay Paree was so spoken of? Before I could form my question,
the solid-looking pink-satin-clad woman, who was now singing
a solo, moved to our table. She stooped to sing in my ear and
then sat down beside me and lingeringly leant against me.
I had a panic-stricken desire to run to Calais: and a wish is
supposed to be father to a deed. But in fact I remained
supporting her with an expression on my face which I hope
looked, from the outside, like a smile. Before she left me, she
put her lips to my forehead and then went off still singing.
Everyone was staring at me and laughing—or at least I thought
so—and I guessed that they were not only enjoying her teasing
but the aptness of the words to her actions. Innocently I asked
Madame Arnaud what her song had been, and unhesitatingly
the reply came: what the singer and I would be doing in the
night. That silenced me. But I soon got over my embarrassment
and I joined in the laughter when Miss Sterling stretched out
her hand to wipe something off my forehead.

Madame Arnaud now suggested that we move on. As soon
as we were outside in the street, I asked to be excused from
going further, as we were so near to where I was staying and
I wanted to walk home. My companions responded to my
thanks with a warm shake of the hand and a cheerful "*Bon
soir*". In bed I decided that gaiety or not-so-gaiety was an
indoor affair after all. What I had enjoyed most that night was
the cold snowy drive round the Place de la Concorde and along
the Quai des Tuileries and the Quai du Louvre.

An old fountain in the top of the Rue de la Mont St Geneviève

V

Midsummer Night in Winter

I ASSOCIATED Paris with gaiety and warmth, for what I had read about it always concerned spring and summer days. Visitors seem seldom to come to Paris in winter, and Parisians just forget to mention that they have such a season. Perhaps winter does not last as long in Paris as it does in London. However that may be, I came in December and found that the winter weather is not at all unlike that of London—plenty of rain; damp, heavy clouds settling above the roofs; occasional thick fogs enveloping the whole city. Only a week after my arrival Paris was engulfed for three days in the thickest fog I have ever experienced. The first French friend I made accused me jokingly of having brought the London fog over with me. I remember reading an old English *Chronicle of the Seasons* which contained the following passage:

. . . a great fog which occurred at Paris, one 12th of November (about 1852), in which the obscurity was such that persons lost their way in the streets, as if they had been blind;—it was necessary to be near a very brilliant light to perceive a trace of it. Fourcroy, the celebrated chemist, described this fog as displaying itself in spiral groups like corkscrews, and that it had a remarkable taste.

I can understand fog occurring in London, which is so full of chimneys and so near the sea, but I was surprised to meet it in Paris. However, it has made me feel that I know more of Paris than most of her visitors as far as the seasons are concerned.

After two weeks' stay, my friend, K. C. Ts'ien, who works in the Statistics Department of Unesco, invited me and two other friends to dinner at a restaurant along the rue des Grands Augustins. I started out early to make sure of finding the way. I walked through the rue Soufflot and the rue Monsieur le Prince to Carrefour de l'Odéon.

In the Boulevard St Germain stand the statues of Broca and Danton. Of Broca I know only that he was a great French anatomist, the father of physical anthropology. From the books

27

I had read on the French Revolution I knew that Danton was one of the revolutionary leaders, and I disliked his association with the rascally Duc d'Orléans who, as a French wit remarked at the time, "would always be afraid to belong to any party where he would not have the chorus-girls of the opera on his side". His joint action with other revolutionary leaders towards the not unreasonable Louis XVI struck me as deplorable. His statue is interesting as being, I believe, the only monumental memorial of the French Revolution to be found in Paris. The French people who erected it must have had their reasons. Very few of the revolutionary leaders had a clean record. Danton, perhaps the best of them, was wronged by his rival Robespierre and condemned to die by the guillotine after being imprisoned in the Conciergerie. Before the knife descended he said: "I have lived entirely for my country. I am Danton till my death; tomorrow I shall sleep in glory." These words survive and distinguish him from his contemporaries. I was told that the site of the statue to Danton was where he had lived and had been arrested.

At the end of the narrow rue du Jardinet I found the Cour de Rohan, a small courtyard, very dark because of low cloud covering the sky overhead. On the right a flight of steps lead up to a balcony and a row of two or three old houses, one of which is believed to be the birthplace of the composer Saint-Saëns. Bare creepers hung on their walls like bunches of rusty black wires, tempting the spiders to add their decorative webs. An ancient well was enclosed by iron railings; its wheel remained, with an end of rope still fastened to the wall. It might have been there for centuries.

A gate led me into another part of the courtyard flanked by a seemingly even older house with windows set irregularly and several small terracotta busts and figures on the window-sills. By the entrance a wrought-iron tripod, much rusted and out of shape, had perhaps enabled old ladies or fat priests to mount their mules in former times, for here was once a mule path. There must have been more room in those days for the mules to move in. In the northern provinces of China two upright blocks of stone are still to be seen in front of many houses. Riders of donkeys and mules used them when mounting and dismounting.

Nobody was in sight and nothing stirred the air of this

centuries old quarter of Paris at that moment except myself. This ancient court reminded me of the old houses with their tiny courtyards along the Royal Mile in Edinburgh. In a small part of Edinburgh's Royal Mile, the Canongate, once lived, simultaneously, no fewer than two dukes, sixteen earls, two countesses, seven barons of the realm, thirteen baronets, four commanders-in-chief, seven lords of session, besides many other eminent men; each house has a story to tell. Why not, then, the Cour de Rohan? Perhaps its stories have been forgotten, for Paris is bigger than Edinburgh and has more than enough current happenings to occupy the people's minds. It was a blessing for me, for my mind is not historical, and my head is already crammed with stories from my travels, besides those told me in my Chinese boyhood.

Beyond the gate an impressively tall stone building with three fancy lattice windows rose up. I said to myself that this must be the house built by Henri II for his mistress, Diane de Poitiers, who had been a mistress of his father, Francois I, too. What charm that lady must have had! I wished I knew more about her. A feature of Paris that distinguishes it from the other capitals of the world is the houses built by and for kings' mistresses. Within my first two or three weeks' stay I had come across so many of these houses that it seemed as if without the kings' mistresses Paris would be appreciably smaller! What interested me about Diane de Poitiers is that she had two kings but one house, while Jeanne Poisson, the Pompadour, had only one king but many more houses than one. Speaking of Diane de Poitiers' attraction for her former lover's son, it was not unusual in pre-Confucian China for a king to make his foster-mother his own queen. This is said to be one of the reasons which led Confucius to evolve his family system, with its stress upon the relationship of one generation to another.

Emerging from the Cour de Rohan, I found myself standing in the middle of the Cour du Commerce. It is a narrow street, a passage rather than a courtyard. When I had been there with a friend a few days previously, a French gentleman, who was washing his new car outside his house, asked if he could help us. He spoke English and was good enough to point out several of the historically interesting houses. At No. 9 had lived the kind-hearted Dr. Guillotin, inventor of the guillotine as a humane method of slaughtering animals, chiefly sheep. That many French men and women were not to escape the destiny of sheep was not his fault. At No. 10 Danton lived at one time and at No. 8 was—and still is—a printing house, the one in which Marat printed his book, *Ami du Peuple*, an incendiary publication designed to ignite the flames of revolution.

Presently I crossed the rue Saint André des Arts and tried to locate the famous Magny, a restaurant in the rue Mazet which used to be frequented by George Sand, Renan, Flaubert, Sainte-Beuve and Gavarni. In vain. As I went eastward children coming out of school were being met by mothers and nurses. Their childish chatter was very agreeable to my ears, though I could hardly distinguish a word of their French. A small house, perhaps a restaurant, at the east end of the road, had red-washed walls like those round the Place du Tertre on Montmartre. They blended well with the darkish yellow stone and pink brick of the houses nearby. Their mellow age seemed typical of Paris even on a winter evening.

The children soon vanished, and I noticed that the road facing the school was the rue des Grands Augustins. In the dusk I could hardly read the name 'Chez Roger', but a large copper sign, 'La Grenouille', and in the window a variety of small pottery frogs, identified the place as that of my dinner

appointment. The entrance appeared to be through an arcade-like passage to the left of the sign.

I was early, so I thought I would look for the big house built by Madame de Pompadour, which I understood was in the rue des Grands Augustins, but I could not locate it.

So, instead, I walked along the Quai des Grands Augustins. The clear lights on the opposite bank reflected without blur or quiver in the Seine banished reasoning from my mind. The water, apparently so still though actually flowing invisibly, seemed to have at its command all the trees, the people sitting on the benches, those leaning on the walls of the quays backed by dreamlike houses, and to be turning them all into silent witnesses of some heavenly procession. There was a subtle spell in the solitary boat anchored right beneath my feet. There used to be more boats anchored by the Ile de la Cité. But this lone one, taking the shape of an almond as if recently-carved out of black marble, added serenity to the scene, for it

contrasted directly with the small ball-like cloud stuck on the
dark-blue sky mirrored in the river. A few bright stars surrounding the cloud could be seen too. I thought what an
admirable composition it would make for a modern painting.
A car passed over the Pont Neuf and the mutter of its exhaust,
clear for an instant, vanished in a few seconds, and the winter
evening closed round me. The cold air pierced my clothes and
I felt chilly.

It was time now for dinner. Returning to the rue des Grands
Augustins, I met my friends under the copper frog. The four of
us, T. C. Chang, Ch'en Yuan, K. C. Ts'ien and myself, entered
by the arcade and found both the first and second rooms full.
Only a few spaces at a long narrow table right at the end of the
third room were vacant. We had not booked in advance, as we
should have done, but K.C., who knew the proprietor of Chez
Roger, explained that two of us could not speak French and
that we therefore wished to sit together. Accordingly three
other diners, two men and a woman, were asked to move along
the long table and we four were able to sit where they had been.
I felt rather embarrassed by this, but K.C. retorted that it was
the manager's idea and that people who came here had no

objection to being moved around; it was part of the fun, and our party might be broken up at any minute.

After the serenity of the quay, I found the room very noisy. There was shouting, singing and clinking of glasses. My eye-balls felt as if they were swelling and my ear-drums dilating. Presently, however, I found myself laughing with the rest. The universal gaiety expressed in a language I could not under-stand, seemed quite irrational. What was it all about? Anyhow the laughter was thoroughly infectious and I secretly con-gratulated myself on the blessing of being able to throw off my habitual sobriety for a while when the occasion demanded. A self-centred and subjective mood often narrows one's vision and causes one to miss half the fun of life.

Presently the dishes K.C. had ordered were placed before us. I felt we were lucky to have seats, for there was now a long queue outside and many intending diners were also standing with their backs pressed against the wall at the entrance to our room. The air was thick and grew warmer as time went on. I examined my dish of frogs. They did not look like the kind that I ate in Shanghai some thirty years ago on my first long journey from home. Nostalgic feeling gripped me.

I had just finished school and had gone to Shanghai to take the entrance examination into one of the National Universities. My grandmother was an ardent Buddhist and always refrained from partaking of any living creature, though she did not press other members of the family to follow her example. Before I left home, she urged me not to try any uncommon dishes if I could help it. Her idea, which derived from belief in reincar-nation, was that those who killed and ate live creatures for food would, when the Buddhist Wheel of Life brought reincar-nation, be transformed into one of the creatures. The idea

 certainly had some effect on my young mind. I stayed in a hotel with a classmate who was in Shanghai for the same purpose as myself. One day a special dish was set before us for dinner. It consisted of *t'ien-chi* or 'field-chicken' (actually frog) so called because these edible frogs are generally found in the ricefields round Shanghai and their taste is said to be like that of a young chicken. They are to be found in other parts of China too, but only people in the neighbourhood of Shanghai and Canton eat them.

Addressing myself to this dish of *t'ien-chi*, not only did I hark back to my grandmother's words, but I was also somewhat shaken by the arrangement of the meat. There were about ten pairs of hind-legs, each a little more than two inches long and the upper part nearly half an inch wide. They were neatly skinned, and their colour and shape were not so very different from human legs. The limbs were paired in a circle round the dish, with lightly cooked green spinach underneath. Some red radishes in the centre covered the ends of the legs. (As I recall that dish now, it resembled the Hollywood star Esther Williams with her 'chorus' of girl swimmers forming a circle in the water, with Miss Williams in the centre as the axis. The effect was of legs without bodies.) The pattern of the dish was quite attractive if one could forget the leg effect. My friend emptied his plate with relish, and without a qualm. I was eventually persuaded to take one or two pieces, but I could not forget Grandmother's warning.

An old Chinese book called *San-T'ang-Ssu-K'ao* tells how an imperial cook once produced a dish of field-chicken for a T'ang emperor, who enjoyed it very much. That night the Emperor slept quite well at first, but later dreamed of hundreds of his subjects, all dressed in bright green, coming to demand their lives from him. Each had a big mouth from which angry grunts emerged, and eyes bulging with anger. The emperor's fear mounted as the noise of their demands grew louder, until eventually he woke up. At once he realised the cause of his dream and immediately issued an edict forbidding the catching of frogs for food. This is probably why many people in China have not since the T'ang period cared to eat field-chicken.

More than thirty years have elapsed since that Shanghai meal, and I have tasted all kinds of food. My grandmother's words no longer worry my conscience. When the dish of *grenouilles* was placed before me at Chez Roger, my immediate reaction was that it looked unfamiliar. There were no pairs of recognisable legs forming a circle round the plate, nor did each single limb suggest a miniature woman's leg. These limbs were far smaller—possibly a third of the size of those I had eaten in Shanghai. They had not been boiled, but fried in hot fat. A thin coating of flour seemed to have been used, and the meat was of a brownish colour—many pieces showing burnt patches. As they were so small, the burnt ones looked like used match-sticks. There were neither green vegetables underneath nor red radishes in the centre, but the dish was sprinkled with herbs and spring onion finely chopped, which imparted a delicate flavour. At least fifty pairs of legs, if not more, seemed to go to a single plate. Thus the number of *grenouilles* consumed each evening at Chez Roger must be enormous.

J. G. Wood wrote in his *Illustrated Natural History*:

In Paris these creatures [frogs] are sold at a rather high price for the table, and as only the hind-legs are eaten, a dish of frogs is rather an expensive article of diet.

It is needful to make a very early visit to the market, 4 or 5 a.m. being about the best time, to see the manner in which the frogs are brought to market. They are generally sold by women, each of whom has by her side two tubs or barrels, one containing living frogs, and the other having a leather band nailed to the side, in which is stuck a sharp, broad-bladed knife. When the purchaser has bargained for a certain number, the seller plunges her left hand into the one barrel, and with a single cut of the knife, severs the hind legs just above the pelvis, leaving the whole of the body and fore-quarters to fall into the tub. The hind legs are then carefully skinned, and dressed in various ways, that with white sauce seeming to be the best, at all events according to my own taste. They require considerable cooking, but when properly dressed have a most delicate and peculiar flavour, which has been compared, but not very happily, to the wing of a chicken. I would suggest that a mixture of the smelt and the breast of the spring chicken would convey a good idea of the edible frog when cooked.

I once spent a whole night at the *Halles*, but I saw no such woman frog-seller as Mr Wood describes. Perhaps it was just as well, for I have no wish to behold such a dismembering spectacle as he described. Being a rather sophisticated Confucianist I sometimes use one of Confucius' sayings for my own purposes. In this case, for instance, I would have used his words, "A gentleman always keeps away from the kitchen", for it would pain him keenly to witness killing and bloodshed.

I have to confess, however, that I enjoyed my dish of *grenouilles*, and so did my friends. The legs had to be eaten slowly, one by one. Even the thighs of these very small creatures did not offer a large mouthful, and enjoyment seemed to lie partly in the satisfaction of leaving the bone quite bare. Knife and fork were useless and we all used our fingers. To employ a primitive method of eating in civilised surroundings is romantic; on the other hand to do the same in uncivilised surroundings would be savage or barbarous. I have no wish to solve the contradictions of human life, but I did long at that moment for a pair of chopsticks. To pick up a single frog leg with the chopsticks and to savour it morsel by morsel while slowly sipping wine, would have been delightful. Undue haste was out of place on an occasion like this.

Before I came to live in England some twenty years ago, I used to carry with me, wherever I travelled, a special pair of chopsticks made of ivory in a fitted case. This habit was a tribute to hygiene, for the chopsticks provided in hotels and restaurants were, I knew, not always to be trusted. In time I became so fond of my own chopsticks as to feel that they possessed a magic power to make the food taste better, just as an artist will have a favourite brush and grow to believe in its magic. I gave up the habit when I came to Europe, and soon took to using knife and fork.

Thinking of my pair of chopsticks, I tried to imagine what would have happened if someone had spotted me using them in that room. Eccentricity is not only precious: it can create commotion. I believe that many of my fellow diners would have demanded a chance to try them! The thought of all the excitement appalled me.

By now our party was as uproarious as the rest. Bottles were drained and some of the bottom of my plate became visible. The commotion in the second room was drawing nearer to us. With a sudden dash, someone broke through and passed our table. All the males present stood up, glass in hand, and gave him a rousing cheer. He was a young man with a thin Fairbanks moustache, wearing a navy blue uniform with thick gold cords at shoulder and waist. Rather slim, of medium height, dapper and rakish, he walked easily, though his shoulders slanted slightly to one side. He did not smile or laugh when he came into our midst, yet he looked naïve and good-natured, as though the whole world was very much to his liking. His perspiring face indicated that he had had a rough passage. He snatched up a single frog leg from a stout man's plate and then began whispering in the ear of a young lady at another table. Apparently he was not acquainted with either of them, yet they both smiled and laughed. He talked, shouted and sang with a serious, long face while the whole room rocked with laughter. It had a comic effect even on me. His glum face might have suggested bad temper, but actually he was making merry all the time. The rest of the room seemed magically bound under his spell.

To my heated brain the young man's unintelligible utterance as well as the clamour of the other diners were neither speech nor song, but something like croaking. The air in the room was getting closer. We were all perspiring.

Buffon says in his *Natural History* that "Before wet weather their [frogs'] voices are in full exertion; they are then heard with unceasing assiduity, sending forth their call, and welcoming the approach of their favourite moisture". Perhaps the croaking noise we seemed to be producing was our way of calling for coolness from the rain.

The thought of frogs' croaking reminded me of my boyhood at home in Kiukiang. As a youngster of about ten I used to spend my summer evenings by the pond in our garden, sitting idly on the garden seat or on the grass and listening to the croaking of the frogs. Not only were their voices agreeable, but the sound of them seemed to produce a cooling effect on mind and body; they lulled me like an old nursery rhyme. The heat in the summer evenings in my native land can be unbearable and we were sometimes unable to sleep until midnight. We had a secluded garden surrounded by a high wall and most of the younger members of our family spent the first half of the night sitting or lying out of doors on bamboo chairs which are rather like deck-chairs. Summer nights in China are usually dry, with moonlight and bright stars. Those of us who liked listening to the croaking of frogs, as I did, would move our stools near the pond, and some would put their seats under the trees or beside the flower-beds and listen to one of our elders telling fantastic stories, chiefly about ghosts and spirits. Those were happy and enjoyable evenings.

That listening to frogs' croaking sounds should be pleasurable may seem queer to those who have never spent a stifling summer night out of doors. Or perhaps the Chinese people are fated to seem queer to other races. Many poems have been written by our well-known poets about the croaking of frogs, and special pavilions have even been erected in gardens with names such as *T'ing-wa-lou*, 'Listening-to-the-frogs Pavilion'.

Sudden Rain in the Place du Panthéon

The poet Ts'ien Wei-chan of the thirteenth century composed a couplet describing his enjoyment, of which the following is a rough translation:

> The colour of the moonlight on the brimming pond is as white as frost;
> A loud chorus of frogs' croaking is like a downpour of rain.

It is not the sound of gentle rain but of a torrent, such as is welcome when a heat wave is at its height. Just before rain the croaking of frogs becomes coarser and hoarser like the beating of drums of different sizes at the same time; just after rain it sounds clearer and sharper as if a number of *muyui*, wooden-fish (a musical instrument which accompanies the chanting in a Buddhist temple), were being played one after another.

I was roused from my reverie by the lively young man in navy blue, who was again starting a song. His head was close to that of a young girl sitting at the long table with her back to us. Then he turned to tap-dancing on a few inches of floor, which made him look more comical than ever. Others joined in the singing, gaily beating time with their arms. One stout fellow jumped on to his chair with upstretched arm, wearing a hat decorated with a white bird made from real feathers. He had

just removed it from the head of a middle-aged woman sitting behind him. Presently he returned to his own seat, which he had nearly lost to two young soldiers in French khaki who had just squeezed into our room. They managed to find a seat at the end of the table. One of the newcomers, as if taking his turn, snatched another hat from a girl nearby. It was pink and shaped like an egg-cup. He crammed his soldier's cap on the girl's head instead. All were in the highest spirits.

Next a noisy chant was struck up: "*Chapeau, chapeau, cha-cha-chapeau*" echoed all round the room. Two tall women with

much-made-up faces and a solidly built man were squeezing in
to take the places of some who were leaving. The man still wore
his hat and was moving inch by inch towards the centre. The
odd song grew louder and louder until the man realised the
point of it and hurled his hat on to the top of a lamp-shade
This brought the song to an end.

No menu was to be had except a large piece of paper with a
list of dishes written in red, pasted high up on the wall. I could

not read the items and anyhow most were beyond my understanding. So K.C. ordered again. We all had our second
course, *cochon de lait*, followed by some fresh fruit.

Newcomers were still managing to squash in, and the air of
the room was now so thick as to render me nearly senseless. I
felt drowsy. Unexpectedly my head bumped against the table
and jolted my neck. The shock restored normal sight to my
swollen eyes; I became wide awake and suggested to my friends
that we should give our seats to some prospective diners who
were still queueing up at the door.

While I was struggling into my coat, a bright young spark
stood up and, stretching out his arm, gave me a most hearty
handshake. But he had caught my arm at an awkward angle
and though I laughingly wished him *"Bon soir"* I was suffering
agony. My companions merely thought I had met an old
friend.

K.C. was the first to reach the door facing the arcade. A
young woman in red was standing just outside. He kissed her
cheek and she put something into his hand. My other friend
followed K.C.'s example. I thought they knew her. Then I
reached the door. The young woman barred my way. With her

left hand she pressed something hard into mine while with a finger of her right hand she pointed to her cheek. I hastily followed the example of my friends, feeling embarrassed that I had needed such a broad hint. The object in my hand turned out to be a small metal *grenouille* painted green. "That's the souvenir. Everyone who has dined here gets one after dinner," remarked my host.

The air under the arcade cooled my skin after the stuffy room, and I drew a deep breath. Outside the arcade it became sharply cold and seemed to penetrate my bones. I shivered. It was then I realised that it was still January and that Paris was only halfway through her winter. Yet I had just spent a midsummer night.

VI

The Mecca of Artists

I FIRST heard the name Montparnasse over thirty years ago in Shanghai, where a number of Chinese art students, recently returned from Paris, had opened art schools of the Western type. Painting in the traditional Chinese style these masters despised; and even our conventional clothes, loose-fitting and comfortable though they surely are, were alleged to be clumsy. Wide black or red bow-ties projected below their chins and obscured their none-too-clean collars. Their miscellaneous jackets and trousers were always copiously stained with oil paint. Their hair remained uncut and their beards unshaven.

This last small affectation means something different in Shanghai from what it does in Paris. To me it is one of the advantages of being Chinese that while the hair on my head grows long, thick and black, the hair on my lip and chin would not get into my soup if I did not shave for half a year. But to these disciples of *art nouveau* it was a source of grief and disquietude that they could not rival the splendid beards of their former art colleagues in Paris. But one cannot alter the physical characteristics of one's race, and the Chinese are not hairy. Even whiskers of the kind generously accorded to Chinese characters in Russian ballet are the product of years of carefully tended growth. Normally, six months of effort is sufficient only to reach a stage of mild discomfort.

Needless to say, these new art schools were all established in Shanghai's French Concession (now abolished), and this part of the city became the Chinese Montparnasse. Spring and autumn *Salons*, even, were held. Young men who had no connection with art, but wished to give the impression of having been abroad, attired themselves similarly. The great difficulty was to get Chinese girls to act as models for life study, especially in the nude; for, according to Confucius' code, to be seen undressed is immoral. The Principal of the first modern College of Art in Shanghai was cruelly attacked by the Press when he at last found an aged Chinese woman willing to be a model in his school. Shortly he was obliged to flee to Japan to escape arrest by the Governor. Gradually, however, things calmed down, and after a few years he was able to resume his work in the College. By that time, if Chinese models were not forthcoming, young French and Russian girls were available, and in fact they proved an even greater attraction. Young men rushed to put on flowing ties and to acquire Western-type brushes and paint. There was little or no understanding of the significance of the nude in Western art, but everyone talked about it with glee and awe. Those who could, wrote articles on the subject and a crop of new art magazines appeared. Confucian scholars nicknamed these art students, *Chu-lo-chih-T'u*, 'nude-chasers'. I was not myself a nude-chaser, though I was always interested in art; at that time I was studying chemistry. It was in one of the new magazines that I first saw the name Montparnasse. It consisted of four Chinese characters *Man-pa-la-ssu*.

When, in 1933, I arrived in England, I visited the London art galleries and saw the works of the Impressionists and Post-Impressionists. The name *Man-pa-la-ssu*, though I still could not pronounce it in the French way, rose in my mind. I began to study Western art by means of books, lectures and my artist friends. I learned how Montparnasse had grown from an uninteresting district into a world-renowned art and literary centre shortly after 1900. Lenin and Trotsky took coffee together in the Rotonde. Modigliani and Utrillo met with joy, clinked glasses, and then fought until they were taken to the police station for the night. Pascin was entertained at the Dôme when he first reached Paris from Munich in 1907. Van Dongen, on returning from Egypt, got himself up as Neptune 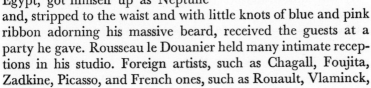 and, stripped to the waist and with little knots of blue and pink ribbon adorning his massive beard, received the guests at a party he gave. Rousseau le Douanier held many intimate receptions in his studio. Foreign artists, such as Chagall, Foujita, Zadkine, Picasso, and French ones, such as Rouault, Vlaminck,

Matisse and others, frequented the district, violently discussing art and comparing their works. In 1923, one afternoon in December, the newly enlarged Rotonde was ceremoniously opened with a speech from the poet and art critic, Gustav Kahn, amid much gaiety and consequence. The owner invited all the guests, mostly artists, poets and their friends, to eat and drink gratis and to look at the works of art hanging on the walls. Some of the artists who founded the Shanghai Montparnasse may have been present on this occasion.

This was the beginning of the flow of people who have since come to Montparnasse, not only from all parts of Paris, but of the world. The bar of the Rotonde automatically became a fine arts gallery housing on the walls and staircases works by all the Impressionists and post-impressionists. Wealthy art-dealers and rich collectors came to see the pictures. Soon the Dôme enlarged its rooms and decorated them brilliantly. In 1927, a third large café, the Coupole, was opened. There were many

smaller cafés, but these three upheld the glory of the place. There one could meet all types of artists, poets and eccentrics. There one could see fantastically dressed men and women. There one went to find interesting characters. There one had chances of all kinds of amusement and entertainment, cheap and otherwise. There one could take life study in studios where all the now-famous artists had been before. There one enjoyed complete freedom. . . . It was no wonder, I felt, that the hearts of those young Chinese visitors to Montparnasse in the nineteen-twenties had been lost. What did they do with themselves? Examining the names of the many artists who had started humbly in Montparnasse, I found only one Easterner, Foujita, a Japanese. I hope their enthusiasm was something more than nudity-chasing.

It was almost another twenty years before I acquired any personal experience of Montparnasse. I got to know it quite well in 1952, by which time, I was assured by many people, it was not what it had been forty, thirty, twenty, even ten years earlier. The street was much like any other big street in Paris, full of cafés and restaurants, but with the old life gone for good.

A few friends thought I might chance to see a strange character or two, but even these would be only mediocre. . . . To lament for the past has never been my habit; I take change as a matter of course. And talk of mediocrity assumes in the speaker a superiority which may not exist. Ignoring the advice I had received, I went to Montparnasse with an open mind.

One morning, after a French lesson in the rue de Vaugirard, I strolled through the streets, without any destination, staring at the shop-windows, watching passers-by, until I came to a sign reading Boulevard du Montparnasse. I followed it. The boulevard was a wide and busy thoroughfare and I felt smaller than I had in the rue de Vaugirard. Crossing the Place de Rennes, I had a look at the old church, Notre-Dame-des-Champs, both inside and out. Directly opposite the church I noticed some vividly coloured flowers in the big glass windows of a shop on the other side of the boulevard, which was too wide for me to be sure of what they were. I went over to look closely and found a ravishing display. I was not surprised to learn that from this florist's shop come the floral decorations of the city.

Presently I reached the point where the three famous cafés cluster. As the Coupole was the nearest, I entered that for a cup of coffee, with the intention of lingering expectantly as long as I could. The coffee was good and refreshing. The house was not full, for it was time for the midday meal. The waiter was as courteous and attentive as most Paris waiters are, though I could not converse with him. In complete tranquillity I sipped my coffee and gazed round. Eyes met mine not infrequently; others, no doubt, were doing the same as I. No one was dressed strikingly; no one talked in an out-of-the-way manner. An hour and a half slipped by. After a second cup of coffee I left. Evidently artists and fashionable poets do not dress up before midday.

The place in which I was staying was within five minutes' walk of the Jardins du Luxembourg. One sunless afternoon I crossed the rue Auguste Comte along the green avenue to look at the Fontaine de l'Observatoire. In the dim light the horses seemed to be fighting the splashing water. As I was close to the Boulevard du Montparnasse I betook myself to the Dôme for a glass of wine. It was after five. There were more people than I had seen in the Coupole at midday. My eyes circled the room like a pair of beamless searchlights and then fell on my own glass, which, I thought to myself, was as normal and well-shaped as any other glass. No difference. People came and went. No one looked eccentric. Everyone was orderly. At about half-past six the crowd thinned out and empty seats appeared. The Dôme provides food, but customers come mostly for coffee and

other drinks. I spent two uneventful hours before concluding that I must again have chosen the wrong time.

Perhaps the 'sights' in these cafés were to be seen late at night?

A Chinese artist friend, Dr. Chou Ling, invited me to a dinner party at his house, 25 Boulevard du Montparnasse, one evening. There were ten of us, all with flat faces except Mrs Chou, who is a Parisian, and her niece. Mrs Chou is a born cook and turned out twelve dishes of real Chinese flavour. I wondered if any Chinese ladies could turn out French dishes as good. The two Chinese ladies present both admitted to being unable to cook these dishes so well themselves.

From our comparison of French and Chinese cooking we passed on to light-hearted exchanges of some of our experiences in Paris. One of the Chinese ladies related how her son of two and half, soon after the family's arrival from Formosa, visited the gardens of the Tuileries and was enraptured with the many marble statues dotted about the grounds. When he saw the pond he wanted to strip off his clothes and bathe in it. "Mama," he shouted, "all these people are going to have a bath, and I want one too." The child's reaction seemed to me appropriate. Many adults—Orientals if not Occidentals—would react more or less in the same way upon seeing these nude statues for the first time. They would miss the artist's vision.

Dr. Chou, who studied art and art history at the Sorbonne many years ago, knows Paris well. He now offered his service as unpaid guide to newcomers who wished to see the night life of the city. As I had been more than three months in Paris, I felt I could rank myself one degree higher than a newcomer, so I made my excuses and left alone.

After half-past nine the traffic on the boulevard was not heavy and there was ample room on the pavements. The neon signs, chiefly of cafés and restaurants, were more brilliant than ever against the dark walls of the boulevard. The night air was fresh and mild. Unprompted, my steps took me once more to the centre of Montparnasse, and I entered the Rotonde. I did not find it very different from the Coupole and the Dôme, except that there were more paintings on the walls. The house was quite full and all the guests were well-dressed. The band was playing and a few dancing couples circled the small area in the centre. Otherwise only the movements of those arriving and departing stirred the smoky air. Laughter broke out occasionally and smiling faces shone when my eyes met theirs. It was  a pleasant and happy crowd. But I felt odd, not under-standing a word of their talk. And I surely looked odd, too, sitting alone all the time. Perhaps I was myself one of the 'strange' figures for others there to see! This alarming thought caused me to leave the Rotonde at half-past eleven, fully resolved to resume my usual habit of travelling aimlessly.

Another month elapsed and my feet were still taking me from one *arrondissement* to another. Easter brought a few English-speaking acquaintances and the temporary suspension of the *silent* aspect of my travels. In a gathering one evening in a Du Pont Café on the Boulevard St Michel, a Bright Young Thing from London laughingly related that she had been searching Montparnasse for days for any kind of strange character or artist, but nothing had she seen until that afternoon. Then, waiting to cross the rue d'Odessa, she heard two women talking in a strange tongue which she did not understand. They seemed to have come from the Far East; one must have been from China—here she threw me a glance—for she wore a long, tight skirt with a high collar, and her hair-do had a Chinese look. She had a huge, flat package under her arm and must without doubt have been an artist. Her companion had a thick roll of black hair coiled on top of her head, a masculine face, and a husky, soft voice. She wore a pair of dark blue  trousers and a man's jacket, and looked fascinating. The narrator could not find enough adjectives to help her description of this unusual pair. Everyone in the group smiled at her triumph but me. I might have done so, considering my own three visits to Montparnasse. But the two ladies the Bright Young Thing had described are my friends. "What one tries to do to others comes back upon oneself," I thought, struck by the truth of an old Chinese saying. Everyone has a comical side which escapes his own notice. The picture of myself sitting alone in the Rotonde late at night for hours came back to me, and I felt sure it had provided someone with amusement. How consistent is the *comédie humaine!*

The Chinese lady mentioned above is Madame Fan Tchun-P'i. She was educated at the Ecole des Beaux Arts under Monsieur Albert Besnard. After having returned to China for many years, she came to live in Paris in 1950. Her companion was Madame Pan Yu-Lin, also a Chinese, educated in Paris about the same time as Madame Fan. She went back to teach in the Shanghai College of Fine Arts for a few years, but returned to live in Paris much earlier than Madame Fan. With years of experience, both know Paris intimately and love her increasingly. The magic power that Paris exercises on her visitors is beyond logic.

Fan paints in oil and water-colour as a hobby, while Pan lives by her work. Their names had often appeared in Chinese art magazines, and it was natural for me to visit them while in Paris. I once made the following attempt at a rhyme:

What an admirable hobby for Fan,
And an honourable profession for Pan!
Neither hobby nor profession for me,
Doodling, doodling, doodling
Is all I can.

Every week Fan and Pan go to the studio at the Grande
Chaumière for life study, though Pan has a fine studio of her
own in the rue Vercingetorix. Contests used to be held at the
Grand Chaumière of Montparnasse for the best models.
Models are not indispensable for artists of the present day as
they were formerly, yet they still draw crowds to the Grande

DESSIN

After a design by Pan Yu Lin
(Original in the Ministry of Education, Paris)

Chaumière. Pan is chiefly known for her nude studies, done in
simple, sure lines with a Chinese brush and very little wash,
sometimes with a few touches of light colour.

One afternoon, at Fan's suggestion, I accompanied her and
Pan to do some life study in that famous studio. We paid our
admission fees and entered the big room. Many artists were
hard at work, sitting in a crescent round a model posed in the
nude. Complete silence reigned. Pan went to her usual seat
beside the platform, where the model stood within an iron
fender. Fan found an unoccupied stool further back. I squeezed
myself on to the long bench at the rear, where my back was
jammed against the wall and my feet pressed the edge of a stool
on which a young girl sat drawing. I made a sketch or two and

then I watched the other students' intense, abstracted faces. Their example infected me and I did another sketch—not of the model, but of an elderly artist nearby, whose long white hair fell to his shoulders. A woman artist lifted her arm to hold her pencil vertically and check her composition. A young man stood up from his seat to try a new angle for his composition. The room seemed already to be full to capacity, but two more artists entered and somehow found seats. I felt rather contorted on my bench.

An hour passed. Another model relieved the first. While they were changing over there was a minute's break and many heads turned. My eyes met those of newly-formed acquaintances from the language school: two Turks, both from Istanbul. We smiled. The second model was younger and better looking, though that was not, of course, the prime consideration. She posed differently, too, and changed her position every five minutes. This was a training for the students in quick reactions to forms and shapes. Sketch-books were turned frequently with a little rustle of sound. I followed the changes of the model for a while and then made a sketch of another fellow student. In the end my sketch-book contained more rough drawings of fellow students than of the model.

About six o'clock the session came to an end. I went to shake  hands with the Turkish fellows. Our French did not permit conversation and they spoke no English and I no Turkish. They introduced to me the people they knew in the crowd and we too shook hands. None of us could exchange a word, but all smiled, and the atmosphere was most congenial and friendly. Inevitably somebody wanted to look at someone else's sketch-book and soon we were all displaying our efforts. I could not escape. There was laughter at my sketches of students at work. The last sketch-book we saw was just a succession of blank pages, which invited giggles. My neighbour on the back bench had done nothing either, but she had been observing the forms and poses attentively. Perhaps she was trying to memorise them. That, to me, would be the best way.

VII

I Bow to Monsieur Henguet

I HAD already been twice to the rue Montmorency in the third Arrondissement. The first time I went to see a compatriot of mine, Monsieur Kia Si-ling, whom I met by chance in a friend's house and who has a leather-work *atelier* in that road, I was at once interested, and Monsieur Kia suggested showing me round his workshop and many other workshops in the district. I found that their chief products were small leather articles—belts, purses, handbags, children's shoes, etc.—and that they also acted as wholesalers to provincial dealers in these articles. There were several *ateliers* besides Kia's in the rue Montmorency, and many more in such adjoining roads as the rue Chapon, the rue des Gravilliens, and the rue des Vertus. We must have been round more than twenty *ateliers*. Some had a shop attached. All the owners were very friendly and hospitable to me, insisting upon treating me to drinks, very little of which could I take. Many of these Chinese have French wives, and I was introduced to a number of their lovely children. The most interesting thing of all to me was that almost every one of these compatriots came from the same district of Chekiang Province along the east coast of China. How this happened is a puzzle. Most of the Chinese overseas, especially those in England and the United States, come from Canton and neighbouring districts along the south coast of China. This is understandable, for in the first place the English trade with the Far East centres upon Hong Kong, and in the second place the American Pacific railways were built with Chinese labour mostly recruited from Canton. In England and America Chinese settlers are generally in either the restaurant or the laundry business. But in France who can beat the Parisian *blanchisserie*? Force of circumstances must have made Monsieur Kia and those who came from his part of the world try leather-work instead. This testifies to exceptional adaptability.

Monsieur Kia was the President of the Chinese Association

of Leather-workers in Paris for the year, and had an idea to start a school for Chinese children in Paris—I mean those with Chinese parents or at any rate Chinese fathers. Thinking that I might be able to help by writing and illustrating some simple books for them, he asked me to dine with him and a few of his friends to discuss the scheme. I appreciated his kindness and praiseworthy effort, but I thought he would encounter serious practical difficulties. Most of the children for whom he wished to provide could have little chance of hearing or speaking Chinese at home, and in school hours they would have to give full atten-

tion to their work. I could only promise to do what I could.

Before I came to the rue Montmorency for the second time, I started out early to have a look round the Square du Temple, which I was told was very old and had played an important part in French history.

I found the square easily. It is now a kind of garden with a green lawn, a small pond, an artificial cascade, and a few trees. Around the square were many metal-framed stalls, and the selling of old clothes was still going on. The roads were full of litter. A few men I met wore bushy moustaches and long beards. The chattering of the women did not seem to be French. They may have been speaking Yiddish, for the quarter between the rue du Temple and the rue Vieille-du-Temple is known as the Ghetto of Paris. All the roads nearby are narrow, like the rue Montmorency, where a car could only just manage to pass through. All the houses looked shabby and old. Sitting down on a bench in the square, I tried to meditate on the little of its past that I had learned. This had been a stronghold of the Order of Templars, an Order which, long before the Crusades, had led small bands of men, half-military, half-monastic, to defend pilgrims to the Holy Sepulchre. At first they followed their principles faithfully; later they grew into a body over-shadowing the Church and the Government; by the thirteenth century they had acquired great wealth in Europe and risen to be a secret society with branches in every country. The French branch built, probably by 1222, the castle in this quarter from which the present square derives its name. Gradually the Templars failed in their mission or forgot it, became corrupt, lived luxuriously, obtained royal privileges without rendering services in return; the Temple became their fortress, where they indulged in debauchery. Eventually King Philippe-le-Bel denounced them as enemies of the State, incited Pope Clement V against them and seized the riches they had accumulated. In May, 1310, fifty-four of the Templars were burned alive near the Abbey of Saint Antoine and on March 11th, 1314, Jacques de Molay, the Grand Master, was burnt on the Pont Neuf, exactly where the statue of Henri IV now stands. I detested the thought that these offenders—if indeed they were offenders—should have been burnt alive. But the history of my own country can match this senseless brutality. In the third century before Christ, China witnessed hundreds of Confucianists being buried alive, not for what they did, but for what they *read*!

My meditation then switched to the end of the eighteenth century, when Louis XVI, Marie-Antoinette, their son and daughter and the king's sister were imprisoned in the Temple. I imagined how Louis XVI passed his time giving Latin and geography lessons to his son and playing draughts. I then moved round a little in order to locate the place where a weeping willow was said to have been planted by the King's daughter, Madame Royale, who was reprieved from the guillotine, and who made a pilgrimage to the Temple on her return to France long afterwards. I was told that the willow lived for many years. But it is no more.

Now I was in the rue Montmorency for the third time. This time I was accompanied by Madeleine Chambert, who came with me to see a theatrical designer. Before we went to call on the artist who lived in this road, Madeleine wanted to show me a medieval house that has not changed since 1407. It belonged to Nicolas Flamel, scrivener, bookseller and reputed alchemist, thought by his contemporaries to have been possessed of the Philosopher's Stone, since they could not otherwise understand how he had accumulated his great wealth. He is supposed to have said: "If one cannot afford a meal, never refuse to give a piece of bread." Such a philanthropic outlook aroused suspicion in the people of the Middle Ages. On the wall and on a glass lamp were inscribed in red the words: *"Auberge-hostellerie de Nicolas Flamel, Batie en 1407, en la bonne ville de Paris."* On the inn card which was handed to us by the woman in charge was printed in red, "1407—85 years before America was discovered". This was presumably meant to interest Americans but seemed to me a crude means of doing so.

The artist whom we came to see is Monsieur Henguet. His *atelier*, only a few steps from the medieval house, was at the top of a spiral flight of creaking wooden stairs, which reminded me of the duelling stories associated with the spiral staircases inside the ancient wynds and closes along the Royal Mile at Edinburgh. I wondered if any ghost had ever walked up and down the wooden steps here.

We rang the bell and a coarse voice called, *"Entrez."* The door opened and immediately a rusty basin fell from the top of a huge pile of objects. The narrow passage was reduced to a bare foot by continuous lines of objects on both sides. No one appeared. Madeleine sidled her way along and I did my best to follow her. Monsieur Henguet was at work in a little room facing us at the end of the narrow passage. He stepped out to greet us in his white overall, raising his two hands covered with plaster of paris to show that he could not shake hands. He looked over seventy, but from his voice and his walk he could not be more than fifty. No time was wasted on ceremony. He expected us to go into his room with him, but I had to leave my left foot outside the door. My friend tried leaning against the door jamb, but in a few moments she was forced outside altogether.

Monsieur Henguet was working on the enormous head of a stage dog. His model was a very small photograph. I was amazed at the immense enlargement. The base of the head was made of papier mâché. Monsieur Henguet kept adding small pieces of linen or canvas here and there by means of thick, liquid plaster of paris, talking as he did so. Fragments of the plaster fell on my hands and a tiny dot on my nose; many more fragments must have landed elsewhere.

Monsieur Henguet told us that from childhood up he had always been interested in making things with his hands. When a model did not turn out satisfactorily, he went to museums and libraries to check the details. He had never received any training; his craft was entirely self-taught. Yet he could supply any object asked for. He never refused a demand, or disappointed a customer. His sole interest is in his work, and if necessary he will labour until any hour of the night. The most trying aspect of his work, he said, is that theatre orders usually have to be finished in a short time, and sometimes many orders come together.

His subject-matter ranges from Peru to China: a human face of any race, a head of any type; bird, beast, fish, insect, plant; even foodstuffs. In a much bigger room than the little one in which we found him working, he took down several huge heads of well-known personalities in the theatrical world of Paris,

and also showed us the photographs from which he had worked. The likenesses were excellent. We could hardly find room for our feet, and it was clear that only Monsieur Henguet himself could put the heads back in place without disturbing other objects.

In yet another room, smaller than the second one but bigger than the first, I managed to find better foothold than Madeleine; but her balance was soon upset again, for she could not stop laughing when Monsieur Henguet showed us in rapid succession the large duck-beak-lipped head of an African tribesman, the tattooed face of a Red Indian, an orange, a well-cooked lobster, and a huge piece of meat looking as fresh

E

as if it had just left the butcher's. I thought of buying that piece of meat to take back with me to England, so that I could keep it in the larder and have a look at it every day. All these objects appeared from nowhere and disappeared without our noticing where they went. Monsieur Henguet takes his work seriously and did not smile or joke at all as he explained the processes point by point. He told us that one minute someone would come asking for the head of a brown bear, the next he would be asked to do the head of the President of the Republic. Madeleine rocked with laughter. That was the jolliest moment we had there. Monsieur Henguet took no notice of us; for he was busy taking out a number of large books to show me. One of them contained many types of old Chinese costumes, which, he said, he copied from time to time.

During this time the door-bell had rung at intervals. First came a young couple who wanted *les bras*, a huge structure in papier mâché with four long arms and hands stretching out in different directions from the shoulders of a short trunk. Monsieur Henguet said that the person wearing this disguise would add his own two arms through the neck-hole. Next came two middle-aged ladies in fur coats who wanted to have the head of a polar bear specially made. The price and date for collecting it were fixed in no time and the ladies went away. Just before the door-bell rang for the third time, Monsieur Henguet's only assistant, a woman, interrupted us to ask what colour she should use for the lower part of the body of a kangaroo. No sooner had Monsieur Henguet told her than in streamed three young people, first a boy, then a girl, then another boy. The girl seemed to be the secretary of some organisation which wanted two complete monkey outfits. From the third little room Monsieur Henguet took monkey heads from beneath a pile of articles on a shelf. Next minute he produced from another pile two one-piece outfits of black and brown hair, which the young men tried on, transforming themselves into a chimpanzee and an orang-outang respectively. "*Ce n'est pas complet,*" said Monsieur Henguet, moving a number of things from one pile to another, and presently extracting two pairs of monkey-paw gloves. Something was still missing. Monsieur Henguet stood thinking. Eventually he turned over a few more piles and handed out two pairs of shoes in the shape of the hind paws of monkeys. "*Ah! C'est parfait!*"

There was something magical about Monsieur Henguet's *atelier*. Madeleine and I found it hardly possible to set our feet down safely, yet many customers came, dressed up, changed back again and went without noticeable difficulty. What interested me most was the apparently haphazard way in which Monsieur Henguet stored his stock and the rapidity with which he found any particular article. I thought of my own rooms in Oxford, where I often fail to find what I want, when I want it. Notes, sketches and books may be mislaid for days. The lady of the family with whom I live often urges me to let her sort out my things and put them in order, but I seldom give way. This is an admitted weakness in my way of living. Monsieur Henguet does not have it and I envy him.

I also envy Monsieur Henguet's unceasing energy and unflagging interest. He tackles each job with care and seriousness, not just with a 'This will do' attitude. He told us that he never lacked work and that he worked on Sundays just as hard as on weekdays. His charge for a piece of work seemed to me quite reasonable and even modest in the face of the present cost of living in Paris. I asked him why he did not charge more. His reply was that if he had been busy thinking how much he should get for his work, he could never have done so much in all the past years. A holy attitude towards one's work!

I asked him why he did not engage an apprentice to help him. This brought forth an outburst against the Government and modern regulations. His type of business, said Monsieur Henguet, with its moderate income, receives no official protection or assistance. As he works entirely by himself, the Government ignores him. He cannot afford to pay Health Insurance premiums for unproductive young employees. In the past he had been able to forget the Government, and he would like to do so still, but Government forms arrived and had to be filled up. Once he had asked a young cousin to help him when he was pushed for time, and during that period he had never ceased to be harrassed by Government officials; much of his time had been wasted in answering questions, and ultimately he had been obliged to terminate the engagement. His only assistant now, the girl we had seen, does only a very small part of the work. A real apprentice would immediately ask how much he would earn; and in Monsieur Henguet's opinion, if one's mind is concentrated on earning, rather than on doing one's work well, one is more of a nuisance than a help. Interest and belief in what one is creating is the first essential. He knew that he could not continue his work for ever, but somewhere in Paris, he felt sure, there must be someone else teaching himself as Monsieur Henguet had taught himself, and willing to carry on the tradition.

Before leaving I bowed to Monsieur Henguet with deep appreciation of the spirit in which he works.

Back to work after lunch

VIII

The True Face of the Butte

I HAVE heard three explanations of the name MONTMARTRE, as everyone now calls La Butte, the mound overlooking Paris: first, that it is a reference to the temple of Mars built on La Butte in Roman days; second, that it is a corruption of the name of Marat, for during the French Revolution it was called Montmarat; third, and most commonly, that it commemorates the martyrdom of St Denis.

The legend tells how St Denis, after being beheaded on this hill by the Roman garrison, picked up his head and, holding it before him, walked round the hill northwards in search of a burial-place for his decapitated self. Reaching a suitable spot five miles north of Paris, he collapsed. The Abbey Church of St Denis now stands on the spot.

Perhaps it is because I come from a non-Christian country and have always admired the steadfastness of the many Christians who have gone to their death for their faith that I found the association of Montmartre with St Denis so appropriate. But I seem to be alone in this feeling, for the thousands of people who come, day and night, to visit Montmartre do not appear to do so with the intention of paying homage to the martyred Patron Saint of France. This is perhaps why there is no official explanation for the name MONTMARTRE and also why the normally statue-minded French have erected no striking monument to the martyr on the hill.

Of the visitors to Montmartre while I was there, everyone had a head on his shoulders. Some were seeking the bohemian quarter of Paris. Some had read that the great feature of Montmartre was the windmills, the sails of which Parisians can see merrily revolving in the wind, a novelty in any city. Some were convinced that Montmartre is a synonym for night-clubs, bars and shows: in Montmartre at midnight one would hear every language under the sun except French. Some believed that Montmartre was not merely picturesque, but the

most historic spot in France: there had been a Roman camp on
the hill; in 978 Otto of Germany having advanced so far
towards Paris sang a *Te Deum* on Montmartre and went away;
at the close of the sixteenth century Henri IV made his headquarters at Montmartre when he besieged Paris; during the
Revolution Montmartre suffered disturbance no less than other
parts of Paris; in 1815 English troops occupied Montmartre for
a while; on March 18th, 1871, the Commune began at Montmartre, and near the old Church of St Pierre Generals Lecomte
and Clément were shot. Many whom I met lament that Montmartre, without Degas, Toulouse-Lautrec, Renoir and the

A side-road near the Place Pigalle

rest, is now 'dead'. The many-sidedness of Montmartre bewildered me; unlike the other visitors, I wandered alone about
Montmartre, more than once figuratively without a head.

My first visit was made with two friends. We came out of the
Metro at the Place Pigalle. The Boulevard de Clichy was as
brilliantly lit with neon lights as Piccadilly or Times Square,
even though many of the lights were not revolving. Before my
eyes had grown used to the glare, my ears were deafened by a
great roar coming from a row of stalls and caravans with
merry-go-rounds and other attractions in between, very

similar to the English fair on Hampstead Heath on Easter Monday or August Bank Holiday. One of my friends began immediately to try to push a heavy weight up a slanting iron bar so that it would hit a small cannon, which would then explode and destroy a picture of an ocean liner. My friend tried three times before he succeeded. His pleasure in his success was promptly damped by a robust young Frenchman who followed him and hit the cannon three times in succession. The owner of the game pulled a long face and all the by-standers laughed loudly. The owner added another weight and invited the young man to try again without paying. The young man took off his pullover, licked his hands, and was again successful. He then picked up his pullover and walked off. Amidst the laughter one old man remarked that this stout fellow would have taken his trousers off if he had been asked to try a third time.

We walked along the row of stalls. The crowd was small and business was slack. In my short stay in Paris I had already seen the same row of stalls at the Place d'Italie, along the pavement of the Boulevard St Michel, and in other places. It seemed to be a mobile unit. If so, it was no wonder the spectators displayed no great enthusiasm.

We proceeded along the Boulevard de Clichy, where the well-known Chat Noir, Deux, and the Theatre de Dix Heures were pointed out to me. We did not enter any of these *cabarets*, as I had been told that to follow the show it was necessary not only to have a sound knowledge of French, but also a knowledge of current happenings in France. I had read how the old Chat Noir used to be a rendezvous of artists and bohemians at the time when the artist and poet Willette painted the sign, a black cat with golden eyes within a silver crescent. The present establishment is too expensive for the old type of customer.

I paid my next visit to Montmartre alone, walking up the hill from the Metro station at Chateau-Rouge. The lofty building surmounted by a great dome on the Boulevard Barbés caught my eye, and I learned that it was the Maison Dufayel, or Palais de la Nouveauté, a department store like Harrods in London or Macy's in New York. I was surprised to hear that the late Monsieur Dufayel, who built it, was the first businessman to start the hire-purchase system of payment which has become so common an arrangement, particularly in the United States. I wondered why he had wanted to add one more dome to the many already in Paris. Probably it was to impress his customers.

Passing through the rue André del Sarte, I found myself at the base of the steps leading to the hill near the rue Lamarck. It was a sunny Sunday morning. Parisian families were sitting on the benches and stone steps, their children running around. The climb was an effort, and I turned back at intervals to gaze at the view. The massive structure of the Sacré Cœur made me recoil when I saw it first. I felt oppressed by its enormous size, particularly by the central dome, which towered over the lower parts of the building. The brilliant white of the structure was to me a little incongruous in the mellow, greyish-blue of Paris. It would fit better, I thought, into New York or Washington. The sandy soil of the hill being too shifting to bear the weight of such an immense edifice, the foundations had to be driven right through the hill. I liked the thought that the church would still remain standing if the hill were to be removed.

I did not at once go into the church, but turned to look at the panorama of the city below. A sea of dark-blue slate roofs was softened by the morning mist to a paler tint. Here and there were rosy and purplish patches, the shadows of red-painted chimneys. The Eiffel Tower was the mast of a huge ship anchored somewhere on the right, while the twin towers of Notre Dame were two piles of hay on a long barge. Other church spires, the domes of the Invalides, the Institut and the Panthéon, partly and faintly visible, were all masts of one type or another, making me feel that I was viewing Chinese junks on a stretch of the Yangtse River. However, the chattering children and their happy shouts from the steps below, together with the noise of a loud-speaker blaring forth in French, English and Spanish a warning to all visitors not to buy post-cards of the Sacré Cœur from street-vendors, but to buy them inside the basilica, shattered my illusion.

I did not want to buy any postcards, but I went inside just the same. A service was on and there was quite a large attend-ance. I was told that the whole interior took the form of a Greek cross, but I could not distinguish it very well with so many people in the centre of the nave. Its construction was begun in 1875, but the walls were still bare, the grey granite was exposed as if newly-cut. It is said to be able to hold 8,000 people. It was

'Love and Be Religious, Montmartre!'

grand enough, but it did not inspire me with awe as did the Cathedral of Notre Dame. I then paid my entrance to the crypt, which contained nothing and was not gloomy enough to depress me like those of many old churches, for it seemed to be still under construction. There was a good-sized model of the basilica, which was placed on a table near the staircase, and someone was explaining its structure to a few visitors. I did not join the audience, for I wanted to find my way up the dome. I managed to get up there with some difficulty, for the ascent was not an easy one. I had a much wider view than the one I had had from the front steps—this time not only southwards, but all around to some distant, hill-like images in the west and north of Paris. Before I descended and left the church I also had a look at the enormous bell, La Savoyarde, ten feet in diameter, weighing sixteen tons, a present from the women of Savoy, the chime of which is said to be heard thirty miles away.

Round the corner of the rue Razais I found myself in the Place du Tertre, practically the highest point of Paris, the centre of the original village of Montmartre and today the Mecca of the Montmartre tourist. As it was early in the day and still winter, there were no tables and chairs set out in the square, but a few children were playing there. I noticed a house named 'La Maison des Poulbots' and remembered that Madeleine Chambert was a 'mother' of the Petits Poulbots of Montmartre. She had told me that the house of the artist Poulbot, well known some thirty years ago for his studies of French child life, was now a home for children. In his lifetime he had arranged Christmas parties for 2,000 children of Montmartre in the hall attached to Le Moulin de la Galette. Each child received a present from the great tree in the centre. Poulbot was helped in this work by his brother-artists, Forain, Willette, Neumont, and by other people interested in giving the less fortunate youngsters of Montmartre a good time. As I watched the children an elderly man appeared with a large bundle of American-looking comics under his arm and began to distribute them. Poulbot in modern guise!

I did not linger long in the Place du Tertre. I wanted to get down to the Place Pigalle, the centre of Lower Montmartre, for I had been told of the gay scene to be observed there each morning. Models, chiefly Italian or French, of different ages, in gay-coloured costumes sit in small groups round the fountain chattering and laughing, keeping their eyes open for prospective employers. Noted artists, and budding artists too, come to prospect, choose a girl, engage her in talk, and soon artist and model leave the Place and enter a café or go to the artist's studio to start work. In the end some models are left without employers and some artists without models, but there is always tomorrow. This model market in the Place Pigalle is quite unique. But I had come on a Sunday, or maybe at too late an hour, for I found myself alone at the fountain.

Artist friends of mine tell me that nowadays they have great difficulty in finding satisfactory models. Modelling is a profession depending for its existence upon demand: upon there being enough artists anxious to draw from the living model and able to pay for the privilege. Few artists can now afford to employ a full-time model, so the best models tend to go into the fashion trade. But a quite different explanation of the scarcity was put forward at a party I attended. An experienced Parisian model was the centre of attraction, not solely because of her beauty, but also because of the striking dress she wore and the way she moved and talked. Someone asked her if she had modelled for certain well-known artists. "Fancy asking me that!" she retorted; and she went on to pour out her grievance against modern art. According to her, the founders of Cubist, Abstract, Surrealist and other schools of modern art had deprived models of their livelihood. She recalled her luxurious, gay and carefree existence when, as a girl of fifteen, she had begun to sit for artists. Her mother too had been a model; and so far from taking her declining state with resignation, had organised with some friends in like case with herself a 'march' from the Place Pigalle to each of the big *ateliers* of lower and upper Montmartre in turn to protest against their unemployment. Those artists who disapproved of the modern trends received them kindly, and their protest created a stir in the art world of the time, but in the end it achieved nothing else. Artists continued to prefer circles, squares and triangles to models; they were *plus facile et bon marché*. Piccasso was her *gros ennemi*. Had it not been for the 'madness' of Picasso, she contended, she and her friends would still be enjoying life with a couple of hours' modelling in the daytime and the evening in a *cabaret*. Now they had sometimes to go hungry. Excited by a few drinks, she made us all roar with laughter when she pulled a long face, kept one eye wide open, shut the other, and twisted her body so as to expose one thigh in a manner suggesting a well-known work by her *gros ennemi*. Snorting with indignation, she remarked that she would long since have killed herself if she had possessed such a face and body. "And would you have invited me to this party?" she concluded. . . .

The long row of glass doors of the Moulin Rouge disappointed me as much as the emptiness of the Place Pigalle. The days of Toulouse-Lautrec are no more. Except for the red-painted windmill above the neon sign, the building might have been a cinema on Broadway. I crossed the Boulevard de Clichy to look at a queer shop-entrance in the form of a Chinese-looking lion's wide-open mouth. It was *Le Ciel et l'Enfer*. To me it did not look attractive enough for heaven, nor gruesome enough for hell; and being, as a silent traveller, concerned with what lies between those two extremes, I strolled on along the rue de Pigalle. The rays of the fanciful and colourful designs which entirely cover the walls on one side glared sharply into my eyes. Every one of the premises was a night-club, a restaurant or a cabaret, and no two had similar entrances. The design of one, for example, is that of a pack of playing cards spread all over the wall and door. New York contains no street to rival the rue Pigalle. Oddly, however, in the one night club I entered the entertainers seemed to have come from the Bowery and the clientele spoke little French. On the opposite side of the street a shop-sign caught my eye: "Piccadilly." The letters were written vertically, but with the two 'c's' and the two 'l's' side by side. I wondered if any English visitors had noticed this.

Pigalle was a French sculptor of the eighteenth century, whose work round the pedestal of the statue of Louis XV in the Place de la Concorde and in the Palais de Chaillot can easily pass unnoticed. He is no longer widely known himself, but the fame of the street named after him extends far beyond the boundaries of Paris.

I visited Montmartre again and again. Once, tired of wandering, I entered the Cirque Mérano, the circus rich in associations with Degas and Toulouse-Lautrec. The programme comprised all the usual turns. The only peculiarity for me was that the clowns spoke French. The laughter of the boys and girls in the audience was infectious, and made me sorry that

I did not yet know any French children. I had never before, I realised, attended a circus unaccompanied by children. The unknown youngsters around me possessed more local colour, I felt sure, than all the *cabarets* and night-clubs of Montmartre.

Emerging from the Mérano, I tried to imagine Montmartre as the pleasant country hillside it had been up to 1830, with vines and windmills everywhere. Two of the oldest windmills still stand, though the sails of both are still: Le Bute-Fin dates from 1245, Le Radet from 1268. A friend suggested that the sails of these windmills have grown too heavy with the tears of the lovers who have climbed their stairs for so many generations to revolve any more. "No one is allowed to go up the stairs now," he continued; "they are unsafe. And it does not matter, for today there are no lovers who shed tears." Any allusion to the topic of love can lead to hours of conversation in Paris. I did not agree with the depressing suggestion that real lovers no longer exist. Modern lovers differ from their forbears only in respect of *speed*. The old tactics of dropping the handkerchief or singing and playing the guitar on horseback are too slow in an era of cars and aeroplanes. Tears have no time to flow!

I should have liked to trace the footsteps of Degas, Toulouse-Lautrec, Renoir, Utrillo and the rest, but although I had long been able to distinguish their work, I did not know what each of them looked like in his days of artistic creation. I wanted to visualise their gait, their mannerisms and their postures when sketching or painting. Now and then I fancied I met Utrillo returning from studying the Sacré Cœur, from the rue St Rustique or the rue Norvins. Of the sketches I made myself round Montmartre, the view I liked best was the faint image of the dome of the Sacré Cœur in the early morning mist seen from the rue de L'Abreuvoir. Utrillo made a picture of the view from almost the same spot as mine, but I doubt if he got up so early to see it.

Despite the number of my visits to Montmartre, Madeleine Chambert was positive that I had overlooked some points of interest, and she asked Monsieur Paul Yaki, author of *Le Montmartre de nos Vingt Ans*, to show us round. Fan Chun-P'i came to make up the party of four. About four o'clock one afternoon we emerged from the Abbesses Metro station and found Monsieur Yaki there to greet us. He has been the

Conservateur du Vieux Montmartre for more than thirty years and every hair of his well-trimmed white moustache has a tale to tell.

He began by telling us that on the spot where we were standing at that moment there once stood the Abbaye des

View near by the Lapin Agile

Dames, various abbesses of which had played prominent parts in their time. As late as the eighteenth century the ruling abbess prevented the territory surrounding her nunnery from being included within the boundaries of Paris. Long before that, Henri IV, whose headquarters were on Montmartre, gave protection to the nunnery on account of the good looks of the sixteen-year-old abbess of his day. Monsieur Yaki smiled as if thinking that Henri IV well earned the name, Le Vert Galant.

From the rue des Abbesses we walked along the rue Antoinette to the Place Dancourt, where we saw a scene made familiar by Utrillo's painting. Facing us was the first theatre to be built and owned by private persons in Paris or in fact in the whole of France. The story goes that after Louis XVIII came to the throne, a young man claimed the crown as heir of Louis XVI. He got some support, but this inspired others to make the same claim, and that weakened his case. At length an old man came forward and said he had adopted the young man from childhood and had papers to witness that there was no basis for his claim to the throne. Out of relief at being thus rid of a troublesome claimant, Louis XVIII decreed that six theatres might be built, owned and run without control from the Government. The theatre before us was one of the six. It was formerly called the Théatre de Montmartre, but later became the Théatre de l'Atelier. In modern times, under the directorship of Charles Dullin, it prospered for more than twenty years and many new and notable plays were staged in it. Since Dullin's death a few years ago it has changed, but business still goes on there.

The March afternoon was dull and rather cold. But on our way up the steps of the Sacré Cœur, the sun suddenly came out and Monsieur Yaki remarked that he had been born in Toulouse, where he had been a good friend of the sun, which had therefore appeared at his request to greet us. I asked how he, a southerner, had come to be the Conservateur of old Montmartre. He replied that after passing the examination for the General Post Office, he had asked to be posted to Paris, either in the Latin Quarter or in Montmartre. During the years he had worked in one of the local post offices in the Latin Quarter his love for Montmartre grew deeper and deeper and he made friends with many of the noted artists. At last he was transferred to Montmartre. I judged by the warmth in his voice when he mentioned *"mon ami,* Renoir" that Renoir had meant much to him. In his book, *Le Montmartre de nos Vingt Ans,* a sketch of Monsieur Yaki by Modigliani forms the frontispiece. Eventually Monsieur Yaki became, what he still is, Le Président de l'Association des Artists du Vieux-Montmartre. At the age of seventy he has one more ambition, to be buried among his artist-friends in Montmartre Cemetery. Unfortunately a plot there costs 150,000 francs (1952) which, says Monsieur Yaki with a sigh, he cannot afford. Madeleine tried to cheer him by saying that so long as one's soul is at rest, it does not matter where one's body lies buried. He did not agree.

At the top of the Sacré Cœur steps one of us asked Monsieur Yaki's opinion of this impressive edifice. He replied that he had got used to it now. He went on to tell us how, during the occupation of Paris by a foreign force in the nineteenth century, the French came from all over the country to pray at the

summit of Montmartre. This is why Montmartre was chosen as
the site of the national war shrine. More than eighty architectural designs were submitted. When the building was
finished and formally consecrated in October, 1919, the artists
of Montmartre organised a demonstration and went round
shouting *"Vive le Diable! Vive le Diable!"* for hours.

Monsieur Yaki pointed out a statue of the Chevalier de la
Barre, sentenced to death in 1766 at Amiens for failing, at the
age of nineteen, to salute a religious procession. The statue is
directly in front of the church.

We turned westwards along the rue Razais. My companions
were deep in conversation in French. I leaned on the stone wall
for a moment. The sun was still high above the horizon, but
its rays hardly penetrated the thick mist which had risen
imperceptibly. The full face of the sun was like a huge Jaffa
orange, tinged with red, which turned the black steel frame-
work of the Eiffel Tower a dull red too. Not a roof or tree-top
was visible below. Among the radiations of the orange sun was
a vertical reddish line soaring up from the cloudy plain. It was
an enchanting picture, but an unpaintable one. Both the circle
and the line possessed life, and any man-made imitation of them
would have lacked that vital quality. My mind suddenly turned
to Chinese calligraphy and I realised once again the truth of our
ancient teaching that the calligrapher should infuse life into his
strokes. The tendency of modern art throughout the world is
towards the calligraphic rather than the graphic, and the
infusion of life into the strokes is of the first importance. . . .

A call to rejoin the others broke my reverie; in a state of
confusion, I could only point to the scene and say: *"C'est joli."*
Monsieur Yaki smiled and murmured: *"Mais voilà cette
curiosité-là!"* pointing to the Eiffel Tower.

We stopped outside the ancient church of St Pierre de
Montmartre in the rue du Mont Cenis close to the Sacré
Cœur. Monsieur Yaki told us that it was built by Louis le Gros
in 1143, and restored in 1593 by Henri IV at the request of
Marie de Beauvilliers, Abbesse de Montmartre. A part of this
church served the Benedictines of the Abbey; the remainder
was allotted to the parishioners of Montmartre. In the eighteen-
eighties, when the demolition of this ancient edifice was
decreed, Willette, with a group of his brother-artists, demanded
its preservation. They made speeches in the Place du Tertre

and in the restaurants, and eventually secured the help of Clemenceau. This, together with the efforts of the Société des Amis des Monuments Parisiens, turned the scale, and the church was saved and reopened for worship in February, 1908. Willette was later elected President of the Associations of Roman Catholics, but, Monsieur Yaki stressed, he remained a bohemian. I was glad to find a city which listened to its artists.

Madeleine knows this ancient church very well. She used to pray in it when she came to attend to business in La Maison des Poulbots. She suggested that we should go inside, wrapping her head in a black silk scarf as she spoke. She pointed out several Roman pillars, said to have been taken from the temples of Mars and Mercury which stood at the east and west ends of the small plateau that crowned the summit of the hill in Roman days. I was particularly taken with a small Roman statuette of a lady sitting amongst her children. The sculpture has been left high up on a wall. It is said that Dante once worshipped within these walls and St Ignatius Loyola meditated while planning his 'Society', which became the Jesuit Order or Society of Jesus.

We passed through the Place du Tertre and the rue Norvins into the rue des Saules. A painting of a rabbit jumping out of a frying-pan on the wall of a rustic-looking house had puzzled me often, and I listened eagerly to Monsieur Yaki's explanation of it. Apparently the artist, A. Gill, used to enjoy his favourite dish in this tavern and made the painting for the owner as a tribute. Friends seeking Gill could never find him except here, so that eventually 'Le Lapin Agile' stood for himself and this painting. Now the painting is the signboard of the tavern and cabaret—a famous one in Montmartre, where artists, poets and bohemians of the late nineteenth and early twentieth century met night after night. Poets came to recite their verses; composers to sing their songs; artists to make known their new works; bohemians to indulge their wit; and so on. Monsieur Yaki knew many of them and was one of the regular visitors.

The tavern is surrounded by a fence which looks like wood but is actually now made of concrete. As we rested against the posts Monsieur Yaki began to tell us a strange tale. While the Impressionists and Post-Impressionists were at the height of their influence, many other schools—Cubists, Fauvists, etc.—were founded in this tavern. Nearly every customer frequenting

it wished to found a new school. One day two young artists
came with a donkey which they tied to one of the fence posts.
They brought several large cans full of oil pigment and fixed
them in a position behind the donkey so that its tail could dip
into the paint. One of the young adventurers then began to
feed juicy carrots to the donkey, while his partner held a large
canvas close to its tail. The more the donkey enjoyed the carrots, the more its tail swept to and fro, making wonderful
strokes and dots on the canvas. The young man who held the
canvas shifted it now and then until the whole space was filled
with pigment. Then the pair took the work back to their
atelier and returned the donkey to its owner. After scrutinising
the canvas from every angle, they decided to call the work
'*Coucher du Soleil sur l'Adriatique*'. They signed it L. Teduab. They
submitted the work to a salon for an important exhibition of
the year and it was accepted. When the salon opened a noted
critic gave it particular attention, with a reproduction and a
long dissertation on its merits. Those in the know laughed with
malicious joy. But this was nothing to the laughter which
ensued when it was realised that one had only to read the
signature Teduab backwards to arrive at the identity of the
artist as *le Baudet*—'the donkey'. Monsieur Yaki remarked
gently that there was always someone to make a joke of things.
Since that time few new schools of painting had been founded
and Le Lapin Agile carries on its business with fewer artists,
poets and composers as habitués. The Bohemian way of life
is more difficult to live nowadays, Monsieur Yaki concluded.

Between the rue des Saules and the rue Saint Vincent, a large
house above the vineyard of the 'Vigne de Paris' was pointed
out to us as the one where Renoir had lived and where he
painted the large canvas, '*Moulin de la Galette*', which now
hangs in the Jeu de Paume. Then Monsieur Yaki took us to
see his friend, Monsieur Platon, *le Potier du vieux-montmartre*, in
his pottery shop in the rue Lepic. Madame Platon was working
at a design on a plate under an old-fashioned oil lamp. We
were welcomed and urged to look round. There was pottery
everywhere—plates, cups, pots—all created by Monsieur and
Madame Platon. Each piece bore as design some landmark of
old Montmartre. The windmills and the basilica of the Sacré
Cœur seemed to be the most popular.

After this short rest, we walked briskly to a small recreation ground for children where there was plenty of sand, but no grass. Some of the children were throwing sand at one another and the dusty air prevented our going too near them. In the centre of the small square there was a new sandstone statue of St Denis holding his head in his hands. The legend says that in his search for a burial-place the saint found a spring here and stopped to wash the blood from his head and hands. The water of the spring immediately became holy water and effected many cures. Monsieur Yaki remarked that many a young man used to take his fiancée on their wedding day to drink this spring water before the couple went to church for the service; the holy water was said to keep a wife faithful through life. Fan Chun-pi was quick to say jokingly that she would tell her three sons to come here before they were married. But Monsieur Yaki disappointed her by adding that the spring had been dry for more than a hundred years and in that time Montmartre had become more infested with night-clubs and cabarets than any other part of Paris. We all wondered why the brides of those earlier days did not insist on their bridegrooms drinking the holy water too!

We then went to have a look at No. 13, rue Ravignan, but only from the outside, for Monsieur Yaki did not know the present occupant. It was said to be Picasso's first Parisian lodging, when, an unknown and penniless young man, he came from Spain in 1904, only a year after I was born. His name in Chinese, Pi-ka-So, became known to me some thirty years ago through the young artists of Shanghai's Man-Pa-La-Ssu (Montparnasse). Now Picasso is reputed to be the wealthiest artist alive. In the whole history of art very few masters have enjoyed so much wealth and fame as he. Quite the contrary as a rule. I think the success he has won by his art has been greatly facilitated, on the one hand, by the more art-conscious or art-minded public of the present age, and on the other by the advancement of methods of reproduction and printing and the uncommon enthusiasm of modern art critics writing about his work, thus rousing the interest of the general public. His versatility still keeps public interest alive, even increases it, and this is something which former masters have rarely attempted. Generally, art comes alive with time; Picasso's art lives in its own time.

The houses along the rue Ravignan are mostly artists'

studios, one of which was occupied by a friend of Monsieur Yaki. He did not know if his friend would be in or not, for he had made no arrangement beforehand. Just the same he went down, through a long corridor, to knock on the door. It flew open and we were soon introduced to his friend by Monsieur Yaki. The studio was full of animals, chiefly wild ones, such as lions, tigers, cheetahs, etc., in oil as well as in stone, wood and bronze. Monsieur Yaki's friend was at work on a large canvas when we came. But the face of the lion, which had just been finished, did not seem to be as congenial and smiling as the artist who had made us so welcome. However, we did not want to interrupt his work for long and soon left him alone. After having said goodbye to Monsieur Yaki and then seen my two companions safely on their way home, I returned to wander by myself.

There was still daylight when the sight of an open gate along the rue Duratin enticed me into a courtyard flanked on three sides by many-storied houses. I made a sketch of them. From outside they were hidden. I was quite pleased with myself at having discovered them. I concluded that most of the other tall modern house-fronts I had seen on the slope between lower and upper Montmartre must also conceal courtyards of the old Paris style. Only a hundred years ago Montmartre was a village of less than a thousand inhabitants. The population must have grown tremendously within this short period. What do all the people do who have no connection with night-clubs, cabarets and restaurants? I seldom saw them in the street; nor did I meet any at that moment when twilight was fading. The roads which we had covered a few hours before were now dark and quiet, except for the occasional running steps of one or two children.

Presently I found myself back in the Place du Tertre. The small square space measuring about forty yards each way and lined with trees was now filled with tables and chairs; a few coloured umbrellas with tassels were open over the tables. The evening was not warm, but neither was it cold, for the bright electric lights and shop signs and the colourful—chiefly red— walls as well as the noisy chatter beneath the umbrellas kept chilliness at bay. Many Easter visitors to Paris had already made their way here. I had a walk round the square and the conversations which forced their way into my ears were familiar.

A huge American car drove into the square. Unexpectedly a taxicab approached from the opposite direction. They faced each other only a step away from Chez Ma Cousine. The taxi-driver stuck his head out of the side-window and poured out a stream of cheerful abuse. The other driver did not answer, being fully occupied with the handling of his very large car in the narrow space. To reverse was impossible. Presently he stuck his head out of his side-window and shouted in his turn. Chefs, waitresses and café hands appeared in every doorway and laughed. It seemed an *impasse*. In the end the taxi-driver managed to squeeze past by drawing up on to the narrow pavement in front of a picture gallery. The huge car moved on to find a parking place and order was restored.

I found a small table and ordered a glass of red wine. It lasted as long as I sat there, enjoying a much-needed rest. The sound of cars coming and going was constant. For a moment I shut my eyes in relaxation without a thought in my head. Suddenly I was woken up by a young man sitting down in the empty chair at my table. He asked me in French if I wanted my portrait sketched. He was about twenty-five, with a thick, brownish beard spreading from his chin up his cheeks to join the hair at his temples and make a complete circle round a thin, pale face, out of which sparkled very blue eyes. His long neck seemed much too thin in the wide-open collar of his American Army-surplus overcoat. I answered that I did not know French and that I was sorry I did not want to be sketched. To my surprise, he replied in fluent English that he was an American from California, where he had many Chinese friends. He hoped I should not mind if he sat and talked for a while. There was no stopping him, anyway. He had been in Paris for about two years, originally studying art. He liked Paris so much that, against his parents' wish, he had stayed on. They did not understand art and had no faith in it. A waitress appearing at this moment, I ordered a glass of red wine for him, though I explained that I myself was not really a drinker. He continued to talk. Later in a whisper he told me how he had to speak French to his clients, as the visitors to Montmartre were mostly English and American, who liked to see if they could make themselves understood in their school French. Business came his way, to be sure. Two years' stay had turned him French in every way. He had not been spotted by his clients so

far, though he still dreaded to meet the local Montmartreer!
He gave me a wink when he said it. As he stood up to go, he
patted my shoulder, saying it had been nice to meet me and
begging me not to give him away. He had already emptied his
glass. Now he took up my glass to finish it for me. He might be
a future Mary Cassatt, though a man. Smilingly we waved to
each other before he was lost to sight. It was a strange con-
clusion to my silent travels in Montmartre.

IX

A Crag from an Eastern Land

S N O W fell in the early morning, heavy rain followed, and now a mad wind whipped me from my post outside the Metro station where I was to meet Francine. While I was wondering whether a fragile young lady would venture out on such a cold morning, she was suddenly there beside me. A bus stopped in front of us at the same moment, and before I knew it we were both inside. She laughed at my suggestion of postponement.

Houses rolled past and men staggered along the pavement against the wind. Our bus moved quickly, but halted often. Through the window I saw a long barge glide through the high arch of a bridge over the St Martin Canal. The barge appeared to be on a level with us, so high was the water. After two more stops we got out and walked some way to the top of a high mound from which we could see the Sacré Cœur in the distance, with two large buildings on high ground, like guards, on either side of the impressive view in the foregound. Francine remarked that she did not mind seeing the Sacré Cœur from a good way off.

I did not know where we were; nor did Francine. But she was sure that we were not at the place she wanted to show me. We stood high enough to obtain a bird's-eye view over Paris. Unfortunately, some low mist concealed a good part of the view, but this had the effect of making the white domes of the Sacré Cœur hang in the air. The mad wind dropped. There were some quite clear patches in the sky. More rain did not seem likely. We circled the mound and followed a winding street downwards. When we reached the main road we discovered that the road we had just descended was called rue Edgar-Allan-Poe. His stories grip me. The statue of Shakespeare in the Boulevard Haussmann occurred to me. Paris is a more internationally-minded city than most.

We were now on the high ground of a park with well-made roads to walk on and fine, tall trees with their bare branches weaving intriguing patterns to look at. The light mist which clung round the tops of trees gave the interlacing branches an ethereal quality. The air was mild and fresh. All material thoughts vanished from my mind. I felt light and alive, not burdened with details, but filled with a mysterious simplicity. We moved on, gazing ahead in agreeable silence. On one side of the road we were following, the ground sloped gradually down to a wide stretch of woodland, which looked inviting. As soon as we came out of the trees flanking our road I drew a deep breath. The whole stretch of woodland became full of satisfaction. Francine was silent; she is a perfect walking companion.

Our steps slackened a little. I pointed out a kind of wintry purple colour among the branches below us. One could imagine a fire inside the woods, for the mist was rising like wreaths of smoke. Francine rubbed her hands and cried, "Let's go there." We quickened our steps to hurry down the slope. The scene became narrower; thick trees and long grass blocked our view. Then my eyes followed Francine's finger, which was pointing to the golden gleam of masses of long yellow tassels on a little willow tree. "What a perfect ornament of early spring!" I commented.

Some distance ahead of us was a bower-like structure. We began to make it our goal. When the road ended, a narrow winding path between many grotesque-shaped and oddly-placed rocks led us to the bower. It turned out to be a copy of the Sybil's Temple at Tivoli. The tip above the round roof was a cross. There must be magnificent views of Paris from this high point of the park, but our gaze and imagination went on into mysterious, mist-veiled infinity.

We did not need to retrace our steps, for a narrow, rocky path led down the cliff to some unexpected scenery. A phrase of the English poet John Keats came to me: "The only way to strengthen one's intellect is to make up one's mind about nothing." I was glad of this impressive sanction for emptying my mind as we climbed down. To our left was the top of the cliff on which the temple stood; to the right the cliff dropped hundreds of feet to a large sheet of water.

I plodded along behind Francine, my feet kicking childishly at stones in the way. Suddenly a loud, hoarse croak sounded from the temple and a pair of ravens alighted on the roof. Was their croak a warning to us or was it intended to draw attention to them? Seemingly neither. Indifferently they dabbed at each other in a kind of playful skirmish. Then one of them stretched wide its wings preparatory to taking flight, and the other did likewise. Ponderously they took to the wing. They dived with speed into the vast space above the lake, then swept upwards in a crescent, and so circled on like falcons. Now they were high over my head, uttering their hoarse croak; now they were below again. Did this mean anything, I wondered? I know that the Greeks and Romans regarded the raven as the feathered soothsayer; the Scandinavians hear it as the oracular voice of the future; some English poets call it the herald of the year; most races see in it "the harbinger of evil and death, the bird of night and of witchcraft, the grim watcher by the gibbet, where swing the bones of the murderer, that amid the

pause of the night wind, as it howls and whistles over the lonely moor, croaks ominous". I do not know what Parisians think of ravens, but I remember that my grandmother used to feel unhappy all day long if she heard one croaking on the roof in the early morning. As a child I believed what my grand-mother believed. As a grown-up I have taken delight in all birds, particularly birds in flight. To try to depict the gracefulness of a bird in flight with my brush and ink gives me infinite pleasure. But why should a raven's croak have upset my grandmother's feeling for the whole day? This puzzles me now as much as the English superstition that the peacock's cry brings bad luck. An English friend of mine declined a reproduction of a noted Chinese artist's painting of a peacock which I innocently wanted to give him not long after my arrival in England in 1933. But in China the peacock is greatly admired, symbolising wealth and prosperity, and it is a favourite subject for the Chinese artist's brush. A single feather from the tail of a peacock is used as an ornament in a tall vase with some flowers. There is something inscrutable in the variations of our human nature.

"Come on," shouted Francine. "Here is a cave." I quickened my steps to catch up with her and explained that I had been

The Crag of Buttes Chaumont in Mist

watching the wonderful flight of two ravens. "Ravens?" she questioned. As we entered the cave she exclaimed, "Oh!" A number of unevenly cut rocks were bound together with cement—except where a large gap formed the entrance. Once inside we found that there were other gaps as well, through which we could see the vertical drop down the cliff to the water surface. It made us shudder. Round the corner a little to the left the daylight was coming in. The supposed cave was turning out to be a short tunnel, artificially constructed to resemble a natural formation. We had been taken in. While inside I felt rejuvenated, for in my younger days I had passed through caves and tunnels just like this in a number of famous Chinese gardens, particularly the one called Shih-tzu-lin, Lion-Rock-Grove, in Soochow. The way the rocks were joined together, the tunnel, cliffs and water, trees and birds—all were similar. I said again and again to my companion, "This is China, not Paris." She had never been to China, but she was pleased, I could see. She loves her Paris dearly, and at the same time has a keen desire to see China after having read about it.

The rocky path continued downwards. We came to another cave-tunnel, a much shorter one. From it an iron gate gave on to a terrace by the cliff, where visitors could stand and gaze at the lake. But the gate was locked. We went on downwards. For a while we saw ahead of us suspended in the air a long, thick, horizontal line on which a few dark dots were moving. It was the suspension bridge which joins the road to the top of the hill Belleville, one of the highest points of Paris, where we had been walking when we saw the Sybil's Temple.

"Let's go up on the bridge," suggested Francine gaily. We might have gone straight to the bridge instead of walking up the hill through the tall trees. But we had purposely passed the road that led to the bridge and taken the next one to the temple on the cliff. "Aren't you glad to have come this way and to have passed through part of China?" My companion smiled her assent.

As we were now on the level of the lake, we moved slowly round it close by the water's edge. The steep, almost vertical, crag provided a different picture at every step we took. Although I am more than double my companion's age, I could have outstripped her lively movements. But the ever-changing look of the crag detained me again and again. The whole scene, with the lake and trees in the foreground and the crag now in the centre, now right, now left, was in some way similar to one near my home, round the crag Hsiao-ku-shan by the northern bank of the Yangtse. It becomes an island when the river is swollen. Hsiao-ku-shan is much higher and on its summit instead of a Sybil's temple is the slanting roof of a Buddhist temple, with green porcelain tiles supported on pillars painted in Chinese vermilion.

Though still clasped by the thin mist, the rugged face of the crag, with the little terrace half way down, was visible, and at its foot a gaily painted boat tied to a small tree rocked a little when the flat surface of the water was gently touched by the soft hand of the wind. On a clear, bright day, the high crag must look imposing and maybe out of proportion in the scene. I was glad that I had not seen it like that.

Presently two little boys of five or six years old began to follow us stealthily. They giggled, as if they found something funny about us—most likely me. I turned to give them a smile, but at once they became shy; one put his tongue out a little and the other wriggled and bent his head, but looked up at me from under his eyelids. They were adorable. I longed to be able to transfer their innocence to paper, with a fir tree on the right and the crag and distant trees on the left.

Leaving the boys behind, we reached the end of the lake and of the crag. An arch joined one crag to another, making the gap between look like a large church gate with no doors. The road we had followed to the temple ran across this arch. Francine took a path to the left and I followed her. A narrow stream of clear water ran alongside the path into the lake. We heard the sound of a waterfall from the shade under a huge rock. Going nearer we found that it was in a cave. The spray of the water could be felt on our faces a little way away and there was a chill in the air. A young couple were sitting near the waterfall and I admired their disregard of the dampness. We had a look round and I made a rough sketch before we moved out again.

A roadside stall was selling something hot to eat. Francine said it was *gaufres*. I had a sudden fancy to buy one for each of us. I found mine rather like a waffle, but crisper. We ate like a pair of youngsters. It was fun to hold something in one's hand, and to give one's lips something to do after their long silence. The chains of 'formality' are loosened in public parks almost everywhere. But Paris seems to have melted all chains as scrap metal during the Second World War.

We had been sitting on a bench for a good while. Aimlessly, as before, we moved on. Neither of us knew the neighbourhood. The roads were good for walking and we seldom found ourselves lacking well-shaped trees to look at. Some birds, mostly sparrows, chirped and quarrelled inside a clump of short bamboo bushes. I particularly liked the shapes of two tall pines and the way, seen from certain angles, their trunks interlaced. I made a rough sketch of them. If a Chinese scholar-hermit in an ancient robe had been sitting inside the little hut near by and a few groups of Chinese orchids had been growing at the base of the pines, the whole scene could have been a copy of a Chinese painting in the familiar composition of the Sung masters.

There was a delicate, delicious grey mist rising over the face of the crag when we came back to the lakeside. We stood on the same neck of land and leant over a railing at the water's edge. The bright-coloured boat was no longer to be seen, for the mist close to the water was quite thick and whitish. As we looked it seemed to begin rolling along over the glassy surface. Then one patch of it grew whiter, turning into a snowy swan followed by two white-and-black drakes. How proud they looked, gliding along! Their assurance seemed to brighten the water and make the lake much wider than before. Their presence gave an elastic quality to the scene; the rugged crag receded several yards into the evening mist and lost its sharp outlines. It was a perfect composition for a painting. The evening mist had now altered the look of the Sybil's temple too. I could imagine now that the roof did slant and turn up at the eaves. The cross became a thin line. For me, this transformation of the temple into a Chinese bower or pavilion added the final touch to the scene.

An occasional quack roused me from my contemplation. The swan had moved away, but the two drakes still played in front of us. They dipped their heads and flicked water over their feathered backs. Apparently they were bathing. My companion chuckled and said that she loved watching them playing in the water. When I pointed out that the drakes were mischievously shaking the crag, she looked at the reflection and laughed. Remarking that the whole scene with the additional charm of the drakes and swan could not be better, I thanked my companion for having been so patient with me all the afternoon. Thoughts of Kiu-kiang, where I was born, caused two little verses in Chinese to form in my head. They can be roughly translated as follows:

> The willow tassels flaunt their spring yellow,
> The bamboo leaves wear a heart-taking green.
> My good companion giggles gently at
> Two drakes disporting themselves in the water.
>
> The crag is like another in Eastern lands;
> Its reflection in the water is more beautiful still.
> If another scene is just as lovely,
> Why should I think of Kiu-kiang?

何 他 倒 怪　　雙 好 竹 柳
必 鄉 影 石　　鳩 伴 葉 綠
憶 亦 情 似　　戲 笑 有 飛
江 佳 更 東　　水 輕 情 嫩
州 麗 幽 土　　浩 盈 綠 黃

It was time for us to leave when the heavenly guardian began to spread a large sheet of black cloth over the crag and the lake for the night. We came out by the main entrance and read on a board the words PARC DES BUTTES-CHAUMONT. After taking a cup of tea in a local café we both felt warm as well as happy. Francine had another engagement for the evening and we parted at the Metro station.

On my way back I tried to remember what I had read about this park. It was situated, I knew, on the Belleville Heights, where the Battle of Paris was waged on March 30th, 1814, while the Allies were pushing down into the city. It then became a waste ground. There used to be an American quarry in it. Some of the materials obtained here were utilised not only for buildings in Paris, but were shipped by the Canal St Martin via Havre to the United States. Many a villa in Kentucky and Florida is built of material from the former quarry at Buttes-Chaumont. Plaster of paris also came from

the gypsum of this neighbourhood. Later the quarter became
desolate and was the haunt of beggars and thieves. Chaumont
means 'bare mountain'. It was Count Haussmann who conceived the idea of turning it into a park. A landscape designer
of the Second Empire, Apland, arranged the layout in 1867. I
wondered whether Apland had just come back from Peking
when he made his design. There was a war in China in 1860-1
during which the French and English armies sacked Peking
Palace. Apland could have been in the army or on some
official mission to Peking. Chinese landscape gardens were, of
course, in great vogue in Europe in the early nineteenth
century. Kew Gardens in London are said to be of Chinese
inspiration. But I think the design of Buttes-Chaumont is more
successful. Buttes-Chaumont is not bigger than the Green Park
in London, but its wild and picturesque features make it appear
much larger. Perhaps Apland had never been to China; if so
it is a phenomenal coincidence that the principle of Chinese
landscape gardening is so evident in Buttes-Chaumont: the
ground kept as natural as possible, and if flat, enlivened by
means of crags, a lake or pond, or even buildings so that the
whole garden cannot be seen at once. I was delighted to have
found China in Paris.

X

Something More in Pigalle

"No, madame, I have not come to see only the gay side of Paris. I want to see all of her."

This was my reply to Madame Joudoin-Prom, who had kindly given a small party for me at her house in the Boulevard Lannes; Madame Joudoin-Prom is the Presidente de l'Union des Cercles Français de Liaison Internationale, and has been doing admirable work collecting funds for the restoration of an old and devastated village, La Rogue-sur-Pernes, east of Avignon. As the head of the Club Feminin de Liaison-France-Americaine, she has crossed the Atlantic many times. On one occasion she was introduced in New York as a visitor from 'gay Paree', but promptly enlightened her audience as to the falsity of this description. Parisians were, in fact, a very hard-working community, she said, and it was a great pity that people who had never been to Paris believed them to be largely cabaret dancers, and that those who did visit the city spent so much of their time in night-clubs and *bals musettes*.

I agreed with her, but silently wondered if she knew that the Chinese have always been regarded in the West as a race of *restaurateurs* and laundrymen. Only a few years ago the Chinese Assistant Secretary-General to U.N., who had a suite of rooms in the Hotel Wardorf-Astoria in Park Avenue, New York, took himself up by the lift one evening and got out at the wrong floor. As all the doors and passages in the hotel looked alike, he did not at first realise his mistake, and tried to fit his key into someone else's door. Before he had pushed the key hole the door flew open and a heartily-smiling lady declared that the Assistant Secretary-General of U.N. was just the person she had been waiting for; and she pointed to bundles of dirty clothes for him to take away to wash.

Like other travellers, I too had been told that Paris had many *cabarets* and night clubs; but what big city in the world is without them? I also knew that for the last hundred years at least Paris had been the art capital of the world. But there was another aspect of Paris in which I was particularly interested, and of which I had heard much less, and that was the work of her skilled craftsmen. It was my wish to search out as many as possible of the old handicrafts still being practised in Paris; and in this I was fortunate in securing the help of Madeleine Chambert. Day after day she took me to see fresh examples.

In England the Industrial Revolution killed many handicrafts, and in America the techniques of mass production hardly allowed any to develop. In my homeland of China we have wonderful craftsmen and an age-old tradition of beautiful handicrafts, but in the last half-century continual disturbances, wars and political instability have made life difficult for workers and the demand for their products has declined. In Paris I hoped to find numbers of the finest craftsmen in the world still pursuing their old occupations, for Paris, in spite of being at the centre of two world wars, has managed to remain herself. My friend Mr. Van Wyck Brooks once wrote me:

I remember what Rodin said about the sculptors in his youth, the 'official' French sculptors from whom he learned nothing. Then he found an obscure stone-cutter, with no pretensions as an artist at all, who knew how to carve a leaf in the great tradition of the gothic sculptors. His point was that the great line has been carried on by the totally unrecognized humble craft-workers.

This remark was an added incentive to me to visit the craftsmen of Paris at work.

One afternoon in February Mademoiselle Moisson, Joan Hendry and I met in Madeleine's office about three o'clock. Our first visit was to a pipe-maker's shop in the Passage des Princes. I had always supposed that pipe-smoking was a largely English habit, for it was Ralph Lane, first Governor of Virginia, who in 1586 brought an Indian pipe to Sir Walter Raleigh and taught him how to use it. So I assumed that England would be the place to find pipe-makers. I am not going to start a dispute between English and French pipe-makers, for I am no smoker of cigarettes, even, let alone pipes. What interested me now was that for the first time I saw a pipe taking shape from a block of wood.

We did not go right into the shop, for we could easily watch the whole process through three huge plate-glass windows facing the passage, which was rather like the Burlington Arcade in London. Three men were at work behind the panes, while further back another man was cutting the wood roughly into shape. Rows and rows of rough-cut pipes lay on a long table. I should have liked to know what kinds of wood made the best pipes—no doubt hard kinds, such as apple or pear. One craftsman then planed the roughly-cut pipe into a smooth shape, cutting it here and there and sand-papering it. The second stage was to bore the hole, while the last and most delicate operation was to fix the two parts, the bowl and the mouthpiece, together and add any ornamentation. I love watching any skilled work done with the hands. I remember watching for hours an ivory-carver engraving religious figurines in a shop window near the Place St Sulpice. He reminded me of the ivory-engravers and jade-carvers in many of the big towns and cities of China, who are eager to show their customers how the work is done, hoping thereby to provide an attraction which will tempt the onlookers to buy. But I do not remember such an arrangement in London, or in New York.

We travelled next by Metro to Blanche et Pigalle, a district of Montmartre. Madamoiselle Moisson led us through a narrow lane, off the Boulevard de Clichy, into a courtyard where the mellow, yellowish-coloured stone of an eighteenth-century building was being repainted pink by two workmen on scaffolding. We went through the house and came out into a small sloping garden at the back. A number of interesting buildings surrounded this, served by a footpath, but there was no thoroughfare to any main road. An unusual quietness pervaded the quarter, in contrast to the noise of the boulevard from which we had just come. "Very few people know this place," remarked Mademoiselle Moisson; "not even many Parisians. Those who come to see Montmartre cast a glance at Clichy and Pigalle and then go on to the Sacré Cœur and sit in the Place du Tertre. But there are many fine houses in this quarter, if one knows where to find them." She pointed out the studios of two well-known artists at the top of one of the houses.

We turned into the stone house and went upstairs to the

third floor. Madame Richaume opened the door to us and Monsieur André Richaume rose from his bench and said he had been expecting us and was delighted to show us his work. Monsieur Richaume described himself as a *"fabricant spécialiste d'archets artisques pour violons, altos, violoncelles, contrebasses"*. He is not tall, but solidly-built, with sharp eyes, a firm mouth, and strong hands and fingers. He was working on a violin bow when we entered, and now in a few words he demonstrated to us the process of making a fine bow.

The first step is the selection of the hair from a white horse's tail. Each hair must be of a good length and of even thickness. One animal's tail may provide only a few suitable hairs and it often takes two or three tails to make a bow. White hair is the best; black hair the worst and the cheapest. No good violinist would care to use a bow with black hair, for it is coarse and uneven and produces a harsh musical tone. A number of specially fine bows were hanging side by side in a glass case behind Monsieur Richaume's workbench. They were all beautifully polished and exquisitely smooth to the touch. They varied slightly in length, because not every performer likes the same sized bow. Every bow had been made to the order of some noted individual musician. I have never before handled a bow, let alone a really good one by a famous maker, and felt a little embarrassed lest M. Richaume should think my interest in his work, which was that of a complete musical ignoramus, was being displayed under false pretences. But I consoled myself with the recollection of how often I have been asked to display my specially made paint brushes (though they are not of my own manufacture) to people who have no idea how to use them for painting and calligraphy.

Monsieur Richaume showed us one bow made with black hair. Outwardly it looked just as finely made as the others, but he laughed as he looked at it and shook his head. It would not surprise me if some of Monsieur Richaume's bows became museum pieces in years to come after being used by the great violinists for whom they were made. He told us that his clients were scattered all over the world and that his bows had been ordered by musicians in Mexico, Argentina, and even Peru. I think he might even have added China, for before the Second World War many notable European violinists played in Shanghai, Tientsin, and Peking.

G

In recent years Monsieur Richaume must have had serious difficulties, for the wood normally used for bows is that known as Pernambuco, which comes from Brazil, and during the Second World War it was unobtainable. But he remarked smilingly that he had had a certain stock of it laid by. But no one had known how long the war would last, and many of his orders from the other side of the Atlantic had been cancelled or could not be met. It was most fortunate, I think, that the war did not bring to an end this family of stringed-instrument bow-makers which, as Monsieur Richaume told us with great pride, had practised its craft since 1750. I appreciated his feelings, for in my country too a craft is habitually practised by the same family for generations. In my home town of Kiukiang there used to be a branch of the Hu K'ai-wen family of Anhui Province that has been making Chinese paint brushes for over 1,000 years. When I was a boy just starting to write, I went to Mr. Hu to buy my first brushes. My father was an artist and always had his paint brushes specially made by this family; he knew the head brush-maker, who in consequence used to show me fine old brushes made by his father and fore-fathers. He always encouraged me to follow in my father's footsteps, and eventually I did. I wonder if this brush-making family is still in existence? It is twenty-two years—twenty-two troubled years—since I was there.

The room in which Monsieur Richaume worked was not large, but was evidently big enough for his needs. His bench, which was like a small desk, seemed to have been specially designed, with racks for all the necessary cutting, measuring and smoothing tools and for the other operations. It was placed by the window to catch the light. Monsieur Richaume said he could not work by artificial light, which cast shadows and prevented him from achieving perfectly smooth surfaces. How fortunate that Paris can provide him with enough sunlight! As we took our leave, I asked how long it took Monsieur Richaume to make a good bow. He replied with a smile, "Until I am satisfied with it!" I could not resist asking one personal question: Had he any other interest in life to which he devoted his leisure time? He smiled again. Making bows was his sole interest; he never tired of making them. He took his wife out for an evening stroll occasionally, but they had no hobbies. Madame Richaume nodded her confirmation. They seemed a completely happy and contented couple living in their quiet backwater in the heart of noisy Montmartre. I felt envious and wished I had singled out one of my many interests and devoted myself to it exclusively; then I might have achieved something.

Outside the Richaumes' premises, Mademoiselle Moisson took us up to the next floor to see another friend of hers, Monsieur René Quenoil, *luthier d'art*, a stringed-instrument maker. Monsieur Quenoil was a tall, rather slim young man in his twenties, with a ready smile and lively gestures. His enthusiasm for his work and his eagerness to show it to us were quite touching.

The first consideration in making stringed instruments is the choice of wood. Some of the finest wood for the purpose used to come from across the Adriatic and was very expensive, but for the past hundred years or so French violin-makers have not been buying it. Four different kinds of wood are used for the various parts: Hungarian maple, Swiss pine, ebony and willow. To achieve a good result, cheap material is useless. Monsieur Quenoil took down from a high shelf two perfectly cut violin fronts, for which Swiss pine is used, to demonstrate the first stage of construction. They looked as if they had only just been cut. He pointed out that each was of an exact thickness and hollowed at a precise angle, and that the two pieces— left-hand and right-hand—had to be joined so that the grain in the wood matched exactly. The back of the instrument is made in the same way, but from Hungarian maple instead. The thickness of the plates varies slightly, the underside being hollowed to a greater degree in some places than in others. The characteristic curves of the sides, which are again of maple, and the acute angles of the corners, of willow, where the curves of the ends and the middle 'bouts' meet, were pointed out to us; the slightest irregularity would be inadmissible. Particular attention has to be paid to the position and shape of the 'sound-holes', through which the vibrations of the air contained in the resonance chambers are communicated to the air outside. The angle at which the sound-holes are cut across the grain of the wood could affect the notes. A great deal depended on the quality and elasticity of the wood used. An important point stressed by Monsieur Quenoil was that the wood must be seasoned for at least forty years, otherwise the instrument may be affected by a slight change of temperature and the pitch of the note altered.

I exclaimed that the wood he was now using must have been bought by his father or even his grandfather, and kept until he was born, reared, and trained to use it! Laughing merrily, he assented. He told us that, like the Richaumes, generations of his family had practised the same craft. He had learned the craft, along with his two brothers, from his father, who in turn had been taught by *his* father. All three members of Monsieur Quenoil's generation were violin-makers in different parts of Paris. He, in his turn, had bought wood and put it by for seasoning for use by *his* children. "How many children have you?" I asked. He laughed again and pointed to a new gold ring on his left hand, saying that he had only been married about a year. Monsieur Quenoil, young as he was, showed as much confidence that his children would follow their father's profession as our Chinese fathers, imbued with Confucius' teaching of ancestor worship! I remembered that many Italian families of the sixteenth, seventeenth and eighteenth centuries were renowned for violin-making, producing instruments which have never been surpassed. I wondered whether the Quenoil family had been making violins as far back as the sixteenth century, and whether they had any Italian connections.

Next we were shown the varnishing of an uncoated violin. Monsieur Quenoil told us that it generally took him about three weeks to complete the construction of an instrument up to the varnishing stage. Many people believed there was some secret about the composition of the varnish and also about the process of varnishing, but Monsieur Quenoil discredited these notions. He makes it himself from a base of linseed oil, natural gums and resins, and turpentine. He emphasised that the instruments must be varnished with great care, but that the obtaining of perfect results was simply a matter of experience. The same, he felt, could be said of any work of art. I heartily agreed. He explained that varnishing could only be done between April and September, the temperature at other times being unsuitable. He did not approve of adjusting the temperature by artificial heat; a violin must be able to stand any temperature and any climate, so it must be made under natural conditions. I thought this a very sound reason. I also think it applies to life in general—life should be carried on under natural conditions!

Monsieur Quenoil told us that the dimensions of the body or resonance chamber of a violin are fixed, but the maker may add decorations or inlay ornaments at the top of the stem above the tuning pegs, and also along the sides of the body. He then went on to say that nothing interested him except violins: he went to study violins in museums and read a good deal on the subject as well. He had a considerable library of books on violin-making, and even suggested lending me some if I were interested, but this I declined with thanks, for my knowledge of French would not have served me well enough. I had never before met a young craftsman so ready totally to immerse himself in his craft as Monsieur Quenoil.

Presently two people in dinner jackets, one quite young, the other middle-aged with a black moustache, both obviously belonging to the world of professional music, came in, and Monsieur Quenoil received them in another room, where he took down several violins for them to examine. They were evidently customers. So after a quick look at Monsieur Quenoil's tools and his work-table we bade him goodbye with gratitude.

My suggestion of a drink was favourably received by the ladies, and we made our way towards the Place du Tertre. My two companions had plenty to say to each other in French, and I was left to think over all I had just learned. I had always imagined the front of a violin to be a single piece of wood, instead of two perfectly matched halves. I could now see that the grain and texture of the wood, and the precise matching of the grain, must have an influence upon the vibrations of sound within the body of the instrument.

The making of a fine violin calls for the most delicate and subtle handling. I do not think we have any musical instrument in China to compare with the violin in point of workmanship, though the *hu-ch'in* is constructed on rather similar principles. Perhaps the Chinese seven-stringed lute, *ch'i-hsien-ch'in*, is the nearest instrument we have to a violin. It is an ancient instrument, one of the few musical instruments which have been held in esteem since Confucius' time some 2,500 years ago. People who can play the *ch'i-hsien-ch'in* are still to be found in China, but they are comparatively few. It has a body three or four feet long and one sound-hole cut at the rear. Its strings are plucked by hand, not vibrated with a bow. Each finger of the right hand is called into play, and the fourth and fifth are always difficult to control until they are well-trained. The fourth and fifth fingers of the left hand are not used. For playing, the lute is placed on a low table specially made for the purpose, or sometimes the lutanist places it on his knees, sitting cross-legged in a bamboo or pine grove. Its construction is similar in some respects to that of the violin. The sides are curved in much the same way, and the acute angles at the corners and the varying thickness of wood in the front (which, however, is made in one piece, not two) are comparable to a Western stringed instrument. The only kind of wood used in making the Chinese lute is *wu-t'ung* (*Sterculia platanifolia*), a tree native to China. It grows up to sixty feet in height, has big leaves similar in shape to a maple, and a trunk which is very smooth and green even in old age. The tree has many literary associations, and from its seed is produced an oil known as wood-oil, which was very much sought after in the Second World War. The grain is very fine and close, and long seasoning is required before the wood can be used for lute-making. Varnishing is also a skilled job, and even when the lute is finished it is left to mature for years before being played.

During my college days, one of my relations gave me an old lute, said to have been in their family for about 200 years. For a year I tried to learn to play it; then I realised I should never become a good player and gave the instrument to a real musician, a Taoist priest, who lived on Lu Mountain in Kiukiang. I suppose by now it may have crumbled to dust. But, thinking of my old *ch'i-hsien-ch'in*, I wondered whether the violin-makers of Europe have ever tried to use this Chinese wood for their instruments. *Sterculia platanifolia* was introduced into England from Japan in 1757, where it is much cultivated, but owing to the cold climate of northern Europe it never grows well, except perhaps in Cornwall. I have been told, however, that it flourishes luxuriantly on the French Riviera and at Monte Carlo. Perhaps Monsieur Quenoil will consider using it one day.

While I was still meditating on *Sterculia platanifolia*, I found we had reached our destination. We stopped at Chez Eugene, Bar Rotisserie, in the Place du Tertre. The two ladies wanted a cool drink of white wine, and I ordered coffee for myself, though the waitress brought me a cup of tea, evidently thinking it would suit me better. I told Mademoiselle Moisson over our drinks that after that afternoon's excursion I was no longer going to join the lament that all the old crafts were dying out.

A Porcelain repairer on the pavement

XI

A Couple of Mooniacs

Monsieur andré paul bastien was a fellow-guest in
my Paris hotel. He was a jolly round little man in his early
thirties, a good three inches shorter than I. He knew how to
talk and seemed always to have something appropriate to say
to everyone who came into the hall, old or young, male or
female. Naturally, he quickly made friends. While talking, his
circular face wore a solemn yet comical expression; he was never
sad; he brought life into the hall whenever he entered it. I was
perhaps the only resident who could not exchange conversation
with him, but we exchanged other things. He gave me a copy
of his published verses, *Au Seuil du Temps qui Fuit*, with illustrations by Schlegel, and I replied with a set of illustrations from
my book, *The Silent Traveller in New York*. When he learned
the object of my visit to Paris, he offered to introduce me to the
night life of the city. I accepted his offer with enthusiasm.

When the appointed evening came, I managed to make
Monsieur Bastien understand that I would like to see an
Existentialists' club if possible. He shrugged his shoulders and
made a wry face as if to say that there wasn't much Existentialism to be found in Paris today, or else that Existentialist clubs
are dull places. I had only a vague conception of Existentialism,
but some years before, just after the end of the Second World
War, a good deal was written about the great vogue of Existentialist clubs in Paris, and how young people, especially,
flocked to join them. The stories I read of the attitude of these
clubmen, their behaviour, and even what they wore, all
suggested the greatest determination to 'exist', if I may be
permitted thus to over-simplify their outlook. I now found it
impossible to believe that a newly established philosophy could
have been forgotten so quickly. Some Existentialist clubs must
still be in existence.

Accordingly, our first call was at a house on the rue St
Benoit. The door was shut and there was no light outside.

Bastien pushed it open, and led the way through a narrow corridor and down some steps. He turned to whisper: *'Une cave!'* The light was dim in the basement, which had a stone floor and bare walls splashed here and there with coloured paints. A young couple were dancing feverishly while two other couples sat watching. All the girls wore tight woollen sweaters and black jeans. One had very long hair hanging down in a 'horse's tail', another had a bush of brownish-black hair like a lion's-head mask. I recalled the witty remark of a Parisian barber who showed me a cartoon in the French daily, *Figaro*, depicting a modern girl's hair-do by the side of a horse seen from behind: "You, I, she, it are animals". The barber had just begun to learn English.

We remained for a while. None of the dancers or spectators seemed to take any notice of us. The club was not really due to open for another hour or two, so we decided to move on.

Our next port-of-call was the Café Anglais in the rue de l'Abbaye. The room here was packed with people—they were sitting on each other's laps, standing and leaning against anything that offered. There may have been a few chairs somewhere, but they were hidden from sight; we were presented merely with row upon row of human backs. Eventually we managed to find a small corner of a wooden structure to rest on, and there we were hemmed in. It was impossible to exchange a word for the din. Bastien lit his pipe and had it nearly knocked out of his mouth by someone's shoulder; but he tilted up his head to blow out the smoke now and then, perfectly at his ease. He seemed quite familiar with the situation and as if waiting for something to happen. Occasional giggles broke out when someone fell off a seat or lap. Spilt drinks were a frequent occurrence, for the only waiter had to squeeze his way between the guests. Bastien grasped him to order two glasses of lemonade.

Guitars began to strum and two voices in the far corner diagonally opposite us broke into a French song. I could not see who was singing, though I stood up and peered across. Bastien did not even try to see, but just listened contentedly.

The music changed to an English folk-song, then to an African ballad. Each song was received with wild applause. I realised that these singers must be Gordon Heath and Lee Payant, two dark-skinned Americans who, I was told, had come to Paris three years ago not knowing a word of French. They were determined to make their way and accepted odd jobs while picking up French songs. Each had a gift for language and a musical ear. In less than a year they were employed as singers in night clubs. Since they had begun to appear in the Café Anglais, the place was crowded every night from nine o'clock onwards. Bastien was now being squeezed off his perch by newcomers, a few of whom spoke American and seemed to be students at the Sorbonne. We decided to move on.

It was unexpectedly cold outside. A sprinkling of snow covered the ground. A full moon was rising above the leafless trees by the north wall of the Church of St Germain des Prés. The quietness of the street and the clarity of the night scene contrasted strangely with what we had just left. As if by magic, I found myself leading Bastien to a nearby square to see how it looked by night. It was the Place de Furstemberg, in the corner of which was Delacroix's studio. This is one of the oldest spots in Paris, a beautiful square of which I was very fond. The street-lamps with their five milk-white balls were lit up. The shadows of the few bare trees were cast by the moonlight on the faded pinkish walls of the houses on the left, one of which was Delacroix's studio. Peace reigned as it must have reigned for decades. Delacroix, who lived here from 1857 to 1863 while working on his frescoes for the Church of St Sulpice, must have appreciated it. It was here that he wrote the lines:

> The choice between being worried and harried all one's life . . . and being abandoned by everyone because one will not submit to constraint. . . .

He cannot have found the choice an easy one.

Bastien gave me a gentle pat on the back as if to show his approval of what I wanted to see. Now it was his turn to lead. Off we went to the Café des Deux Magots, opposite the Church of St Germain des Prés. A whimsical thought came into my mind as we entered. I took out a piece of string which happened to be in my pocket and hung it under Bastien's nostrils to represent long whiskers. He grasped my meaning at once and

Activities in the tranquil Place de Furstemberg

burst out laughing. I was showing off my limited knowledge of French, for the word *magot* means 'grotesque Chinese figure'. If I was to be one of the *deux magots*, Bastien should be the other, I thought.

The Café des Deux Magots was said to be the place where the infant Existentialism was nursed to maturity. During its infancy the chief doctor and his assistants were to be found there day and night, while the adorers flocked in to pray and worship. They came in all kinds of eccentric attire; here, if anywhere, one would find the Existentialists, so I was told. But Existentialism had evidently passed from maturity to decadence some years before. The chief doctor and his assistants had all received rewards with honour; they came here no more. After the *garçon* had brought us coffee, my eyes wandered round the room. It was full of people. All looked leisurely and well-dressed; there were many charming ladies in fashionable evening frocks. A young artist, with a black moustache and beard and dressed in an American Army-surplus coat, had just finished a portrait of one of them. The rest of her friends fought to have a look at it, and as each seized it in turn, he or she burst into loud laughter. Their commotion attracted all eyes.

It was nearly midnight when we came out on the street again. Our two shadows, one slightly taller than the other, cast by the bright moonlight, moved over the cobble-stones at a steady, brisk pace. I blindly followed Bastien as he made one turn and then another; I had long lost all sense of direction and did not know where we were. No word was spoken, but we turned our heads to exchange smiles now and then. Most of the lights in the shop windows had been switched off, but a few fanciful coloured neon signs remained alight. They indicated night-clubs.

Bastien wore his usual air, unchanged since we came out; he looked contented and not at all bored. He still occasionally lifted his head to puff out smoke or make a little sizzling noise when he sucked at his pipe. I could hear it clearly, for there was no other sound in the street. We met no one; the side-streets down which we turned did not seem to suit motorists.

There was one moment when Bastien kept his face turned towards the dark, bluish sky for so long without blowing out smoke that I thought he must be composing poetry. At another he seemed to be reciting some old *ballade*, perhaps by François

Villon or another of the great French poets. I secretly wished he had a bushy beard under his chin like Victor Hugo's, or that he had not brushed his hair back so neatly, but had let it grow into a massive mane, like that on Balzac's head. How fine he would have looked in a cloak of gaudy colours in the eighteenth-century French style! Then, what an event it would be for me to walk with him side by side in Paris so late at night!

But this was pure speculation. For all I knew, Bastien may have been cherishing a wish of another kind. Perhaps he would have liked *me* to be transformed into a figure in a silk gown with my hair coiled round the top of my head, a pair of slanting eyes, and long whiskers that dangled over my chest as if I had just walked out of a Watteau painting. Or he may have imagined me as the original of one of the two grotesque Chinese figures we had seen in the Café des Deux Magots, who left his chest bare and his fat belly sticking out to represent the Deity of Contentment!

When we started out, my thoughts roved freely about our surroundings; later they were all concentrated on the bright full moon. Many beautiful lines and poems about the moon, by our greatest poets since the fourth century, came into my mind and I recited them to myself while we moved along. They seemed to take me back to my homeland, and I felt that I was roaming about with one of my oldest and closest friends, possibly Sun Mo-chien, a poet and artist, in the ancient city of Nanking or Peking. Bastien was not now the grotesque Chinese figure I had imagined him in the Café des Deux Magots, but a congenial soul known to me for years. At last, on recalling a poem called 'The Traveller's Moon' by Po Chü-I (A.D. 772-826), I came back to earth.

> I, a traveller, came from the South of the River
> When the moon was only a crescent.
> In my leisurely moving about
> I have now seen the clear light in full thrice,
> At dawn I follow the steps of the remnant moon;
> When night falls I stay with the sickle moon.
> Who says that the moon has no feeling for me?
> She has chased me for hundreds of miles.
> In the morning I set out for the bridge of Wei-Shui;
> In the evening I enter the route for Ch'ang-an.
> But I wonder about to-night's moon:
> In whose home will she again be a traveller-guest?

客從江南來　來時月上弦　悠悠行旅中　三見清光圓　曉隨殘月行　夕與新月宿　誰謂月無情　千里遠相逐　朝發渭水橋　暮入長安陌　不知今宵月　又作誰家客

白居易客中月

I felt suddenly homesick. Fortunately, just at that moment Bastien turned his head and gave me one of his friendly smiles. We wandered on, making calls at various clubs. Eventually we became new members of the Club du Vieux-Colombier and were ushered to a table. My companion explained to me by gestures that since we had none of the fair sex with us we did not need a bottle of champagne in an ice-bucket, but that two glasses of lemonade would suffice. The *garçon* lost interest in us at once and never came round to us again until we summoned him before leaving.

It would be difficult to describe the place, for the walls, the furniture and the decorations were all lost in semi-darkness. The lights were so dim that it seemed as if we were all huddled together and surrounded by a great darkness. The chairs we sat on and the tables we leaned on were dark, and so were the beams and pillars. Most of the members, including us two new ones, wore dark clothes. Even the few coloured sweaters on the girls looked dull. Only a few searchlight-like rays, though faint, were moving up and down, here and there, from the reflection of the highly polished brass instruments that were being played by the band. The players were on one side of the dance floor, which occupied the centre of the room. There were tables in front of the band. We ourselves were at a table on a slightly raised platform. I was still absorbed by the novelty of our enterprise, but I found the band hard to bear, directly after the quietness outside. I asked my companion if the music was French. He shook his head and went on smoking contentedly.

Lively and expressive gestures occurred occasionally. Confused murmurs of pleasant voices roved round the room as if they had legs. Presently all the dancers in the centre returned to their seats except two: one a tall, dark-skinned young man and the other a pretty, rather diminutive girl in a grey jumper and black jeans and with a horsetail hair-do. This pair then began to dance with quicker and quicker movements, while the band played faster and faster. They stamped, they jumped, they whirled round and tugged at each other roughly, keeping time to the music, which blared out at its highest pitch. Their movements were hypnotic. Those who stood near the dance-floor began to move their legs automatically; some swayed their bodies too. The rest of the onlookers, even down to the *garçon*, behaved differently. But my companion remained unruffled, still sitting contentedly and smoking his pipe with a little sizzling noise. I imagine the whole performance was a kind of Apache dance. Unexpectedly Bastien gave me a smile and exclaimed: "*Americaine!*" Then he knocked the ash out of his pipe and resumed his former manner. A stir went through the room as two flashily dressed girls, not exactly elegant, but certainly very striking, entered. They seemed to be on friendly terms with most of the company, for they smiled and waved to other dancers in all parts of the room. Their presence had an enchanted, exotic air. One of them must have looked to Westerners more Chinese than I did, for her pencilled eyebrows were drawn tilted up at the edges. This sort of thing always makes me feel embarrassed. Her companion wore large gold ear-rings and a huge gold necklace like a Spanish gipsy. Both had bright red mouths. No sooner had they been shown to a table than they were carried off to dance.

After another couple of dances, an elderly, gently-smiling, dark-skinned man, with contrasting white hair, eyebrows and moustache, stepped to the edge of the platform and bowed. He held a glittering brass trumpet. Everyone applauded. Some even whistled. Bastien wrote a few French words on the bill by way of explanation to me, then gave me a gentle pat on the shoulder and remarked, "*C'est bon!*" The elderly musician began to play an air on his instrument which, unlike all the music that had preceeded it, was soothing even to my ears. Presently the rest of the band joined in with a soft accompaniment. Dancing began again. A deep pink flush suffused the player's face, turning his dark skin to mauve-brown. He became more energetic, the dancers more lively, the atmosphere very stuffy. My surreptitious glance at my watch, which told me it was ten to two, was observed by my companion, who settled with the *garçon* and we rose to leave. The trumpet, the music and dancing which I had just witnessed seemed quite familiar to me; they reminded me of what I had seen in New York at the Apollo in Harlem. There was nothing particularly French or Parisian about them.

The air was sharp with frost when we reached the pavement, even colder than when we had left the Café Anglais. It was now

early morning, and the street was completely deserted. The thin layer of snow had frozen on the ground. The moon had risen higher; her rays extended over a wider area and everything they touched—such is the translucent quality of moonlight—looked wet. On the other hand, our two shadows, accompanying us closely on our walk, had become shorter and oddly shaped. I felt there was something uncanny about them. We were conscious of the sound of our own footsteps, and I was also conscious of the faint sizzling noise from the pipe of the persistent smoker.

We were returning by a different route and I had no idea of our whereabouts. I was still ready for any adventure, not at all tired, and as before enjoying the clear tranquil night scene

under the moon. Bastien remained as unruffled as ever. He had
faithfully fulfilled his promise—"just to show you the night life
of Paris"—and had expressed no personal feelings, nor tried to
influence mine. We went happily on. Presently I recognised
the Place St Sulpice, then the tall railings of the Jardin du
Luxembourg. At one point we simultaneously approached the
railings to look through at the moonlit park. The thin snow
on the ground distinguished each tree trunk from its neighbour
and the moonlight singled out the multitudinous twigs and
branches above. The garden had become more spacious than I
remembered it in daytime, and there seemed to be more trees
in it, some of them far, far away. The scene was quite insub-
stantial—a fairyland. Suddenly Bastien exclaimed: *"La lune
est très belle et très claire!"* To which I quietly assented.

At the thought of Bastien composing a verse in his head
again, I recited to myself the following poem of Li Po (A.D.
701-62):

How often does the moon appear in the sky?
I hold up my cup awhile to ask a question:
We know we cannot reach the bright moon,
Yet she always follows us about.
Her brilliance is like a flying mirror reflecting the red palace door-
    way.
After dispersing the greenish vapour she unfolds her clear light.
We only know that she rises from the sea at twilight,
And vanishes in the clouds at dawn.
The White Hare pounds his mortar from autumn to spring there,
Ch'ang-O lives there alone, companionless.
Man of today cannot see the past moon,
But to-day's moon shone on men of the past.
We of the present and they of the past are like flowing water.
Yet all have gazed at the moon in the same way.
My only desire, when singing and drinking,
Is to have the moonlight forever reflected in my golden cup!

An ancient Chinese legend says that there is a white hare in the
moon forever pounding in his mortar the elixir of immortality,
the precious drug stolen from her husband by Ch'ang-O, who
then became the Goddess of the Moon.

By the time we reached our hotel it was well after half-past
two, but we were both still quite fresh. Bastien knocked out his
pipe and patted me on the shoulder as if to say: 'There. I've
done it for you.' I shook his hand warmly and we parted with a
whispered *"Bon soir"* and crept to bed.

The Jardin de Luxembourg in Snow

Lying awake, a strange feeling compounded of fear and relief obsessed me. I was brought up in China, where the beauty of the moon has been praised and sung by famous poets for hundreds of years, and I have always had a great passion for the moon. In the part of China where I was born we could see the moon on fifteen nights in every month. For the first year or two of my stay in England I craved for the moon and often recalled her beauty. But gradually I ceased to talk about her, partly because there was seldom a chance of seeing her in a country where the sky is so often clouded, and partly because I read in the newspapers of several cases of moon mania. It was said that moonlight, and especially the light of the *new* moon, affects the minds of certain people, who in consequence go about attacking and even killing others without knowing what they are doing. They behave quite normally when there is no moon. The odd feeling that possessed my mind in Paris that early morning was that I might not have been able to record our adventurous night if either of us had become a moon maniac. But the fear soon left me, for to both Bastien and me the moon is a familiar companion. Perhaps we are *mooniacs*, a word which is not to be found in the *Oxford Dictionary*, and which means 'moon-lovers'.

青天有月來幾時，我今停杯一問之。
人攀明月不可得，月行卻與人相隨。
皎如飛鏡臨丹闕，綠煙滅盡清輝發。
但見宵從海上來，寧知曉向雲間沒。
白兔搗藥秋復春，嫦娥孤棲與誰鄰。
今人不見古時月，今月曾經照古人。
古人今人若流水，共看明月皆如此。
唯願當歌對酒時，月光長照金樽裡。

李白 把酒問月

XII

Man Traps?

I OWED my admission to the august establishment of Christian Dior to the kindness of Madame Odette Arnaud, who arranged for me to see the last of the three shows of the spring-summer season. Curiously enough, the day of the show, February 28th, was graced with bright sunshine after many days of dull cloud and rain. The sunlight penetrated through the twigs of the trees and printed a pattern on my unassuming suit and on the pavement where I stood outside the entrance to Dior House, waiting for my hostess.

A number of guests, many in mink coats, were already beginning to arrive when Madame Arnaud joined me. We were then assigned one of a group of black-clad girls carrying pencils, pads and programmes, who led us upstairs and showed us our seats. The luxurious rooms, with their gilded ceilings and chairs typical of the Quartier Champs Elysées, were rapidly filling up. I felt rather timid, self-conscious and even awkward at the sudden turning of faces when we entered, for I realised that the connection between Dior House and my flat face was quite remote and that my presence was likely to cause surprise. Besides, there appeared to be only three other men besides myself in the whole room! "We have been given good seats," remarked Madame Arnaud. I smiled and replied: "Yes. I am benefiting by the honour bestowed on you."

I was told that it was not easy to obtain an invitation to a Dior show. Most of those present had paid for their invitations a long time ahead, either as prospective buyers or mere spectators. Those 'in the trade' had had to pay more than the other guests and must submit to restrictions concerning the reproduction of the models. "It is forbidden to make sketches or to take photographs of the models presented; unauthorised publicity given to original models makes the offender liable to prosecution; any unauthorised copy constitutes an infringe-ment liable to penalties", read the footnote on one of the two printed programmes. In the one a few lines of description were provided under the various headings: Tailor-mades, Mantles and Cloaks, Dresses, Hats, Colours, Materials, Silks, Em-broidery, Furs, Jewels, Belts, Buttons, Gloves, Shoes, Um-brellas, Stockings and Hair Styles. The other contained a list of names of the model clothes in the collection, 186 altogether, with twenty-three furs in addition.

Now the show was ready to begin. One of the girls in black standing near the entrance to the room read out in French and then in English the name of each dress and its number on the list. No sooner had we heard the first announcement than we saw a tall young lady wearing the gown in question walking with mannered gait forward and slightly sideways from one end of the central space to the other. She then turned and walked back in the same way, moving sideways and swirling her longish, finely pleated skirt, which gave the effect of a huge Chinese fan being opened swiftly and with a circular motion. With one more swish of her skirt she was gone. All this happened in less than a minute, but the novelty of the experience made quite an impression on me. I had not been to a fashion parade like this before, nor had I ever concerned myself with ladies' dresses. Dior's name first came to my notice through an accident to an Oxford girl undergraduate, who fell off her bicycle in a busy street when her 'New Look' skirt became entangled in one of the wheels. Dior did not design his 'New Look' for cyclists! The dress which I had just seen in the parade was an afternoon gown in a soft, pink woollen material. The oval face of the elegant mannequin, full and ivory white with a slight tint of rouge, underneath a small closely fitting hat of pinkish white feathers, completed the charm and dignified gaiety of the outfit.

While I was trying to appreciate the various points, the next dress appeared, on a different mannequin, and was quickly followed by a third, a fourth, and so on. My head began to ache, for my non-professional mind could not grasp quickly enough such a bewildering display of styles, colours and materials, while my attention was often distracted by the movements and comments of the onlookers. Someone fingered the dark grey silk of a dignified evening gown skilfully held in place, smooth and stiff, as the wearer came round, and remarked: "What lovely material it is!" Another whispered to one of my neighbours, "*C'est ravissant!*" when a three-piece suit in fine black wool appeared with hat, gloves and umbrella to match. But on the whole there was a tense silence in the room: at times one could almost feel the fashionable ladies holding their breath! Many evening dresses appealed to me with their dignity and elegance. I was especially impressed by the delicacy and tastefulness of two afternoon frocks, *Fleur des Bois* and *Cœur de fleurs*, which had many tiny flowers embroidered here and there over the skirt in different colours, with tiny green leaves, on a white ground of soft linen. They were evidently intended for garden parties and other outdoor functions; for young wearers and those young in heart. Another dress that gave me particular pleasure was made of printed silk with a pattern in the Chinese style—large pink peonies with leaves in broad brushwork, and designed by my friend, Miss Chang Chien-yin, for a London fabric company.

The title or name that Monsieur Dior gave to each of the models intrigued me very much. Most of them were names of well-known writers and artists of France, Great Britain and America, past and present; some were named after cities, such as PARIS, LONDRES, NEW YORK, MADRID, and so on. For instance, No. 1 in the list was called ALEXANDRE DUMAS

FILS, *robe soir, boléro,* and No. 18, BERNARD SHAW, *robe soir, paletot.* I was rather surprised at the latter. Though I have read more of Shaw's work and seen more of his plays on the stage and in film than of the other writers in the list, yet I failed to find a connection between his sharp wit and sense of humour and that evening dress and cloak. Perhaps it was too subtle for my layman's eyes. Although many of the French literary figures were not known to me, I thought I could see why Dior had not presented any creation in the names of Victor Hugo or Balzac, for both of them sounded too manly for feminine clothes. The name of the poet Alfred de Musset was chosen for an evening dress with cloak in plain grey silk, hinting perhaps at that poet's inclination towards Wertherism. Yet another great French poet, Charles Baudelaire, was not cited, probably on account of his morbid imagination and subjects, which had no place in the world of fashion. This would also explain why Edgar Allan Poe was not included in the list, though other American writers, such as Eugene O'Neill, had their place. But why, then, was the author of *A Streetcar named Desire,* Tennessee Williams, associated with an afternoon frock and cloak? Many contemporary writers, such as Christopher Fry, Noël Coward and Somerset Maugham, appeared, though their connection with the various garments was too deep for me. However, a tall mannequin wearing a yellowish-grey silk gown did suggest to me the haughty, elegant air of Oscar Wilde's ladies, while another in a black *fourreau soir* well conveyed Ibsen's grim invention. The grey, dignified dress named after LONDON had its counterpart in the loose light one named NEW YORK.

I admired a dinner dress called *Nuit de Chine* in stiff black silk, with a pair of dragons embroidered in gold on each side of the bodice. It was full of dignity, in which the Western style blended admirably with its Chinese decoration. Somehow, I felt, this could not have come from a Chinese hand, nor was it intended to suit a Chinese lady. What interested me in this dress was the choice of black for the ground colour on which to place the Chinese decoration in gold. As black reflects no light, it offered a contrast of tone and made the gilt ornaments embroidered on it stand out more distinctly than they would have done on any other colour. Most colours would distract from the golden-yellow and confuse the eye. White, for instance, which is essentially luminous, would form little contrast of tone with the gold, which is itself luminous. On a white ground the Chinese dragons would have looked insignificant and the point of naming the dress *Nuit de Chine* would have been lost.

The whole question of colour in connection with the show impressed me most favourably. Colours are dangerous to any artistic creation unless very judiciously employed. Monsieur Dior showed a cultured taste in his choice and the combinations of them. Black seemed to be his first favourite. It was used in a number of gowns and costumes, and was evidently planned for women with pale or fair complexions, both of which black supports and heightens. Grey was probably chosen for the same reason. Several mannequins were in white, which looked well on a fresh-complexioned wearer. Two frocks in delicate green were charmingly appropriate for fair ladies. Neither strong green nor bright orange was employed, for both colours would be too vivid for elegance. Dark red appeared more than once; the gowns of this colour betokened a restrained gaiety, suited to large receptions or other formal occasions.

The dress and the wearer complement each other. Monsieur Dior seemed to have selected his mannequins for his various creations with the utmost care and thought. All of them were elegant, fairly tall, and attractive, though each was of a rather different type, and had a special charm of her own and a pronounced individuality. Dior's choice seemed to have been based on the suitability of the girls for his different styles of dress rather than on their standard of beauty. I was told that they were not all French, but that some had come from Scandinavia, Switzerland, and even the United States. I also learnt that they diet themselves strictly and are not to be seen in any of the ordinary restaurants.

One of them was a striking blonde with an oval face, fair complexion and blue eyes, neither so big as to overbalance the nose and mouth, nor so small as to render the face lifeless like a Japanese mask. With such a face she only needed a quiet dress to set it off. Throughout the show she seemed only to wear three colours: lustreless white, pale grey and blue. Both white and grey exalt the colour of a fresh-complexioned face by raising its tone; blue allies itself favourably with white and pale flesh tints. Another mannequin had a totally different face; hers was not oval, but angular, the bones of the cheeks, of the brows and of the ridge of the nose being marked, though not prominent or obvious. It was a characteristic face, indicative of individuality and self-possession. Her skin was a little dark, her hair deep auburn, and her eyes brown, with long black lashes. I noted with satisfaction that Monsieur Dior dressed her in black, dark red, yellow and scarlet, violet and blue-green, all of which contrasted in colour and brilliancy with her face so as to heighten its natural colouring and contours. There was yet another mannequin who had an Oriental face with slanting eyes, high cheek-bones and jet black hair, though she was rather too tall for a Chinese or Japanese lady. Her distinctive features were admirably set off by gowns in strong colours and beautifully printed silks with colourful designs. Despite my ignorance of feminine fashion, I have learned a great deal from Monsieur Dior's fashion parade about the delicate relationship between the colour of the dress and the complexion, features and figure of the wearer. It is clear that a fashionable creation is designed for a certain type and not all types.

While the show was on, some little incidents attracted my attention. Although the day was bright and sunny, every window was tightly shut. By the time a number of dresses had been shown, the air in the room had become stuffy, close and warm—very warm for those who had fur coats round their shoulders. Removing the furs did not seem to ease the situation, so someone asked for a window to be opened a little. Immediately those who were sitting with their backs close to the window protested. I suppose the air of a still-wintry Paris could be disagreeable, but what surprised me was the sudden vulgarity of voice and manner in this exchange of words among such a well-dressed crowd.

An elderly couple were sitting in the front row opposite to us. The lady often rested the large programme on her knees, while she jotted down some notes. Unfortunately, the programme sheet was swept on to the floor, not once but several times, by the swish of the mannequin's skirt. The close air of the room caused the lady's husband to drop asleep now and again. From the beginning he had shown little enthusiasm in the parade: when roused to pick up the paper time after time, his annoyance was apparent and intense. Human nature cannot be concealed by whatever finery we may wear.

A young-looking mother had brought her daughter of thirteen or fourteen with her. The mother, neatly dressed in black with a beautifully-made flower of velvet and dyed feathers on her lapel, smiled appreciatively at each of the models displayed. She would turn her head and murmur a few words to her daughter, whose response was given placidly with an occasional turning-up of the corner of her lips in a sort of half-smile. The mother, with her sophisticated understanding, might have made some witty remark. But her daughter's reaction towards the display interested me. Having a good-looking face, delicate in texture with a slight rosy flush over her cheeks, the girl seemed rather shy and innocent. She was not actually bored by the parade, but she was restless, and fidgeted from time to time. She may have liked some of the dresses inwardly, but outwardly she seemed to be completely indifferent to them. At thirteen or fourteen she probably had not yet experienced the feminine urge to beautify herself.

The show had lasted more than two hours, for the collection was a very large one and even then we had not seen every item on the list. We followed the crowd down the stairs. When we finally reached the show-rooms on the ground floor, Madame Arnaud wanted to see the Marquis de Moussabrè, Christian Dior's joint-manager, who was responsible for the arrangement and management of the parade and who had kindly invited us to view it. While waiting, I mingled with other guests in looking round the show-rooms. I noticed that several ladies had started to try on some of the newest hats which we had seen in the parade, and that some had already made purchases. Eventually in came the tall, handsome Marquis, who doubled his kindness by offering to take us for a quick look round his whole establishment. He regretted that it was already closing time and that we might not find many of his employees still at work. On the way he told us something of the history of Dior House. It was established in 1946 with a staff of eighty, and the first dress show was held there in February, 1947, to launch the 'New Look'. Now there were over 1,000 employees, occupying three houses and twenty *ateliers*. We visited the order-room, packing-room, and despatching-room. In one *atelier* many young midinettes were still working on some designs; in another the head, a man, of the *atelier* was moulding the bodice of a dress on a wooden bust while a few needlewomen watched him.

"The heads of all departments are men" we were told. In the third I saw a large number of wooden dummy heads on a long desk to be used in the modelling of hats. At the sight of a large collection of wooden busts in various sizes on the shelf of yet another *atelier*, I murmured to myself that Monsieur Dior has been creating according to the natural figure of all possible types of customer. In other words, Dior is in command of a vast number of women and rules them with the wand of his originality.

Lastly, the Marquis revealed the efficiency of his management in the spacious and spotless kitchen, with all its modern devices and gadgets. There was as good a canteen for the staff as any I saw in the cities of the United States. He smiled slightly and remarked with satisfaction that the workers in the Dior organisation had no need to take their meals at places like the Restaurant la Questche on the rue des Capucines, which is chiefly frequented by Paris *midinettes*. Dishes were rattling, and footsteps resounding on the stairs, so we bade him *"Au revoir"* with thanks and took our leave.

Throughout the evening my head was full of *robe soir, robe d'aprés-midi, robe diner, manteau, blouse, chapeaux, parapluies*, etc. My eyes were now gazing at a lovely grey flannel suit, now a graceful evening gown in deep purple silk with a cloak of the same colour on an auburn-haired mannequin, as if I was sitting in Dior House again. Sometimes, after spending an hour or two at an art exhibition, I try to shake off the whole impression of what I have just seen, for a while, simply because the pictures I like best tend to become confused either by those intended to shock the spectators or by those which are just a conglomeration of crude colours. In a day or two the jarring elements are forgotten and I can then concentrate on the pictures I have really enjoyed. None of Dior's creations had shocked or startled me; nor had I seen any harsh or displeasing colours. The whole show had impressed me with its refined taste, without the slightest suggestion of vulgarity.

Thinking about vulgarity I suddenly remembered an old Chinese story about a *parvenu*:

A man of low taste became suddenly rich and built himself a large house, which he filled with many valuable art treasures and curios, books, and paintings of all kinds. He invited his friends and the noted personalities of the district to come and see them, and was quite modest about his collections and willing to take advice. To one visitor he said: "Please be so good as to point out to me anything you find not quite appropriate and I will take it away." After a close examination, the visitor remarked that every object in the collection was very beautiful and exquisite, except for one item. Naturally, the collector was curious to know what that could be. Presently came the answer: "Your honourable self!" I could not help thinking of the rich *femmes du monde* who would buy and wear Dior's lovely creations. Would the same be said of them?

An English expert on the fashions of today, James Laver, once remarked that woman is the mould into which the spirit of an age is poured. But without doubt there is more than one type of mould. Moreover, a human mould is not an impersonal thing; the *femme à la mode* has a spirit of her own which evades definition. Madame Ancelot wrote about 'A Leader of Fashion' a hundred years ago as follows:

> For who can say how or why that Queen of Fashion, the *femme à la mode*, is placed upon her throne. It is not beauty, the only incontestable power of woman, that ensures supremacy—for the most beautiful often pass unnoticed. It is not wit or talent, those invisible spirits, which control all others—for very often the idol of the day has none. It is not rank, that superiority which pride no longer admits, for the capricious goddess has never owned its claims; and palaces have been before now deserted for the *boudoir* of a Ninon de l'Enclos. It is not wealth, for fashion frequently, without the least consideration, covers with ridicule the glittering gold, of which vanity makes such parade. There are no sure means for attaining to the pinnacle, nor rules for keeping it, when gained.

A fashionable gown requires personality in the wearer: two equally charming 'moulds' attired in equally fashionable outfits would give an entirely different impression.

In the China of the old days, we kept to strict conventions in women's dress as well as men's. For instance, it was customary for women to take their age strictly into account when choosing the colour of their gowns. No girl under twenty would wear plain black, deep purple, or brown, while those over fifty would never dress in pink, red, or delicate green for fear of appearing frivolous. Many modern Chinese girls ignore the old rules and, despite their different natural colouring and physiognomy, dress in Western styles and colours with lamentable results. Monsieur M. E. Chevreul once wrote that "it is only the dress of women with white skins that is susceptible of being studied in detail". Certainly Christian Dior's creations are chiefly for women with white skins.

I used to hold the view that in beauty and artistic value there is little difference between the art of the West and the East. Now I see there are exceptions. Only art in its purest form, apart from all considerations of physical structure, can have a beauty and aesthetic value that will appeal equally to Westerner and Easterner. But a creation of fashion that can look beautiful on a Westerner will not necessarily look the same on an Easterner. I think this may be due to a somewhat different ideal of physical beauty deriving from the different racial physique.

The following incident is perhaps an illustration of it. On one of my visits to the Musée du Louvre I accompanied an

American-Japanese friend of mine. His parents were both Japanese, but he had been born in America and has lived there ever since. When we came to the gallery containing the original statue of the Venus de Milo, my companion passed over her without even a glance and made straight for the door. I rushed after him and dragged him back, saying that he ought not to miss seeing the world-renowned beauty. Shaking his head, he replied, "Too big; too tall!" No amount of persuasion would make him look at the statue seriously.

We Chinese have our own Venus de Milo, or ideal feminine beauty; she is the Goddess of Lo River. We admire her not from a beautifully sculptured piece of statuary but from a masterly poem. Most educated people learnt it by heart—always remembering a number of lines if not the whole. A certain scholar, Liu Poyu, was very fond of reciting this ancient

Ode to the Goddess of Lo River, and once remarked with a sigh in front of his wife, "What a beauty to have for a wife!" His wife retorted at once: "What do you mean by praising the Goddess of Lo River and insulting me? When I die, I shall become a water-spirit." That night she drowned herself in the river. Some nights later Liu Poyu dreamed of his wife telling him that she had become a goddess and reminding him of his desire to marry one. Ever after Liu Poyu never dared cross the stream for fear of being carried to his death. The river ferry not far from where Liu Poyu lived was called thereafter 'Ferry of the Jealous Woman'. Whenever women crossed the river by this ferry, they had to spoil or crumple their beautiful clothes, lest the spirit of the 'jealous woman' should cause a heavy storm to rise and overturn the ferry-boat. Fortunately, there is no jealous river-spirit in the Seine, or Monsieur Dior's mannequins would have endangered their lives in crossing it.

It is said that many Westerners regard fashionable clothes as 'man-traps', but to us Chinese they seemed to be describable as 'woman-traps'.

One of the prophets of Paris flood showing sign of worry

XIII

None of My Business

THROUGH the good offices of Mademoiselle Josette Vidmer, secretary to Christian Dior, I was able to visit the workrooms of Monsieur and Madame Rébé in the rue Danielle Casanova, near the Place de l'Opéra. The Rébés specialise in embroidery, chiefly for the Christian Dior Company.

Madame Rébé herself ushered us in. Slim and elegant in black silk, with big gold-knob earrings, gold brooch, bracelet, and ring all catching the light, she harmonised perfectly with the bright, sunny room into which she led us. I became uneasily conscious that my creased clothes and lack of sartorial style, and even my Oriental face, had no business in such company. However, Madame Rébé's friendliness and the modest way in which she said she had not much to show us that day overcame my hesitancy.

First, some large coloured silk scarves with embroidered designs were spread before us. The subtlety of their colour combinations enchanted me. Then Madame Rébé took us round the workrooms. On all sides *midinettes* were at work. I was particularly interested in a girl who was embroidering tiny flowers and leaves, every sprig different, all over a long white silk skirt. There seemed to be no guiding marks whatsoever on the skirt, yet the girl stitched away unhesitatingly. When completed, the skirt must have looked as if handfuls of tiny flowers had been freshly picked, tossed at the skirt, and held there by their own little thorns and stalks. I remarked that I had seen two skirts like this in the Christian Dior Spring-and-Summer Show, and Madame Rébé smiled with pleasure.

In his catalogue Christian Dior gave names to the two flowered skirts, but they seemed to me inexpressive names, and in my own mind I called them *Pai-Hua-Wu-Yi*, 'Dancing Garments of a Hundred Flowers', or simply 'Madame Li-Chuan'. There is a story of the time of the Han Dynasty, about the first century B.C., of some silk presented to the Emperor Wu which was said to possess a magnetic effect upon flowers. Any flower that touched it stuck fast. The Emperor had a dancing garment made of it for his favourite lady, Li-Chuan, and she danced in the dress under the flowering trees in the Imperial Garden. By way of applause, flowers were thrown at her, and they all stuck to the dress. The Emperor was delighted and named the gown *Pai-Hua-Wu-Yi*.

Another *midinette* was embroidering a design in gold ribbon on a black silk frock. I say gold ribbon, for the material was not the gold thread I remember Chinese girls using but a ribbon-like gold cord, very thin and not more than a millimetre or two in width. Madame Rébé explained that great skill and patience were needed for this work because the edge of the gold cord was sharp and could easily pull the black silk out of shape. I watched the girl stitching away with a sure hand quite as quickly as I remember Chinese girls embroidering with gold thread. When Madame Rébé translated to her that I had said her skill and patience excelled those of Chinese embroidery girls in Soochow and Hunan, she smiled and murmured, "*Merci, monsieur.*" My remark led Madame Rébé to tell me that in her girlhood she had lived in Shanghai and Peking for many years. She remembered seeing Chinese women doing embroidery. Their work, she said, was "*magnifique*".

My thoughts sped back to Soochow, a great silk-embroidery district near Shanghai. Some twenty-five years ago I visited it and the surrounding countryside with a few friends on a sightseeing excursion, for its scenery is as famous as its embroidery. Outside one of the peasant huts we visited, some girls sat in the brilliant sunshine embroidering a coverlet of pink satin stretched on a wooden frame. We watched them at work. When we started on our way again, we heard chattering behind us and found the girls by our side with long bamboo poles and sedan chairs, inviting us to let them carry us on their shoulders to the nearest viewpoint. We were all young fellows, strong and fit, and the thought of being carried by girls struck us as funny (though in China there is no term corresponding to 'the weaker sex') and we declined. But they were unwilling to return to their embroidery, even when we suggested paying them something for their offer, and eventually it was agreed that they should carry our parcels and the clothes which the heat drove us to discard. I was puzzled by this combination of two opposite types of work, the very delicate skill of embroidery and the heavy, muscular labour of carrying a sedan chair. The girls seemed to feel no incongruity between their tasks, no matter in which order they were performed. I know that, although I could drop work on a 'fine-stroke' painting to dig in the garden, I could not do the reverse.

I should have liked to ask Madame Rébé if she ever encountered these adaptable peasant girls, but she was showing some hats to my companion, and my thoughts roamed again—to the Province of Kiangsi, where I was born. In north-west Kiangsi a famous clothing fabric, made of fine hemp fibre, is produced. It has been known for centuries all over China and even outside the country. As it is used to make garments for wear in warm weather, it is called 'summer cloth'. It is cool, for the air can pass through it easily; yet it is opaque. There are several varieties, differing in accordance with the thickness and colour of the fibre. The cheaper varieties are made of thick fibre with an occasional brownish or black streak. The best cloth is pure white and made of the finest and lightest fibres, with a surface as smooth as silk. The most flawless lengths of summer cloth are embroidered with flowers and other designs from Nature, and have always been very highly priced. In my boyhood I often heard how summer cloth was made. The fibre was sorted by young unmarried girls between the ages of sixteen and twenty. Only they, it was thought, had sufficient delicacy of touch and singleness of mind to select the best fibres and to work out the designs, for they had no domestic worries; they did not, in those days, even have to concern themselves with selecting a life-partner. Everything was seen to by their parents. So their minds were pure and unperturbed—that, at least, was the theory—and they could concentrate on choosing the best fibres instead of the best husband. Time has changed all this. Chinese girls of today are generally not as patient as their sisters of the generations gone by. I wonder for how long a Parisian girl of sixteen can maintain an unperturbed mind? Perhaps I am unjust, since there are so many *midinettes* in Paris. But *midinettes* are exceptional; no other city in the world possesses such a specialised class of needle-workers.

Involuntarily I asked Madame Rébé if any of her girls were married. "Yes," she answered. "Some. But why?" An awkward

moment for me was happily eased by my companion's exuber-
ant admiration of a 'simply beautiful' hat adorned with
daisies. Madame Rébé held the hat in her hand, raising it
and lowering it, holding it nearer us and then again further
away so that we might enjoy the full effect. Madame Rébé
remarked that in her workrooms they loved "*La belle Marguerite*". In her opinion Paris is the world centre for ideas on dress
design. Frocks, hats, sunshades, gloves, valises—the best ideas
all came from Paris. Ideas bubbled up incessantly within
the boundaries of the city of elegance. Ten or twenty miles
outside it, the fountain dried up. People from all over the
world came to Paris to feel the ideas, to pick them up and work
them out. And, of course, people also came to fight and
struggle for them. She spoke of a friend who thought she could
do well in New York, but after a year there her ideas were all
used up and she had to come back to Paris to gather some
more, intending to return in due course to the United States:
she was still in Paris. "I do not know why only Paris has new
ideas," continued Madame Rébé. Whatever the reason, it is a
fact, and it applies to other arts than those of dress. Paris is
the modern world's Mecca of art.

The arrival of Monsieur Rébé brought back my straying
thoughts. He had a happy, round face with a neatly trimmed
white moustache. Apologising for having been detained, he
proceeded to tell us that though spring was only just on its
way to Paris, all the spring-summer fashion shows were already
over. He would soon be going to Greece and Italy to collect
material and to form new ideas for the autumn-winter fashions.
"To find new ideas about dress," he continued, "is not easy.
They must arise out of full knowledge of the past, the present,
the climate of the place, the conditions of the wearer, the
material to be used, etc." He then related that he had formerly
worked under his father, who had a business in London.
After returning to Paris, he had started a business of his own,
and now spent all his time working with his wife at new ideas.
During the Coronation of King George VI he opened a
business in New Bond Street, London, and fashioned new
creations for the occasion. He was now hoping that he and his
wife would be invited to bring new ideas to lead London
fashions for the Coronation of the young Queen Elizabeth II.

My companion and I now thanked the Rébés for their kindness. She went on to another engagement, while my legs took me slowly past the windows of the shops in the rue de la Paix. Now, any shop-window in Paris, big or small, can detain a passerby. Many a time I walked slowly, feasting my eyes, along the Avenue de l'Opéra, the rue de la Paix, the Place

View from the Palais Royal

Vendôme, the rue de Rivoli, the Faubourg St Honoré, the rue Royale, the Avenue des Champs Elysées, and all round the Rond-Point. As I have mentioned already, modern art movements, particularly Surrealism and Abstractism, have influenced many kinds of design and decorative arrangement, but they have had little effect on Paris fashions. To my amusement, however, I did see a window dressed in Cubist style—squares, circles and triangles made of thick iron wire providing the background effect. Who are the customers at whom all this design is directed? I could never make up my mind.

The next day I went to see the famous statue of St Catherine, the patron saint of the *midinettes*, in the Boulevard de Bonne Nouvelle. On November 25th all the *midinettes* gather round the Archbishop of Paris outside the church of Nôtre-dame-de-Bonne-Nouvelle. Nothing of this kind was happening on this day. I wandered round a little disconsolately till I found the restaurant, La Questche, on the rue des Capucines, which is

I

said to be the luncheon place of the *midinettes*. It was full of women, mostly young and all well-dressed. There is no doubt that *midinettes* do understand how to use the products of their trade. I tried to overhear their talk, but their swift-falling words were too much for my ears.

Still thinking about fashion ideas, I remembered reading in a book published more than 100 years ago an amusing account of the origin of bonnets. Bonnets were first worn by a French *midinette* to whom Nature had given such a large nose that street urchins would follow her, laugh at her and call her nose by the most uncomplimentary names. She created the bonnet, with its overhanging brim, to escape their ribaldry. The disguise proved effective, and other French women no prettier than she were quick to adopt it. She soon made money. Slight differences of colour and trimming followed, but the general shape of the bonnet remained constant. Gradually those who disdained the bonnet because they had beautiful faces, or anyhow were not as plain as the inventor of that headdress, found themselves in the minority and began to lose their monopoly of the attention of the gentlemen. Ultimately they were compelled ignominiously to assume the headdress of their ugly rivals. Thus arose the bonnet fashion, which was to cover the European continent and to cross the English Channel and even the Atlantic Ocean.

The same book furnishes the alleged origin of another feminine garment. An English butcher of the thirteenth century married a wife who, born loquacious, grew after their marriage so ceaselessly talkative that she was not to be endured. The butcher therefore made a pair of stays and put them on his wife with the object of shortening her breath and thus stopping her chatter. The stays proved effective and the butcher was soon the envy of his friends, who began to copy his invention and, like him, enjoy peace at home. Before long there was scarcely a wife in all London who was not wearing stays. So universal at last did stays become that in self-defence the ladies made a fashion of them. So the story goes. Doubtless the 'fashionable' stays were more comfortable than those designed by the butcher. Both these stories seem to me to possess something of the truth of myth.

The former Chinese preference for small feet in women, which became nation-wide and caused agony to a great many unfortunate girls, is said to have begun in a similar way. Centuries ago a young man loved his wife so excessively and jealously that he was in constant fear that she would run away from him. In the end his jealousy drove him to the cruelty of forcing her to bind her feet so that they became smaller and smaller. The agony she endured, which constantly brought tears to her eyes, did not move him to mercy. Gradually the wife got used to her bound feet, and was able to walk, slowly and carefully, but with complete serenity. She was certainly entitled to sympathy for the torture she bravely bore. In fact, she earned praise and love from her husband such as she had never been accorded before. Her natural beauty of face was enhanced in his eyes by her new way of walking, with her arms slightly outstretched to keep her balance and her feet moving in tiny steps delicately and gracefully. By degrees she even forgot the pain and enjoyed the increased admiration, not only of her husband, but of his friends. Many laudatory verses were written about her beauty and her gait, and she eventually became an object of envy. Innumerable young women and girls proceeded to die of the pain caused by binding their feet, just as modern Western girls are prepared to suffer in the interests of slimming. Yet the fashion spread. Gradually no young man of good family and literary reputation in China was willing to wed a girl whose feet were not small. Accordingly, parents, especially mothers, saw to it that their daughters' feet were small in order to improve their prospects of marriage. It was found best to start the treatment while the girl was still of tender age; between the ages of five and ten was usual. Verses in praise of small feet were constantly written; paintings of famous beauties with incredibly tiny feet circulated; drinking games in which the tiny embroidered shoes of these beauties were used as wine cups were devised; in the end the binding of feet was taken for granted, just like the wearing of stays.

Occasionally broad-minded and enlightened men protested against the imposition of this unnatural suffering on womankind, but without much result. There is a well-known Chinese satirical novel entitled *Chin-Hua-Yuan*, written some 200 years ago and still in print and widely read, in which a chapter describes a 'Country of Women' where all the common practices of the sexes are reversed. Bearded men do the domestic work while women engage in politics and rule the country; men's feet are bound while women stride about on feet of natural size, and so on. In the story three Chinese, a scholar, a philosopher, and a merchant, leave China for a world tour and visit by chance this Country of Women. The merchant is the youngest of the three and his exceptionally handsome face is noticed by the 'King' (a woman) of the country, who decides to make him his 'Queen'. So the merchant is seized by the King's men (all women) and driven to the Palace. Before the royal wedding can take place, his feet have to be diminished, in obedience to the King's orders. This takes a month or two, and the young man suffers agony which he is certain will kill him. When at last he is led, pale and feeble, to the female King, he is admired and loved exhorbitantly. The detailed description of his sufferings made generations of readers laugh, but it did not shake the grip of the foolish foot-binding fashion. Not until China was invaded and defeated by Western powers about 100 years ago and the sight of Western women with big feet became familiar in our towns did Chinese men became reconciled to seeing their women with normal-sized feet. The opportunity was avidly seized by the women: bound feet were unbound and daughters were thankfully relieved of the misery of ever starting to bind their feet. Gradually bound feet disappeared from the cities of China and even from the countryside. Western civilisation did this undoubted service to China's womenkind. And now some Chinese poets and scholars have sought new subject matter and inspiration in *large* feet!

Twenty years ago, soon after my first landing on English soil, I went round several church bazaars at Christmas time and saw displayed for sale small embroidered shoes made of Chinese silk. They were of a size that could only have been worn by women with bound feet. The story was that they had been brought back from China by missionaries and traders. The intention in exhibiting the shoes was to arouse interest in Chinese customs, and the proceeds of the sale were to go to save Chinese souls. I was amazed and amused. Since the outbreak of the Second World War, small embroidered Chinese shoes have been seen no more in church bazaars, either because of the impossibility of importing them or because of the huge number of other souls evidently in need of saving.

At this point I remembered an incident I had witnessed in Montmartre a few days previously. A young couple were descending the long flights of steps from the summit, singing and laughing. When still a good way from the foot, the young man executed several flying steps like a ballet dancer and entered a tobacconist's shop, presumably to buy some cigarettes. The young lady, left alone, caught one of her high-heeled shoes on the edge of a step, pitched forward, and rolled

down the stone stairs screaming and moaning. The young man dashed out at once and running to her kneeled down and kissed her face and hands tenderly, evidently not knowing what else to do. The young lady could no longer even moan; the steps and ground were wet, for the rain had only stopped shortly before; her suit acquired a new pattern. An elderly Parisian offered to call a taxi, but the young man said no, and the elderly man moved away. So did I, for I could not converse in French and if the elderly man could do nothing, how could I do more? But it seemed that after all the young woman was not seriously hurt. How did the fashion of wearing high heels start? It occurred to me that pairs of smart high-heeled shoes might be turned to good account at bazaars in China, for the benefit of—— But suddenly I remembered my sister starting to wear high heels some thirty years ago, and I realised that this wouldn't do. The object of binding feet was to secure what was considered an elegant manner of walking. Would that be so very different from the object of wearing high-heeled shoes?

Oh, Fashion, Fashion! What extravagances are perpetrated in thy name! Thou art none of my business.

XIV

A Pair of Powerful Hands

I FIRST met Napoleon some forty years ago in a Chinese
school textbook, which told me that *Na-p'o-lun* was a great
man of France who won many battles, made a code of laws
and did other famous deeds. The names of the battles were
transcribed in Chinese characters and sounded very odd. I
had not the slightest idea where the battlefields were; indeed,
I did not even know where France was. At the age of ten it
never occurred to me that I should ever want to see Napoleon's
tomb or the Empire he had ruled over somewhere beyond the
horizon. Hero-worship formed no part of my education, and I
did not pay any attention to the importance which the textbook seemed to attach to Napoleon. But now as I walked
about Paris I felt the presence of the Emperor in every corner
of the city, as though his unseen, powerful hands had moulded
it. In this he is unique. Rome, for example, is not stamped with
Augustus, nor Peking with Genghis Khan.

Only a few days after my arrival a French girl insisted upon
pointing out to me the big letter 'N' on the pedestals between
the arches and underneath the parapets of the Pont au Change.
A little later, when travelling to Sèvres with another French
friend, our autobus passed the Arc de Triomphe de l'Etoile
and I was urged to look back at the group of sculpture adorning
the wall of the arch. Seen from a certain angle, it formed a
silhouetted image of Napoleon being reprimanded by someone.
Had I not already become familiar with his face from many
paintings and statues I might not have grasped what my friend
meant, for the likeness was only suggested. Of course, this
unfortunate arrangement can only have been discovered long
after the erection of the arch, and must have been far from
the minds of the sculptors, who were concerned to exalt the
great Emperor. The groups of sculpture on this famous arch
represent episodes in the history of France from the Revolution
of 1789 to the peace of 1815. In front are four colossal groups

representing, respectively, Triumph by Cortot, Peace and
Resistance by Etex, and the Departure by Rude. Though this
arch was begun under Napoleon, after the design of Chalgrin,
to commemorate the victories of 1805-6, the Emperor never
saw it finished except as a small model in wood. Nevertheless,
he passed through it when his coffin was brought back from
St Helena on December 15th, 1840. I was most interested to
learn that the foundations of the arch were constructed on
solid pillars of stone, sunk twenty-four feet deep into the Paris
soil, which had been found too loose to support the weight of
the enormous monument.

Facing the Arc de Triomphe de l'Etoile is the Place de la
Concorde, so named by Napoleon. And facing that, straight
through the Tuileries Gardens, stands the Arc de Triomphe du
Carrousel, designed on the plan of the Arch of Septimius
Severus at Rome and erected by Napoleon's architects,
Percier and Fontaine, to commemorate the victories of 1805.
Both fronts are decorated with four columns of the Corinthian
order supporting the marble figures of fighting men. The
present quadriga, the work of Bosio, on the top of this arch
succeeded the chariot and four bronze horses of Lemot which
were removed from St Mark's Square, Venice, by Napoleon,
who later returned them to their original place. This is a clear
instance of Napoleon's powerful hands at work.

After the Revolution the Louvre, I was told, degenerated
into a communal house for barely self-supporting artists and
other indigent people; it was filthy, with washing of all sorts
hanging out of the windows. One night in 1806 Napoleon
ordered the ancient palace of the French kings to be cleared.
He also gave orders for the construction of the section to the
west of the oldest part of the Pavillon de Rohan. When I
stood in front of David's painting of Napoleon at his Coronation
I could see his powerful hands actually moving as I recalled
the words of the Duchess d'Abrantes: "When it came to his

Bird's-eye View of the Champs Elysées from the Musée du Louvre

own crown, he (Napoleon) hastily took it from the Pope's
hands and placed it haughtily on his own head—a proceeding
which doubtless startled his Holiness." I learnt that part
of the Louvre had been opened as a museum before Napoleon
became Emperor, and since then the palace has been chiefly
known as the National Art Gallery of France. The whole world
was ransacked for pictures representing all the schools of
painting. There are pictures belonging to the former Kings
of France, the Italian paintings of François I, the Flemish
and Dutch and French paintings of Louis XIV, as well as gifts
of famous collectors and the purchases of the State. Immense
contributions came from Napoleon, who brought back great
works from every country his armies overran. He was not
only busy with his legs and feet, but tremendously so with
his powerful hands. But I must acknowledge that, apart from
his brilliant mind, active legs and powerful hands, he had
intelligent and artistic eyes. Perhaps it was in this that he
differed from the other great conquerors, such as Alexander or
Genghis Khan.

Some say that Napoleon brought the body of Cleopatra to
Paris and that she is buried in the gardens of the Bibliothèque
Nationale. This is only legend, but I liked it. The story goes
that until 1870 three mummies which Napoleon brought back
from Egypt were kept with the rest of the Egyptian antiquities.
Unexpectedly, the bands round one of the mummies broke
and revealed a woman's figure "of a Greek cast of countenance
and adorably beautiful", as was testified by Monsieur Morteuil,
formerly General Secretary of the Library. Monsieur Morteuil
and his friends took her to be Cleopatra and called her so.
Unfortunately, Cleopatra and her companions had to be
rushed into the cellar for safety during the disturbances at the
time of the Commune in 1871. Absolutely air-tight conditions
were not available there and the humidity caused decom-
position. When the mummies were brought to light again,
the decision had to be taken to bury them all in the gardens at
once. On a cool spring night Monsieur Morteuil, holding a
lantern, led the funeral procession. No more was heard of the
mummies. I agree with Monsieur Roland-Manuel that "This
story is too pretty to let perish. Let us believe in it until it is
contradicted by some further discovery. If it should happen
that the authentic remains of Cleopatra are discovered in

Alexandria, it would be sad: it would seem to me that sweet
enchantment had departed from the library." Modern science
has made our life too clear-cut and unromantic; a little mystery
makes life more interesting. I wish Monsieur Morteuil had set
up a bronze plaque or tablet of some sort to mark the site
where it could be alleged the renowned beauty of Egypt lies.
The gardens would be full of people paying homage.

Though the history of the Comédie Francaise does not
begin with Napoleon, it was he who signed a decree in 1800
by which the theatre became state property, and later he
gave it its present constitution. He was a sincere lover of the
drama and an ardent admirer of the plays of Sophocles,
Aeschylus and Euripides. Again, it was Napoleon who made
the Hôtel de Ville the seat of the Prefect of the Seine and the

Council. The most conspicuous reminder of him is the bronze
statue poised on the top of the Colonne Vendôme in the
beautiful Place Vendôme. This is said to have been erected
in 1810 by the Emperor with the metal obtained from melting
1,200 cannon taken from the Germans. It is an imitation of
Trajan's Column in Rome and is 155 feet high. Its bas-reliefs
again illustrate the principal events of the campaign of 1805.
Though it suffered destruction and the present statue is only
a replica of the first one by Dumont, the 378 sheets of bronze
forming the castings are so perfectly adjusted that the whole
column appears to be one mass of solid metal. This must be
credited to the skilful hands of the French craftsmen, not
to the powerful hands of the Emperor. The present rue de la
Paix, opened in 1806, was originally named rue Napoléon.

Napoleon's order to erect a 'Temple of Glory' to the soldiers of the *Grande Armée* on the site of the Church of the Madeleine in 1806 was not fulfilled, though he is often mistakenly claimed as the creator of it. Nor was his grand scheme for improving the Bois de Boulogne carried out, but during his reign many new trees were planted there.

One kindly old Parisienne pointed out to me the Hôtel de Metz, where the Emperor used to lodge before he became famous, another dragged me to see the room at No. 3, rue d'Antin, where Napoleon was married to Josephine. I myself tried to locate the Café de la Régence and the Café Corazza which Napoleon frequented as a captain. He must have had many haunts in Paris known to his contemporaries. Time has erased some unimportant marks of his powerful hands, yet I still felt them strongly at work.

After much persuasion, I went to see Napoleon's tomb at the Hôtel des Invalides. Not that I had anything against seeing his tomb, nor the impressive building, but I felt bewildered at being reminded of his death while he still seemed so very much alive everywhere. I got out at the Metro station Duroc and first walked through the rue Duroc to see the monument to Pasteur at the Place de Breteuil, not far from the Pasteur Institute. The great bacteriologist stands on a pedestal surrounded by the figures of grateful women bringing their tributes, and a figure of Death vanquished. It is a good statue, serving its purpose.

I then sat on a bench for a while meditating on the Place de Breteuil, which seems to have had a connection with the saving of life for a long time past. The monument to Pasteur stands on the site of a famous artesian well formerly surmounted by a decorated column 130 feet high, constructed by the engineer Delaporte. It was pulled down in 1903. This well was begun in 1834, at the cost of the city of Paris, and completed in 1841, and had a depth of over 1,600 feet. The work was carried out by the mechanical engineer, Monsieur Mulot, and proved to be an expensive undertaking. Before locating the water, Monsieur Mulot had dug for seven years without success. At last, on February 26th, 1841, he struck the greensand, which contained sparkling water. Suddenly the water rose in a torrent which flooded the adjoining premises. The neighbours, far from resenting this inundation, gave vent to exclamations

of joy. Although drenched, they shared the general enthusiasm
displayed by the rest of Paris. The discovery was then considered a great triumph of human science. From that time
until the modern water supply was introduced, the well
furnished daily 1 million litres of water, which was stored in
the reservoir that formerly existed near the Panthéon. The good
it did to the inhabitants must have been immeasurable, yet
no memorial to Monsieur Mulot is to be found here. Pasteur's
work must have saved countless lives, particularly women's
and children's and is still saving them and will continue to do
so, not only in Paris, but throughout the world; yet the
monument to his life-saving work is negligible in comparison with the monument to Death at the north end
of the Avenue de Breteuil. I looked up at the gilt dome of
the Hôtel des Invalides with a feeling of the injustice of the
past.

I walked towards the Hôtel des Invalides along the Avenue
de Breteuil. The fine double carriage-way with grass and
flower-beds down the centre, looked newly made, but was
in fact laid out in 1680. With such a 300-year-old example,
it is not surprising that there should be so many spacious roads
with turf and flower-beds in other parts of Paris. The dull,
sunless morning did not help the houses on either side to look
younger; the overpowering gilt dome of the Invalides made
them look dowdy. The beautiful gate and tall iron railings
attracted me as I approached them, and I liked the fine
façade of the building. Presently the morning clouds dispersed
to reveal the blue sky, and stronger sunlight glinted on the
dome and made it sparkle so that its golden rays illuminated
everything around it. It was an astonishing sight.

Having paid the admission fee and entered, I felt more
subdued than awed. The building was not as spacious inside
as I had expected, nor was it designed like the nave of a church,
as one would have imagined looking at it from the outside.
Much of the interior was taken up with tombs, twelve colossal
statues and fifty-four flags arranged in six trophies. I looked
at the altar beyond the barrier of red rope, but I was chiefly
interested in the circular space directly under the dome.
This was an open crypt, said to be only twenty feet deep and
thirty-six feet in diameter, with the tomb of the Emperor.
Everything planned with his powerful hands had been on a

grand scale, but his body lies in the centre of a circle only thirty-six feet in diameter.

I leaned over the balustrade and looked down. There is room enough for people to move around, but the whole structure lacks grandeur. The design of the sarcophagus,

which is carved in Finland granite, the gift of the Emperor Nicholas of Russia, is simple, but I doubt if it can be described as classical. The curvilinear movement of the lid, with the suggestion of softness which curves always impart, was not in keeping with the weight, power and prowess of the Emperor lying beneath. Red Finland granite is said to be very hard to carve; the craftsmanship of this sarcophagus, although I felt it was more suitable to a palatial hall than a tomb, was admirable in itself. The ox-liver colour of the stone imparted a solemn effect, but it made me feel cold. There seems to be an ancient notion that the coffin of an Emperor should be larger than that of an ordinary person. But this sarcophagus lacks the scale appropriate to an Emperor, let alone Napoleon. When I recalled all that I had found of him in Paris, I felt disturbed that his death had not been more fittingly commemorated. I felt empty and cold; the feeling of powerful hands was quite lacking. I made haste to go. I did not try to see any of the Napoleonic relics, nor to discover

the whereabouts of the Musée Historique. I saw a notice
directing me to the Musée de l'Armée, but that was a place
I had no wish to see. (I have lived in England for nearly
twenty years without ever bringing myself to visit the Imperial
War Museum in London.)

I followed a lady visitor out through the corridors and
courtyards and found myself facing the cannon on the terrace
overlooking the Esplanade des Invalides. Thence I strolled
slowly down the middle of the Avenue du Maréchal Gallieni.
The spaciousness of this esplanade revived my pleasure at
being in Paris. I love the spaciousness of Paris streets, the wide
avenues, gardens, and long vistas. Indeed, I think that this
aspect of the city is the one which has impressed and pleased
me most. Paris has made the best possible use of space, and
that is why I like walking there better than in most of the
cities I know.

My thoughts went back to Napoleon's tomb. His own wish
has been fulfilled, for he stated in his will: "I desire that my
ashes repose on the banks of the Seine, in the midst of the
French people whom I have loved so well." The Hôtel des
Invalides, in which he rests, was not his creation. It was built
by Louis XIV to house his old soldiers in the way that the
Chelsea Royal Hospital in London was built for English
Pensioners. And I could not help feeling that a tomb of that
nature would have been better situated outside the city, like
the Pyramids of the great Egyptian kings.

In my own country, on the outskirts of the City of Hanchow,
there is a wonderfully simple yet impressive tomb of a great
Sung general Yueh Fei, who lived at the end of the twelfth
century. Yueh Fei, when he had won battle after battle against
invading enemies, was betrayed by a treacherous prime
minister and put to death. His noble character, courageous
life and undeserved death acquired a great moral meaning
for the Chinese, and they have been paying homage to his
tomb for the past 700 years. I went there several times when I
was a college student. I think the bare simplicity of the huge
tomb, with its spacious hall in front, commanded our reverence.
Among modern shrines I like the Lincoln Memorial in
Washington best.

My walk had now taken me to the Pont Alexandre III,
the widest of all the bridges over the Seine within the Paris

boundaries. The gilt horses and figures surrounding the four pillars at either end of the bridge dazzled my eyes as the sun caught them. The vistas of the bridge are magnificently planned to lead up at one end to the Grand Palais and the Petit Palais and at the other to the Esplanade and the Hôtel des Invalides.

I rested my arms on the parapet and looked at the river. The waters of the Seine have been flowing at least as long as the waters of the Yangtse which wash the southern shore of my hometown, Kiukiang, where, at the beginning of the third century, a famous general, Chou Yü of Wu State, defeated the fleet of Wei. The general, a young man at the time, is said to have had a pair of powerful hands and to have won many victories for his Emperor. When I was a boy I used to play along the riverside. At Kiukiang the Yangtse is so wide that I could never see the farther shore. A small tugboat took an hour to cross over and back. Big fleets of war junks could sail to and fro and engage in battle as in an ocean. It was at a point a little below Kiukiang that Chou Yü is said to have laid the massive iron chain from shore to shore to trap the fleet of Wei. Many historical sites associated with him in my home town were well-known and often visited by me. Chou's wife, renowned as a great beauty, was the younger sister-in-law of the Emperor; a road named after her was still in existence when I left Kiukiang some twenty years ago. Su Tung-P'o, a great poet of the Sung dynasty, wrote a memorable poem about the young general when he came down the Yangtse from the Gorges and passed the battlefields along the Red Cliffs a little above Kiukiang. Every Chinese scholar for centuries has learned the poem by heart. The following is a translation by my friend Mr. Ch'u Ta Kao, but the powerful music and rhythm of each line cannot be rendered in English. We often recite it after a cup of wine:

The waves of the mighty river flowing eastward
Have swept away the brilliant figures of a thousand generations.
West of the old fortress,
So people say, is Lord Chou's Red Cliff of the time of the Three
　　States.
The tumbling rocks thrust into the air;
The roaring surges dash upon the shore,
Rolling into a thousand drifts of snow.
The river and the mountains make a vivid picture—
What a host of heroes once were!

It reminds me of the young Lord then,
When the fair Younger Ch'iao newly married him,
Whose valorous features were shown forth;
Amid talking and laughing, he put his enemy's ships to ashes and
   smoke.

While my thoughts wander in the country of old,
Romantic persons might smile at my early grey hair.
Ah, life is but like a dream;
With a cup of wine, let me yet pour a libation to the moon on the
   river.

大江東去浪淘盡千古
流人物故壘西邊人道是
三國周郎赤壁亂石崩雲
驚濤裂岸捲起千堆雪江
山如畫一時多少豪傑
遙想公瑾當年小喬初嫁
了雄姿英發羽扇綸巾
笑間強虜灰飛煙滅故國
神游多情應笑我早生華
髮人間如夢一尊還酹江
月

蘇軾念奴嬌赤壁懷古

The moon had not yet come out over the Seine as I leaned on
the parapet of the Pont Alexandre III, and I had no cup of
wine, but many of my hairs are grey. Glancing back at the
Hôtel des Invalides, I recited this poem to myself.

Sunset over the Pont Alexandre III

XV

More Powerful Hands

CERTAIN parts of Paris exhibit the works of another pair of hands than those mentioned in the last chapter, but a pair that are tender as well as strong: the hands of Auguste Rodin.

His statue of Victor Hugo, near the Théatre Français, in the spacious gardens of the Palais Royal, was erected in 1909. At the south end of the central gardens running down the Boulevard Raspail and the Boulevard du Montparnasse, his massive but strong and aloof statue of Balzac, erected in 1939, seemed to have turned the great novelist into a stage-announcer on the performance of his *Comédie Humaine*. But the bronze group, *The Burghers of Calais*, in the Place Richelieu made a deeper mark on my mind than any of the host of other statues and monuments in the gardens of the Tuileries and the Luxembourg and many other places. Not that this sculpture is more beautiful or 'better' than the others, but it speaks clearly and I can understand its meaning without racking my brains to discover what it actually represents.

The great monument—the one to Gambetta—is very fine, and no visitor to Paris should—or can—miss it, for it stands in a wonderful position facing the Arc de Triomphe du Carrousel in the middle of the road leading to the Louvre. But for me it is only a rather anonymous monument in gleaming white marble. I remember that the flying, tossed, and ruffled frockcoat of the figure is so beautifully executed that I imagined Gambetta to be an actor! Otherwise it says nothing to me. As for the other statues and monuments of Paris, many of them are of kings and queens of whose history I knew little or nothing. Others are startling nudes. The rest are either allegorical or symbolical or mythological; and whichever it happens to be I am puzzled. In the end I did not even scratch my head when I came upon a fresh statue, but merely said to myself, "Another statue."

When I first saw *The Burghers of Calais* I moved over to glance at it, but remained to gaze for a long time. I was deeply moved by the way that each of the six men in the group seemed to convey some emotion that I had myself experienced. At that time I did not know the burghers' story, nor did it occur to me then to find it out. I saw that these men stood at the most critical moment of their lives, when they were faced with a life-or-death decision. Each figure expresses agony, sorrow, and urgency in its own way. All six men are hard pressed, but they are too tense for hysteria. And they are not angry; none of them betrays the slightest sign of hatred. In their circumstances, it was evident to me, such feelings would have been futile. Their minds are made up and they will accept the consequences of their decision.

No one who has experienced a moment of real crisis—has been forced to make a decision under threat of death—could fail to be struck by this bronze group, even if in complete ignorance of the story behind it. Nevertheless, the story makes the sculpture more poignant. The six burghers face death in order to bear, with the keys of Calais, a petition for mercy to the harsh King Edward of England, who had besieged the town for eleven months (1346-7) without breaking the resistance of the starving inhabitants. These six simple and honest citizens, non-belligerents, would have been hanged had not the gentle Queen interceded for them with her not-so-gentle husband.

When the sculptor first displayed this group, a warm controversy arose. I think I can see why the work was not at once acceptable. Many of Rodin's contemporaries at the end of the nineteenth century were still deeply prejudiced in favour of the traditional rendering of a patriotic or heroic subject; for them the hero had to be outstanding—some sort of superman. His hands must be firm, his muscles strong and tenacious, his gestures mobile but powerful; his facial expression generally as if he were shouting; he must never be meek or hopeless. Rodin's vision saw far ahead of his contemporaries and he meant his work to be universal, impersonal (meaning above prejudice) and eternal.

The burghers of Calais were not supermen, nor even particularly unusual men: they were simple men with a clear conscience and the resolution to act upon a balanced judgement. The world must have produced many other such men, ready to perform a self-sacrificing deed in circumstances of emergency. Wherever wars have been waged such modest heroes have existed, and seldom have monuments been erected to them. I could relate many parallel stories from the history of China. This bronze group by Rodin is the only great monument in Western art which could stand on Chinese soil and there be permanently revered. This is because of its universal quality.

How can the universal quality of this group be defined? I think it lies chiefly in the *naturalness* of the postures of the figures, particularly in the expressiveness of the hands. The bearded fellow, who is the leader, declares: 'If I die in the quarrel to save the rest, God will pardon me; wherefore, to save them I will be the first to put my life in jeopardy.' His head, slightly bowed, shows him deep in thought for the agony of his fellow-beings within the city and of his own agony, which will follow swiftly on his speech. Both his hand and arm are drooping as naturally as would any old, fatigued hand and arm. There is no strength left in them after the struggle to reach the decision, and no hint whatever of heroic attitudinising. Though feeble of limb, he stands fast and firm in a philosophic posture, as if thinking that the remnant of his already long life is a small sacrifice for the rest of the citizens. The burgher on his left shows more determination than the others, for he holds the key and has been chosen to hand it to the English King. His deep-set eyes stare intensely, awaiting the ordeal, but show no ill-will or hatred. His lips are tightly closed, the upper one sunk instead of curled to denote anger. His body is erect, his arms straight, and his fingers grip the key. He too, clearly, has no thought of looking like a hero. The burgher behind him clasps his head tightly in both hands. He is called the 'weeping burgess'; I do not know if it was the sculptor's idea to call him so. To me he is not weeping, or regretting his decision to join the group; an unbearable agony has assailed him, following his decision, and he holds his head in his hands, each finger expressive of the violence of his feelings. It is a natural and understandable attitude in one who, in the prime of life, is making the supreme sacrifice. But he is not faltering or shrinking. The same can be said of the fourth figure, who cannot help looking back at his beloved town, rubbing his eyes first, believing that he will never see it again.

The last two, brothers, both young, are expressing their

decision firmly, the one by stretching out both arms and hands, as if to say that there is no other hope for Calais, and the other by raising his right hand, as if declaring that his is the only way.

This wonderful group is only one of many Paris sculptures made by the powerful yet tender hands of Auguste Rodin. I had seen some of his work in England and America before I began to make a fuller study of it at the Musée Rodin in the Hôtel Biron on the rue Varennes, where the originals or the replicas and studies of most of his best work are to be found. I came to this museum twice. My first visit was made with a few friends on a warm afternoon in February, and after a quick look-round I had to follow them out of doors. At that time I thought it would have been better for my companions if Rodin's wish to have his works suitably arranged in a public garden among trees and flowers had been fulfilled.

I came again alone one early afternoon in late March. There were very few visitors, and I moved at ease from one exhibit to another. Here I saw *The Man with the Broken Nose*, *The Age of Brass* and *The Crouching Woman*. Here I saw many busts of notable men and women, such as Victor Hugo, Clemenceau, Shaw, Madame Rodin, the Duchesse de Choiseul, and so on. Here I saw the studies for *The Burghers of Calais*, *The Shadow*, *The Three Fauns*, and also the studies for *The Gate of Hell*. I saw a number of Rodin's drawings and sketches from which he worked up his sculptures in stone and metal, hanging on the walls behind the sculptures. I greatly enjoyed the vast quantities of plaster casts in the adjoining chapel. Later I saw the entire work *The Gate of Hell* (though it was never completed) in bronze (1880-1917) with *The Three Shadows* on the top and *The Thinker* in small size directly underneath, set close by the wall of the garden near the chapel. I sauntered slowly along the garden path, sorting out all I had just seen. The twigs and branches of the trees were covered with tiny green and yellow buds, but the dark straight trunks brought a sense of coolness and subdued colour, which helped to calm and clear my mind.

I was now near the big pedestal of stone on which sits the great bronze figure of *The Thinker*. Rodin must have made a special plaster copy of it from the studies which he did for *The Gate of Hell*, and several bronze copies of it must have been cast, for I saw one in Columbia University in New York.

It was set in an enclosure of evergreens not far from the back of the house. I brushed the dust from one of the steps below the pedestal and sat down with my back to *The Thinker*. A suitable spot to think in, if ever there was one! After two hours of gazing at the exhibits inside the building and the chapel as well as the complete *Gate of Hell* in the garden, my mind was a welter of muscles and limbs and postures projected into me by this great modern sculptor. While I was contemplating his art, although his actual figure eluded me, I felt his presence, particularly his pair of powerful hands, as if he was still there to smooth or to add a lump of clay here and there. I wondered what Rodin looked like. I imagined him with a grotesque head and a big bump sticking out of his forehead, as we generally portray our great thinker, Confucius. But to judge from his self-portrait, the space between his rough hair and his drawn brows was narrow. How did he, with such a narrow forehead, conceive the ideas of *The Burghers of Calais* and *The Gate of Hell*?

I thought of him as very strongly built, tall, with firm muscles and powerful hands, able to twist stone and metal at will. But, according to the description of his friend, Camille Mauclair, he was of medium stature, gentle-looking, with a big head and prominent nose, flowing beard, small bright eyes and often reticently folded mouth.

I thought of him as crude, tough, forceful and even ironical, as suggested by his monumental statues of Victor Hugo and Balzac and his head of Baudelaire. Yet I found that he was simple, precise, reserved, courteous and cordial without excess, according to Mauclair, and as revealed by his bust of *Puvis de Chavannes* and *Mozart* and also from the *Muse for the Whistler Monument*.

I thought of him anguished, terror-stricken, and free of implied moral censure and convention in such works as *Caryatide, Sorrow, She who once was the Helmet-maker's Beautiful Wife, Despair, The Flying Figure* and *The Prodigal Son*. Yet, on the other hand, such works as *The Kiss, Thought, The Eternal Idol, Mother and Dying Child*, and *Brother and Sister*, showed him to me full of passion, love, gentleness and grace.

I thought how extraordinary it was that he should have achieved so much work in his lifetime without human entanglements or interruptions, or rather by strong will and determination despite external encroachments. I thought of how he managed to keep a cool head despite his great popularity, of how he silently withdrew his statue at the time of the Balzac quarrel, and of his slowness of speech and his pauses in conversation to reserve his energy for his work.

Above all, I thought of his intense interest in the human *hand* as seen in his remarkable studies of hands, which so conspicuously serve to reveal the meaning of his works. He must have regarded hands as symbols. In his own hands lay the power to realize what he imagined. All the hands he carved were full of character and significance, expressing more than any other parts of his works, as for example the hands in *The Kiss, St. John the Baptist, The Thinker,* and *The Burghers of Calais; The Hand of God,* or *The Creation,* upholding the beautiful forms of Adam and Eve; *The Cathedral,* a work of two hands joined with fingers outstretched and pointed upwards symbolically; and *The Secret* suggesting something held tightly between two hands—all are expressive and full of tenderness. If he found that a particular work did not need the aid of hands, he hid them, as in the statue of Balzac, where they are concealed by the cloak, or he left them unfinished as in *The Three Shadows.*

I have read some translations of Rodin's remarks on his own work and they came back to my mind while I was sitting thinking. He said: "I have invented nothing, I only rediscover, and it seems to be new because the aim and the methods of my art have in a general way been lost sight of. People mistake for innovation what is only a return to the laws of the great statuary of antiquity. It is true that I like certain symbols. I look at things from a symbolical view-point, but it is Nature that gives me all that." Again, he said: "Nature is ever full of fine form, of design; yet so many pass by and see nothing, and copy old things, or work on preconceived notions of Nature; and all the while Nature is there, full of delightful new forms, in the stalk of a flower, in a bud, in a human limb, in a passing action in the streets." Again: "Nature is so much greater than people think, and there is so much to be got from Nature than people usually get. But Nature is God, and one can only get what Nature has to give by real communion as with God; by close devoted study alone with Nature; by returning always perseveringly to Nature, and by going to her with a mind entirely free, devoid of all preconceived notions, be they reminiscences of antique art, old Italian masters, academic teaching or other accepted theories; without any conventionality or other ideas, but with a mind and eyes naïvely and honestly open to receive what Nature has to give. Then, and then only, will Nature give up her secrets: we must learn to love, and worship and believe ere she will yield all she has to give; she is the only teacher, and only through fidelity to her and reverence for her can we hope to progress." Discharging criticism of his work being unfinished, he remarked: "There is no finish possible in a work of Art, since it is Nature, and Nature knows no finish, being infinite; therefore one stops at some stage or other, when one has put into one's work all one sees, all one has sought for, all one cares to put, or all one particularly wants; but one could really go one for ever and see more to do."

All these remarks of Rodin seem to me to express the idea underlying Chinese art in general and Chinese painting in particular. I have explained this principle of Nature fully in my two books, *The Chinese Eye* and *Chinese Calligraphy*. Nature is the religion of Chinese artists. We—particularly our artists—are called 'Nature-worshippers'. A Chinese philosophy, Taoism, says: "Life in close harmony with Nature is the only real life." We are taught to live with Nature and speak with her and identify ourselves with her. By continual observance and by projecting ourselves into the life of Nature, we are able to present the feeling of natural things. It is said that Rodin often compared human beings to animals and insisted upon their resemblances; thus, Falguiere was for him a small bull, Clemenceau a tiger, and so on. Chinese artists often compare flowers, birds, and beasts to human beings.

A frivolous story which I had read somewhere returned to my mind. A wealthy *parvenu* visited the great sculptor's studio and remarked: "Oh, *Maitre*! How do you manage to create such *chef d'oeuvres*?" "Easily, Madame! I take a block of marble and chip off everything I don't need." Yes, but what was it that he *did* need? Anyone can chip pieces off a block of marble, but not everybody knows what he wants to achieve thereby, and when he does know there arises the question of technique. Does technique in art have a value of its own?

Rodin is said to have regarded technique as only a means to an end; but he did not underestimate his own technique. He said: "One must have a consummate sense of technique to hide what one knows." He thought no artist should *neglect* technique, the means of embodying feelings and ideas. Whether technique has a value in itself or not is of no great importance. I admire Rodin's art for his thought, for his principles and, last but not least, for his mastery of technique.

I then looked round at *The Thinker* and wondered if he would agree with what I had been thinking. He had no time for me, and I waved him 'goodbye'.

Before I stepped out of the courtyard, a shaft of sunshine caught the gilt dome of the Hôtel des Invalides over the wall between the trees. I then realised that it was not far away. I have written about Napoleon's powerful hands and now about Rodin's. That these two pairs of powerful hands should have been so close to one another seems to me an interesting co-incidence. After his death in 1917, Rodin bequeathed his works and his house to the nation. The present Musée Rodin is, in fact, the house where he lived for many years. Did he particularly choose to live near Napoleon's resting place? But Napoleon's powerful hands can be seen no more for they are encased in red Finland granite in the Invalides; Rodin's are still about the house and the garden of 77, rue de Varennes!

XVI

The Angry Soup

"The *Halles Centrales* are Paris and France," a French friend surprisingly affirmed. His reasoning was that as, to the French, food is a passion—almost a *ruling* passion—and food has for centuries been supplied by the central markets, to which sellers and buyers come not only from Paris but from all over France, it was not an exaggeration to say that the central markets *were* Paris and France. Moreover the site of the *Halles* has been an assembly point for the French people for hundreds of years: festivals, demonstrations, fires, riots, the great Revolution itself, have all started here. It was here, in a sense, that the history of Paris and France was made. Fortunately, my French friend did not expect me to know much about French history, and he was kind enough to enumerate and direct me to a number of places of interest in the neighbourhood.

I found the Church of St Eustache without difficulty. Its façade looked very fine, but I could not get a full view of the whole church, which is closely surrounded by houses and the tall iron pavilions of the markets. It must have been more accessible when its erection began in 1532. I was told that it took 102 years to finish. It is late-Gothic in style, decorated with Renaissance carvings. The spacious interior supported by lofty pillars surprised me, for it was not like the inside of any other church that I had seen in Paris. It breathed an Indian or Persian air, I felt. I was interested in the tomb of Colbert by Lebrun and the marble '*Virgin*' by Pigalle.

The Passage de la Reine de Hongrie was hard to find. It lies very close to St Eustache, but I missed it several times. It is only a little alley, and its road-sign is somewhat defaced. There is nothing arresting in the short double row of common and uninteresting houses, but the lane has a long history. It lies at the southern end of the rue Montmartre, and the walls of some of the houses are said to be at least 200 years old. The passage is named after one of its former residents, Julie Bêcheur, who

achieved notoriety shortly before the Revolution of 1789. She
led a delegation of market women to present a petition to Marie
Antoinette. The Queen remarked to her: "You bear a striking
resemblance to my mother, the Queen of Hungary." From
then on she was jokingly known in the *Halles* as 'La Reine de
Hongrie', until at last the nickname supplanted her real name
and she lost her own identity. This was a not impossible event
in the France of those days, though nobody would take that
kind of fanciful remark seriously now. Two hundred years ago
a French Queen was a Royal Queen, high above and different
from the rest of humanity.

I remember reading in tales of the old Imperial China that
whenever the Emperor or Empress emerged from the Forbidden
City of Peking no ordinary folk were allowed in the street, and
all shops had to close and cover their windows with wooden
shutters. If anyone had the good fortune to catch a glimpse of
the Imperial face through the chink of a door, he would
treasure that moment all his life. An Emperor hunting on the
outskirts of Peking once chanced to touch the hand of a peasant.
After this incident, the peasant's hand was carefully wrapped
in long bands of imperial yellow silk and its praises were sung
by all the neighbourhood. No one else was allowed to touch
that hand, for to do so would have been to insult the Imperial
head. The peasant had reverently to worship his own hand,
sitting indoors all day long. It is recorded that although he died
of starvation from neglect of his farm, he died without regret!

Julie Bêcheur, too, may have had her head turned by her
contact with Royalty. From being a simple market-woman, she
may gradually have come to imagine herself to possess some
sort of royal blood in her veins. I doubt if the head of Marie-
Antoinette falling under the guillotine troubled her for an
instant. Nor would she have realised the cause of her own tragic
end; she was executed for her supposed sympathy with the
Royal Family. Nevertheless, the authorities of Paris after the
Revolution remembered her, and through her nickname she
has lived in this alley to the present day.

Two writers whose account of this incident I have read
consider Marie-Antoinette's remark to Julie Bêcheur infamous,
because it led to her death. I dislike this kind of wisdom after
the event. Marie-Antoinette was a most unfortunate person.
It must have been very difficult for her to decide what to do

when a delegation of market-women came to demand help from her. She knew well that she was the main cause of the French people's anger, for she was not French. Yet she accepted the delegation democratically. To the great Palace of Versailles, where the Court etiquette had been worked out to the last detail, and whose fashions led the world, came suddenly a flock of uncouth market-women. Many another queen would have inflamed the women and probably caused the great palace to be burnt down. Marie Antoinette poured forth her senti-mental words—words such as only women would heed—to turn the dangerous situation into a light-hearted one. Her words not only saved her own life, but the lives of many others in the palace, and prevented a lot of damage. What a diplo-matic stroke! And what great insight into the psychology of women! Unfortunately, the age in which she lived was out of tune with her, and she was doomed to die. But I have a soft spot in my heart for her. It was she who made Julie Bêcheur's name known to me.

My next move was to find No. 11, rue de la Ferronnerie, opposite which, on May 14th, 1610, King Henri IV was assas-sinated. He was on his way to the arsenal to visit a minister, the celebrated Sully, when his coach was suddenly brought to a standstill. The day was very hot and the King, having taken off his cloak, was dressed only in a light costume of black satin. There were six attendants with him in the coach, but none of them was able to prevent the assassin, Ravaillac, from plunging a dagger into the King's body. That was 300 years ago. Today nothing unusual was happening along the rue de la Ferronnerie.

The Place des Innocents is a close neighbour of the rue de la Ferronnerie. It is that rare thing in Paris, a square, with a green lawn and trees, similar to the squares in London, but with the addition of a beautiful fountain in the centre. Only a father and his two small daughters were there when I visited it. The children were pointing at the fountain while their father explained the stone carvings. I found out that the original fountain which used to be attached to the former Church of the Innocents (demolished in 1783) had been constructed in 1551 by Pierre Lescot and decorated with bas-relief sculptured by Jean Goujon, one of the victims of the Massacre of St Barth-olomew. The present square and its surrounding streets used to be a cemetery, but in 1788, for hygienic reasons, all the bones from the old tombs were removed and deposited in the disused subterranean quarries which were to become the 'Catacombs of Paris'. The fountain in the centre of the present square was a later arrangement and its decoration was only a replica of the original, which is now kept in the Louvre.

After the demolition of the Church of the Innocents, the square became the Marché des Innocents, and was used as a provision market, many stalls of which were covered by large umbrellas fixed in the ground. In 1813 the Paris Corporation constructed wooden galleries to replace the umbrellas, and later the galleries were replaced by brick buildings. These were demolished in 1855. It is said that the old market was the gathering-place of ruffians who swindled customers and robbed passers-by. Many of the dealers were old women who would treat a poor customer quite fairly, but would behave outrageously if a young man of striking appearance stopped to buy an apple or orange and was unwilling to pay the exorbitant price they demanded. They would pour out curses and bad language which no decent folk could bear to listen to. Before the reconstruction of the markets there used to be a good many low taverns in the neighbourhood, including the one called the 'Paul Niguet', which was the abode of rag-pickers and famous for its terrible *vin bleu*. At that time this quarter was regarded as one of the most filthy in Paris; but in 1952, I found it one of the airiest, where I felt free to walk at my ease among honest and industrious, if not invariably cheerful, workers. I felt glad to have been born in the present age.

Had I been born 100 years ago, it would not have been so easy for me to visit Paris, and if I had, I might have become a curio to be shut up in a golden cage and carried about by French noblemen as an entertaining object who could say a few words in Chinese for the amusement of the Court. I should not have been allowed to leave the house and would never have been able to wander alone like this in the Marché des Innocents. Or, if I had managed to escape there, my long pigtail, even my long whiskers if I had any, would perhaps have been tied round the handle of one of the large umbrellas or a pillar of the wooden galleries, and my Chinese gown might have been torn to pieces simply because I could not understand the curses and slang being hurled at me. My relief at having been born in the present age should encourage all those who lament the past and persuade them to open their eyes and see more (for instance, *les halles*) of contemporary Paris!

On leaving the Marché des Innocents, I proceeded to explore the immense metal structures of the great markets of Paris, the *Halles Centrales*. The rebuilding of these markets began in

After Gustave Doré's "Consequences of the London
Exhibition of 1862"

1854 from designs by Baltard, whose name was given to the short road, the rue Baltard, which divides the two sections of the markets, the eastern group of six square pavilions and the western group of four. All ten pavilions are made of iron and zinc, after the plan of a Paris railway station. Each pavilion has 250 stalls, four metres square. There are 2,500 stalls altogether. I was told that many traders leave their goods lying on the pavements and some even in the middle of the roads. I just could not comprehend how the people of Paris consumed so much food every day. New Yorkers always like to say that they have the largest things in the world, but I never remember seeing a market there as big as the *halles* of Paris. The population of Paris is said to be half or even a third of that of London or New York: so it seems that each Parisian must consume at least two of three times as much food as an inhabitant of the either of the other cities! Though I could find no account of the eating capacity of a Parisian of today, that of two well-known figures of the past in the Parisian world of art and literature has been recorded. Louis David, a famous French artist, created a baron by Napoleon, once ate for his *déjeuner* four dozen Ostend oysters, four mutton chops, one beefsteak with potatoes, two whiting, half a dozen smelts, four large bunches of grapes, as many peaches and enough bread for an English family of eight, a bottle of burgundy, two-thirds of a bottle of Sauterne, a small glass of curaçao, and coffee; while Honoré de Balzac was seen by one of his publishers to devour at one meal 100 oysters, twelve cutlets, a duck, a brace of partridges, a sole, a number of sweets, and a dozen pears.

I was interested in the appropriate name, Antoine Carème (the man was one of Napoleon's cooks), used for the road which traverses the whole length of the *halles*. Did Napoleon impose his cook's name on the road or did some later admirer choose it?

There were a number of metal carts full of meat-bones standing by the side of the rue Rambuteau facing the Church of St Eustache. Before I turned into a nearby street I saw two ill-dressed fellows, both unshaven, climb up into the carts one after another and search hard and deeply. They looked

Good French food creates some embarrassment on the staircase of a small pension

like members of the Clochard Club. I then had a look at the round house, 'Bourse de Commerce', on the rue de Viarmes. All the doors were closed, but more metal carts, empty ones, were standing outside in rows. Two more ragged fellows and a woman were resting in the shade with bundles of their findings beside them. At another street-corner a small crowd had gathered and was silently watching something. I joined it and saw another ragamuffin, busy packing an overloaded wheel-barrow. It was not a proper barrow like those which fruit-sellers use, but one he must have made himself from odd pieces of wood. Its two little wheels were hidden beneath a mass of broken boxes, piled one on top of another. He was trying to tie them on with odd pieces of string picked up after the market had closed. The string was giving him trouble; while he made a knot in one place another would come undone. Nevertheless, he seemed determined to have the load well packed before he set out through the boulevards. He could have made his task easier, but the pockets of his well-worn overcoat were already so full of things that they looked like the puffed-out eyes of a Chinese goldfish; besides which, some large parcels were tucked inside his coat. His arms and legs were not quite under control. The hair on his head, lip and chin was bushy and uncombed; his red cheeks told me that he was in his early forties. He did not seem to mind people watching, though none of us lent him a hand. However, we refrained from laughing at his various efforts. I made a quick sketch and left.

At the corner of the rue Sauval I paused a good while: Molière was born here and was named a child of the *halles*. He introduced the *halles* to the literary world. I know little about Molière, but the sound of his name catches the French ear as readily as that of Shakespeare does the English.

It took me almost the whole morning to complete my round of the *halles*. I was not more disappointed at having missed seeing the markets in full swing than at not having encountered a goatherd in the nearby streets. I had particularly chosen an early spring morning, for I had heard it said that every year in the spring there came to Paris little flocks of goats led by Béarnais goatherds. They would parade the streets with their bells jingling and the goatherds playing their pipes. Leaving their stables on the outskirts of Paris in the early morning—about six o'clock—they would return home, after doing their round, by midday. The goatherd generally wore a beret of the southern pattern, for he came from the Pyrenees and the Basque country beyond. Natives of Paris had a passion for goat's milk and always welcomed the herds; many of them would wait specially for their supply and have bread ready to feed the animals. The milk was often consumed on the spot, while it was still warm. It did not need boiling and could not be impure. This bucolic sight was common in Paris as late as just before the war. I lingered, but no goatherd or goat appeared: the Second World War must have banished them.

In a small gathering of friends I mentioned casually that I intended to spend a night in the *halles* to see the marketing through. I said I should go there after 11 p.m., and stay until morning. I also wanted to taste the famous onion soup. I did not imagine that anyone I knew would care to sacrifice a warm bed to accompany me, but to my great surprise two ladies, one Scottish and one Chinese, expressed their wish to join me. They knew Paris very well, but had never been to the *halles* at night.

I hesitated to accept their company as I was not sure if they would care for my way of loitering. However, the date was fixed, and both came along with undaunted spirit. We reached the Central Markets by the Metro at half-past eleven. Most of the lights were lit and a few people had already begun to busy themselves on their allotted spaces, but there was little to detain us for more than a casual glance. We roved round the side-streets. These quiet, dark alleys depressed me, and I began to feel guilty at having dragged the ladies here for nothing. At one corner two big lorries arrived, with another following behind. They stopped. Several men jumped down and immediately began to unload vegetables on to the pavement. The street light was not strong enough to expose the unloading clearly, but I found their movements in the semi-darkness interesting. Their faces being hidden, they could have come from the markets of London, New York, Shanghai, Addis Ababa, or Havana.

One of my companions learned that the markets would not be in full swing until four or five o'clock in the morning; the other proposed we should sit in a café for a while. Contrary to what I had read, we found very few cafés, and those we saw were closed. However, we eventually found a very tiny one. It had only two tables right at the back and its long counter down the centre made it look even more cramped than it actually was. An old-fashioned stove with its chimney going up through the ceiling stood close to the table at which we sat. There was only one other customer when we came in; he stood by the counter, glass in hand, smoking a cigarette. He looked at us with the air of one well acquainted with the quarter, yet he did not seem to be a regular market trader. Our request for coffee had apparently set the middle-aged proprietress into action; she had to start the stove going. It seemed to me that she had only opened the café a few minutes before and that her customers were likely to require wine rather than coffee. She had two assistants, a young man and a girl, both of whom looked happy and smiling; they were probably exchanging remarks about our unfamiliar faces.

Presently a commotion arose at the door. In came six men and three women. Only one of the men wore a jacket; the rest had rolled-up shirt-sleeves and stood with their elbows leaning on the counter. They must just have finished unloading a big lorry, for they seemed in need of something to quench their thirst. They drank and drank without speaking a word. They were all stout and strong, with hairy arms, except for one pale thin fellow, who seemed unable even to raise his head. He looked overworked and short of sleep, yet he drank even more than the others. The three women made a group of their own and never stopped talking and laughing. By degrees the men were drawn into the women's discussion, and I detected a quarrelsome note in their voices. The atmosphere was getting too hot for us, and I regretted having picked on this café. We could not leave, however, for the proprietress was still busy preparing our orders.

Whether or not it was owing to our presence, when the noise became unbearable the proprietress, though she did not look especially sturdy, courageously sent the men and women out of the café and shut the door behind them. She then came and sat down beside one of my companions, explaining the trouble and chatting familiarly, while my other companion put the finishing touches to some sketches she had begun a moment before. Though I could not understand the French conversation, I could see that it was on our account that the proprietress had been worried. She seemed to be expressing disgust at the sort of patrons for whom she had to run the café. Presently she got up to re-heat our coffee and to lay more cakes and boiled eggs before us. I learned that her helpers, the smiling young couple, were her daughter and son-in-law, who had only been married three months. When another group of men came in, followed by two of the former women, I suggested to my friends that we should make a move. The café's original customer was still there when we left; his glass was only half empty and he had not uttered a word all the time.

Now the rattle of wheels grew louder. Various types of lorries and some strange-looking vehicles blocked the corners and streets. More people were unloading, unpacking, arranging and rearranging the goods on their stalls. We saw vegetables of every description piled on the pavements and in the roadways. They were all neatly arranged in some sort of pattern; the love

L

of pattern seems to be in the French blood. Cabbages, lettuces, melons and tomatoes were heaped up in great quantities. I was interested to see big bunches of leeks also arranged in a pattern, each single leek being washed clean so as to show the long white end with its thin white tassels. They looked like a pile of jade or ivory rods, rather pleasing to the eye. I do not think I have ever seen leeks *washed* for sale in London or New York. Transactions were taking place while we moved along. The discussion of the quality of the foodstuffs and on prices seemed to be conducted by men, who darted here and there in black berets and unbuttoned yellow or grey coats. By each stand stood a woman—quite a solid-looking one as a rule, whether old or young—with one hand inside the huge pocket in the centre of her dark-coloured apron or else holding a paper pad and pencil in the expectation of working out calculations. Very few of the women wore anything on the head, not even a beret, but I saw one old woman wearing a black felt cap shaped like an English tea-cosy, not very different from the sort of cap worn by many men in the north of China. I moved under a lamp-post to make a quick sketch of her.

The next section we came to was full of fresh fruits, chiefly oranges and apples. These, like everything else in the market, were neatly piled up singly and in boxes. Their colours under the electric lights were mellow and made us long to touch or bite. Broken boxes, paper, straw and litter scattered on the road indicated the great activity which had been going on. The section dealing with the sale of eggs was in a similar state.

Suddenly my companions realised that they were treading on wet ground, and moved away quickly. The smell of the fish market nearby was not to their liking. While they moved on, I stopped to have a look at the different kinds of fish for sale. There were many freshwater fish, including carp, which I like particularly, and which are not to be found in any English market. I noticed boxes and baskets of snails, mussels, oysters and many other kinds of shell-fish. I remember seeing two restaurants close to the *halles* which specialise in dishes of snails, each of which has a large carved or clay-modelled snail as a sign. I did not notice any frogs, nor did I see women frog-sellers, of whom I had heard.

The noise of bones being sawn entered my ears. I turned aside to avoid seeing what was going on, but instead found

myself facing rows and rows of beef and mutton carcasses. Each
hung in the manner of Rembrandt's 'Slaughtered Ox', one
version of which is in the Louvre and the other in the Glasgow
Art Gallery, both masterpieces of that great painter. But
though I love all the works of this master, these two examples

are exceptions; it is the subject-matter that is disagreeable to
me. Inside the meat pavilion a few men were working in pink
caps, a fashion said to date back to the days of the Burgundians.
I later joined my companions to gaze a while, from the
opposite side, at five men wearing white overalls spattered with
blood.

The section which attracted us most, particularly my companions, and where we spent much time, were the flower
markets. They seemed to cover a much wider area than other
sections; they had invaded every possible nook and corner. Box
after box was taken down from lorries and small carts and laid
on the pavements and streets. Men and women were busy
unpacking the boxes and arranging the flowers on the stalls.
They were chiefly white, pink and red carnations, and tulips of
various colours, as well as many kinds of roses in bud. As it was
only the middle of March and still rather cold in Paris, most of
the flowers had come from the South of France. I noticed on

one stall piles of little bunches of violets, primroses and other
wild flowers, which might have been picked in the Bois de
Boulogne and the outskirts of Paris.

My companions moved about independently, making close
inspections of flowers on particular stalls. I preferred to view
the scene as a whole—the selling, buying, wrapping and un-
wrapping, with men and women gesticulating, discussing,
shouting and moving about while the colours of the different
flowers appeared through the gaps between their bodies, arms
and even legs. It was a fascinating sight, this daily mass activity
devoted to something beautiful. One elderly fellow with a big
white moustache had climbed on to a wooden stool to arrange
some tropical-looking flowers, possibly 'birds of paradise',
round the top of a pole. A number of holes had been pierced in
the pole and the lower ones were already filled with flower
stalks; he was not filling the upper ones. Not only did his
conspicuous position on the stool attract attention, but his
comic yet scared facial expression with the occasional shrug
of his shoulders, as he stretched his arms ever higher, invited
laughter. The orange-yellow flowers with spade-like leaves
seemed to print a pattern on his white apron. He might have
been a self-employed human advertisement, like the London
'sandwich men', giving his performance nightly. I watched his
antics with interest.

There must have been more people
in the flower sections than in the
others. We had seen quite a number
here on our first round, and now
more and more were arriving. In
other parts, such as meat and fish
markets, wholesale dealers with
perhaps a few retailers were the
only people to be seen. In the
vegetable and fruit sections, the
number of wholesale and retail
dealers seemed about equal; but
in the flower sections there
was another class of people—
presumably spectators, like us.
After a few minutes, however, one of my companions suggested
that we should wait to buy some cut-price flowers, and I

realised that the other recently arrived 'spectators' had come for the same purpose. There were more women than men, and some of them were fashionably dressed, with sparkling jewels on their heads and hands. A few of the sellers were buxom and mature, but many more were young and slender. Curiously enough, they all wore close-fitting black skirts, as if this were their uniform. The skirts of the younger women had hundreds of pleats and they spread out and twisted gracefully as their wearers moved about.

The *Halles Centrales* were the scene of non-stop activity from midnight to six o'clock in the morning and even an hour or two later. We saw the arrival of the lorries and carts as well as their departure. Later came people with small wheelbarrows, basket-carriers and many porters with ladder-like wooden carriers sticking up on their backs. The last was the most striking sight in the whole market. I have not seen this method of carrying goods in any other city. They waited, they carried, they moved, they vanished, and some of them still waited. Eventually they had to go away without earning anything; but they would be back again early the next morning.

About six o'clock we felt very tired, but each of us carried a big bunch of flowers wrapped in paper. I had bought two dozen pink and red carnations; my companions had made different choices. Yet the markets were still full of activity. Many were packing up their goods, resigning themselves to having some left unsold. The pavements and roads were now full of brown paper, tissue paper, broken boxes and baskets. The porters had gone, but another type of person had taken their place and was busy collecting broken boxes, gathering unwanted leeks, cabbages and potatoes, or searching for stray apples, tangerines, and oranges. None took any notice of the flowers being trodden into the road.

A few yards away I saw two tall, stout men talking together in the midst of a crowd in which their size made them conspicuous. They looked like the fat wrestlers in an old Japanese print and they must have been two of *les forts de la halle*, strong men of the market, supposed to be able to carry incredible weights on their shoulders.

A year or two earlier, one early morning in London, I had visited the fruit markets of Covent Garden and seen fruiterers walking steadily along with towering piles of baskets on their heads. This method of porterage is, apparently not used in the *Halles Centrales.*

I think the market women were the most interesting of the people there; stalwart, self-composed, indefatigable, masterful. They must be very efficient. While engaged in the business of receiving or selling, directing operations from some high perch, marking multitudinous produce or giving orders in raucous voices, they never ceased talking. I wished I could have understood what they were saying. But perhaps I enjoyed watching them talk just because I did not understand them.

A night spent in the *Halles Centrales* is incomplete without a meal of onion soup. I was told that the *restaurateurs* at the *halles* used to have the special privilege of remaining open all night. This attracted a multitude of people who either had no fixed abode or had no desire to return home. They came to take soup flavoured with cheese and braised ham, and to drink chablis. It was first a custom and then a tradition. On one occasion, in December, 1859, the police recorded that over 150 cabs brought people to the *halles* from all parts of Paris between midnight and five o'clock in the morning. On another occasion after a big ball at the Opéra 600 people arrived within an hour and a half. They attended *cabarets* and filled up all the restaurants. Such a crowd moving about swamped the *Halles* workers. This proved a hindrance to the marketing, and on that account the police prohibited most restaurant proprietors from keeping their cafés open the whole night. The few restaurants which were allowed to remain open were intended chiefly for the people who bring goods in from the countryside. Lorry-drivers and other workers, after disposing of their merchandise, clean up, change, and have a bite before setting out on the return journey. They are a very different type of patron from those who frequent the cafés and restaurants in other parts of Paris, and I was urged to see them if I had a chance. Some visitors still come occasionally for the onion soup, as a treat and a link with tradition. A French friend of mine even suggested that I should buy a bag of chips fried in horse or donkey fat while I wandered round the *halles.* Horse and donkey fat may be as good as butter or lard, I suppose, but I wish I had not been told that they were used for those chips.

My companions and I enquired at a number of small cafés

but none of them sold onion soup. We were rather surprised and thought the Second World War might have stopped the tradition. Eventually we found a side entrance to the Père Tranquil, the back of which is a restaurant, and a young waiter informed us that they sold good onion soup. After having given our order, soup for three, I went to the front of the building, which is a bar, and had a look at the customers. They were all quiet and sober, as if anxious to comply with the name of the café. Two other tables besides ours were occupied, one by a stout fellow consuming a large dish of beefsteak with piles of vegetables and other good things, but no soup; the other by a young couple drinking their soup with evident enjoyment.

Presently our soup arrived, with a bottle of white wine. My companions beamed at me, and, tasting their soup at once,

made little noises indicative of great satisfaction. It cheered me to think that I had not, after all, dragged them out for nothing. When I lowered my head to look at my own bowlful I saw that it was boiling hot. Moreover, it did not look like normal soup, for the liquid part was completely covered by a puffed-up mass of something dark brown-grey which did not look at all like onion. As I hesitated, a little bubble in the middle grew bigger, emerged on the surface and really looked as if it were angry at my hesitation. I felt I had to break up the floating lump and taste it, with some of the liquid. It gave me a shock and an uncomfortable feeling inside, but I could not tell my companions. Fortunately, they had already drunk half of their soup and thought it went extremely well with the wine. Two-thirds of the soup was a solid mass of cheese with chopped onion boiled or steamed in it, and I detected a trace of braised ham. For the past twenty years I have tried unsuccessfully to cultivate a taste for cheese. My failure has been a great handicap to me in my travels, and especially so in Paris, for the best French dishes seem nearly always to have some cheese in them. Many of my compatriots love cheese; I seem to be the only exception. To avoid embarrassment, I have forced myself to eat a little now and then, but I have never done so with enjoyment. There must be something in my tongue which is allergic to cheese. This onion soup in the *halles* was too much for me. The more I looked at it, the more angrily it seemed to look back. I never finished it, and I still recall it as 'the angry soup'.

XVII

Other Wild Animals

"I WENT to Normandy for my holidays," Francine wrote to me just after Easter. "My uncle, aunt, the dog and I spent two days, Sunday and Monday, motoring from place to place—Rouen, Honfleur, Deauville—through miles and miles of sunny meadows and beaches and blossoming apple trees. The four of us ate plenty of shrimps, lobsters, mussels and other wild animals whose names I don't know. . . ."

I read with particular interest of those 'other wild animals'. I had thought that only we Chinese ate 'queer' animals. Not that I have ever tasted dragon's liver or phœnix's marrow; but I have many a time had bird's-nest soup. *Yen-wo*, or 'Bird's nest', is not an appetising name, and I have to confess that it is not figurative; the soup really is, as its name implies, made from the gelatinous nest of a bird, the bird being a species of swift or swallow, *Colloclia brevirotris*, found on the south China sea-coast or imported from India and Burma. It is supposed to have a tonic and invigorating effect, and certainly, if well made, it is a tonic to the digestion. That I like bird's-nest soup does not, however, mean that I am able to eat *any* unusual dish, however well cooked. Before I came to live in England, I travelled quite widely in China and found the food differed according to the locality; whatever was grown, raised or found in a district formed its diet, for communication and transport between places far apart were virtually non-existent, and even when ingredients were the same, the preparation and cooking often differed. This is much more interesting for a traveller than the uniform foods offered today in every modern town and village.

I must confess that I cannot claim to have eaten everything prepared in any

Snails used as designs in the dining room decorated by Victor Hugo

Chinese kitchen, nor are all Chinese dishes to my liking. But it is true that, although there may be many foods which a particular Chinese will not eat, there are none, I think, that will surprise him. Ancient Chinese books affirm that almost everything on earth has food value—plants, birds, fish, even fossils; it all depends on the cooking.

The French have a great art of cooking. While I was in Paris, most people I met talked about food and most books on Paris I could lay my hand on were full of names of restaurants. Being a Chinese and no cook, I am unable to pass judgement on French cooking; but I do want to express my interest in things cooked and eaten.

Monsieur Jacques Martin was introduced to me through a compatriot of mine whom he had met in London and with whom he had spent a few days sightseeing. He is a young engineer, devoted to his work, whose office is near the church of Notre-Dame-de-Lorette in the Ninth Arrondissement. He wrote telling me to meet him outside the church, for he could only spare half an hour for his lunch. Paris was very new to me then, and it was only after a struggle that I managed to get to the appointed place, and unfortunately I waited on one side of the church and he on the other, so that we missed one another. I thought he must be able to spot my Chinese face, while I could not distinguish him in the huge throng of French men coming and going past the church. Perhaps, being an engineer, he was very exact and particular about time, and had dismissed me as an unpunctual and 'inscrutable' Oriental.

After a month or so another letter came from Monsieur Martin inviting me to dine at his home in Courbevoie, outside Paris. There was a small diagram attached with directions how to get there. He seemed to imagine that after a few weeks' stay my knowledge of French must have improved so much that I could easily find my way about, even outside Paris. However, with an effort I managed to arrive at his house, punctually this time. I was warmly received by three smiling faces: those of Jacques and his mother and father. Neither of Jacques' parents knew English and we could therefore only exchange smiles. But I must admit that I was beaten in the natural art of smiling by the mother, for she could smile on and on as long as I was in the room.

My presence that evening must have been an unusual

occasion. The delicious odour of specially-prepared dishes was wafted into my nostrils from the kitchen where Jacques' mother had been busy with the dinner for a long while. Presently the cloth was laid and we each sat down at one side of a good-sized square table. There was a great variety of dishes on it and very little space was left unfilled. Though the food was cooked differently, the appearance of the table reminded me very much of a family dinner in China to which special guests had been invited. Monsieur Martin opened one bottle of wine after another, while his son spoke French and English by turns with a few Chinese words now and then. I particularly enjoyed the food in a big dish in the centre and Jacques' mother smiled more broadly than ever when, like Oliver Twist, I asked for some more of it. She told me the dish was called *Oiseau-sans-tête*. I grasped her meaning at once and asked what kind of bird it could be. They all laughed, for it was not a real bird at all, but was made of tender meat—pork—shaped like a bird's body without a head. The meat was so well prepared that it had lost its original taste and been transformed into that of a young roasting chicken. The whole dish reminded me of a very famous restaurant in Shanghai where only vegetable dishes were served. It was run by a Chinese Buddhist Society and was patronised by many wealthy Buddhists and abbots of big monasteries. Buddhism forbids the killing and eating of animals, and Chinese Buddhist monks are vegetarians. In this restaurant a specially skilled cook performed wonders with vegetables, producing dishes called 'chicken', 'pork', 'ham', 'fish', etc., but all made of soya-bean curd. Their texture, shape, colour, and in some cases even their taste were exactly like meat or fish. Only their ingredients were entirely vegetable. I was taken there once by a relative when I was a boy. I remember wondering why anyone should want to make 'false' chicken, meat, and fish, but a youngster was not allowed to ask such questions, or was not answered if he did.

From the dish of *Oiseau-sans-tête* our conversation drifted to other French specialities. I told the Martins that I had had some *grenouilles* at 'Chez Roger'. Then Monsieur Martin mentioned a few small but attractive restaurants round the Central Markets, particularly the expensive one, 'A l'Escargot d'Or,—La Vieille Renommée'. I said I had noticed the signboard during my night wanderings in the Central Markets. I remembered the great gilded snail made of plaster of Paris hanging above it but I had not mustered the courage to go inside, for at that time I had never eaten snails. The look of an *escargot* always makes me feel uncomfortable, though many Chinese are very fond of snail dishes.

We continued to talk about the *escargot* for a while, and  Jacques even told me that Paris itself was a sort of snail—that is, the plan of the city resembles a snail in shape. He attempted an explanation, but by then my thoughts were somewhat confused by the delicious wines which had been pressed on me and I could not follow him. The evening was a most enjoyable one.

A few days later I was at a party in a friend's house. The host, a compatriot of mine, did all the cooking, and I looked forward to some tasty Chinese dishes. To my surprise, a huge dish piled high with masses of hot *escargots* was set in the centre of the table for the first course. Five out of our party of seven were French, and I was sitting between two Parisiennes. I was about to help the ladies when they insisted on helping me. A kind of needle was laid in front of my dish. I did not know how to begin, and, not wanting to make myself conspicuous, I dallied till I could copy my neighbours. Then I used the needle to pick out the contents of the shell, and let it slide into my mouth. A picture of the creature's slow movement suddenly obsessed my mind, and its movement inside my mouth seemed even slower. It had a slight flavour of garlic and a feeling of rubber. One guest was making a whistling noise as he drained his shell. The rest of the company was eating with apparent enjoyment and chattering away in French, while I kept chewing my piece of rubber. My host reminded me that this was one of the chief delicacies to be found in Paris; the others chorused agreement. I nodded and smiled. I had not realised before how difficult it could sometimes be to smile. There must have been more than 100 *escargots* in the dish, yet they all disappeared before I had struggled through my third. I was immensely relieved when the next course proved to be *Po-chia-chi*, a well-known Cantonese dish—pieces of the tender flesh of a young chicken cooked in boiling water only.

After that dinner, I recovered from the taste of the *escargots*, but their shape haunted me. They came into my dreams at night—not only one *escargot*, nor two or three, but numbers of them. One was moving over my lips, one glided by on my right cheek and there were many on the sheets of my bed. Later I noticed several on the wall and even one stuck on the electric

light bulb. They looked harmless and friendly, yet I could not understand why they should have suddenly become so attached to me.

They continued to occupy my dreams for several nights running. I happened to describe my experiences to one of my French friends over a cup of coffee. *"C'est bon!"* he exclaimed *"On le mangera quand on l'essaie bien"* ("You will eat them if you try hard enough"). His theory was that I was not familiar with the appearance of snails and that they had come into my dreams so that I should get to know them better. As soon as I was used to them, I should enjoy eating them. This was not

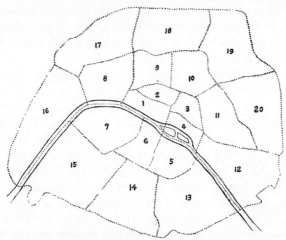

quite the reply I had expected, but it was an ingenious one. He also remarked, as Jacques Martin had done: *"Paris est un escargot."* From a pencilled map of Paris he showed me how her twenty *arrondissements* were arranged round the Seine in the shape of a snail: fourteen on the north bank and six on the south. The whole arrangement forms a kind of spiral, the first four *arrondissements* being grouped in a square on the north bank; the fifth, sixth, and seventh, numbered from east to west, being on the south bank, the eighth to twelfth encircling the first four, the thirteenth to fifteenth again on the south bank, and the remaining five comprising an outer ring on the north side. Indeed, *un escargot parfait!*

While on the subject of snails, I cannot help recalling a series of drawings in *Humour Magazine, Le Condense de l'humeur français,*

After a cartoon from *Humour Magazine, Le Condense de l'humeur français,* No. 22

No. 22, *Fevrier,* 1952, which entertained me highly. The title of the drawings was "*Les origines de la Bicyclette selon Darwin*". There was a sketch of two snails and an identical sketch of two cyclists bending forward over dropped handle-bars, and wearing caps which made their heads look like those of snails. I have copied them in my illustration.

I am told there is a British Snail-watching Society, and I have seen some British coats-of-arms borne by seafaring knights

—Sir Andrew Barton's, for instance— showing snails. In 1790 an English token halfpenny was struck at the Mint with a snail on its face. But in general it is not a creature in which the British are interested. Many Chinese eat snails, yet very few of us would make it a topic of conversation. It was only in Paris that I encountered the *escargot* in 100 forms— in plaster, in ink-drawings and in shops. I have also seen a crystal snail beautifully carved by the contemporary French artist Sabino. Only a Parisian humorist would have seen "*Les Origines*

de la Bicyclette" in the shape of an *escargot*. And only the town-planners of Paris would have arranged their city in the shape of an *escargot*.

The snail is quite a familiar figure in French folk-lore. For instance, I have read a translation of a fairy story with a snail motif. It is called 'Prince Vivien and Princess Placida' and comes from a collection of stories entitled *Nonchalante et Papillon*. Prince Vivien manages to rescue a poor little gazelle, which is being hotly pursued by a large green lion. He kills the lion and its owner, a horrible giant. Then the gazelle asks the Prince to lift her up and mount with her on the back of a huge snail. At first the Prince refuses, for he thinks it is a joke and that it would take them a year to get to the Green Castle. But eventually he takes the gazelle in his arms and climbs on the back of the snail, which glides along very peacefully, absolutely declining to be hurried by frequent digs from the Prince's heels. In vain does the gazelle represent to him that she is enjoying herself very much, and that this is the easiest mode of conveyance she has ever discovered. Prince Vivien is wild with impatience, and fears that the Green Castle will never be reached. However, they arrive at last, and everyone in the Castle rushes out to see the Prince dismount from his singular steed. To his astonishment, the gazelle suddenly changes into a charming Princess, and he recognises in her his pretty cousin Placida, who greets him with her usual tranquil sweetness.

So it was a huge snail which had carried the gazelle and Prince Vivien to their happiness. The snail is a nice, kind-hearted creature in the eyes of French children.

XVIII

An Old Bridge called 'Neuf'

EACH of the two dozen or more bridges across the Seine has its distinctive charm, but the New Bridge, 'Le Pont Neuf', which is in fact the oldest bridge, is my favourite.

It has long since ceased to be the important thoroughfare it once was. There are stone seats built into the recesses in the parapet on either side, offering rest to those who, like me, prefer to see this part of the city on foot. I took full advantage of these seats and was grateful to their sixteenth-century designer. Modern bridge-builders forget that there are still people who walk and linger. Paris, like any other European metropolis, has its busy side, but her pavement-café seats, her free benches along the boulevards and avenues, quays and waterfronts, above all these seats on the Pont Neuf, show that she is not all hustle and bustle.

Sitting on the Pont Neuf, I watched Parisians taking their cats for an airing. The cats sat peacefully on the parapet as long as their owners desired to gossip. To me the conversations sounded so lively as often to be indistinguishable from heated arguments, but the cats showed no concern.

Once eight children came with a middle-aged woman who might have been either their nurse or their mother. They climbed and clustered on to one of the seats, eagerly shouting when they saw a fisherman catch a fish or a boat pass by. Their excited movements required more space for their arms and legs than was available, and one or other was constantly being pushed off the seat. The woman had a busy time keeping them in hand. Though the children were all lively, their activities did not disturb but rather enhanced the carefree atmosphere of the place.

On another occasion a young couple sat down directly opposite me, and I watched, astonished, their laughter turn to quarrelling, until finally the girl was left weeping and the man strode away. That, too, did not destroy the atmosphere. I suppose that love-making is so universal a practice that even 'lovers' quarrels' strike the ear and eye no more disturbingly than the cries of children.

In the dusk, before the bridge lamps were lit, I caught glimpses of figures clinging so closely together that their heads became fused and they appeared to have only three eyes between them, or even only two, with a deep scar on the forehead! Their garments, too, took on unbelievable shapes. It was a revelation. Cubist and other new forms of modern painting began to seem much less grotesque to me. Inventors often attribute their inventions to accidental happenings in the course of their work; no invention seems to arise from nothing. I believe that Picasso used to live near the Pont Neuf, and in his early years in Paris was often seen on the bridge. He may have seen such visual illusions as I did.

One morning I found myself in the Place Pierre Curie at the south end of the Pont Neuf. The names of Paul and Marie Curie had been known to me since I studied chemistry in my college days. Monsieur Curie met his death in this square in 1908, when a six-ton dray ran over him. The square was named to commemorate the wonderful benefit to mankind resulting from the discovery of radium by him and his wife. Pierre Curie died in his fiftieth year, and I was amazed to learn that he never went to school in his life. The slope from the bridge bed down to the Quai des Grands Augustins could, I realised, be very dangerous for crossing when heavy lorries pass to and fro.

M

I liked the old red-walled houses at the west corner of the rue Dauphine and enjoyed looking at them from various angles when my eyes travelled between the houses into the darkness of the rue de Nevres. The light from the quay did not penetrate its narrow length and the houses on either side were tall. I remembered reading somewhere that Madame Sans Gêne, the washerwoman who was to become the wife of a Marshal of France, lived in the rue de Nevres and washed her clothes in the Seine. I do not know her life-story, but I know the story of a most beautiful Chinese washer-girl, Hsi-shih, who lived by the side of a great lake during 'the period of the Warring States' some 2,500 years ago. Her beauty was remarked by a minister, Fan Li, who suggested to King Kou-chien, of Yueh State, that she should be presented to their conqueror, Fu-ch'ai of Wu State. The washer-girl quickly became the favourite of Fu-ch'ai, who gradually neglected his state affairs and lost control over his

ministers and generals. They all became corrupt and ruined. This fell exactly into the design of Kou-chien, who soon rose again to crush his conqueror. It is clear that one should never underestimate the power of a woman, not even a washer-woman.

After making some rough sketches I moved on to the bridge and rested for a long while. Easter was approaching and, with the sun already high in the sky, it was now quite warm.

Waking from a little nap, my mind became active but my eyes remained half-closed. I was thinking of the days long before the Pont Neuf came into existence. According to an old map of Roman Paris which I saw in Hilaire Belloc's *Paris*, there were six islets in the river. The Romans created the town of Lutetia on the largest of them—the one now called Ile-de-la-Cité. From this island Paris grew. For many centuries it was the centre of Paris life. The early kings of France lived on it, and then the Palais du Louvre became essential.

It was decided that the new bridge should cross the two westernmost islets, the Ile aux Vaches and the Ilot des Juifs. This was costly. Many books told me that the Pont Neuf was completed by Henri IV; but Belloc writes:

He (Henri IV) continued it, but he neither began it nor ended it. The first mention of such a project is in 1379, the next is the memorial of the University and the St Germain's quarter to Henri II in 1556; the first attempt to realise it, the commission of 1577-8, that took advantage of a drought in the winter to drive the first piles in the low water of the narrow arm of the stream. It was a time not only of drought, but of extreme penury. Only the year before the exchequer had been so low that four great rubies of the reliquary in the Ste Chapelle were sold by the Crown, and it is no wonder that the work—already refused by Henri II on the ground of expense—went slowly in the reign of his unfortunate son and namesake. Henri III, his eyes red with weeping for his favourite, came with the Queen-Mother to lay the first stone when the pier next the southern bank was at the level of the water; but during all these last eighteen years of the Valois nothing was done but to bridge the narrower of the two arms of the Seine, and to fill in and unite with the Cité the little islets that support the centre of the Pont Neuf and became the Place Dauphiné. . . .

I remember seeing in the Musée Carnavalet a design with a label which read: "*Anonyme, Ecole Française, Vers. 1570: le Pont Neuf (Projet non-exécuté)*." It looked a finer design, more in tune with the architecture of the Palais du Louvre, than the one which was carried out. It was rejected perhaps on the score of expense. I do not pretend to be a student of architecture or of history, but I was interested to know that a king wanting to build a bridge could not afford to do so, and that the Crown was forced to sell four great rubies of the reliquary in the Ste Chapelle to keep the exchequer going. I have now lived a long time outside China, and these facts did not seem to me incredible, but many Chinese contemporaries of mine would think them so. Our emperors exercised absolute power over the nation's revenue; whoever was poor, they were not. I was born in the last few years of the Manchu Dynasty under the wretched Empress Dowager Tsu-Hsi. She used the nation's nearly-exhausted treasury, not only to build the extravagant new Summer Palace of the City of Peking, but also to train a group of fanatics called Boxers, who brought upon Peking the ruthless reprisals of allied foreign forces. If we had had a different conception of our imperial head, that Empress

Dowager could never have held power and Peking Palace might have been saved from wanton attacks. Our conception of absolute power being vested in the ruler of the country continued even after China became a republic. The President, artificially elected, was an emperor under another name. Nobody could question his use of public funds. An annual budget was an unheard-of thing among the people. I could not but admire the French for having seen to it so early in their history that the king should not ruin them.

Rising from my seat, I walked towards the Quai des Orfèvres. Leaning on the parapet there, I turned my back to the Seine and gazed at the whole width of the bridge. I tried to imagine it crowded with people coming and going, lingering and sitting. In the seventeenth and eighteenth centuries it was the pitch of pedlars and hawkers of every description, who lined both sides and shouted the attractions of their wares. It was also a show-ground for jugglers, newsvendors, dancers, singers, and strolling players whose activities Molière enjoyed as a boy. Presently an unusual smell began to fill my nostrils and I wondered if one of those vendors of sausages, fried fish or pancakes had been conjured up again by my concentration on bygone days.

At first I saw nothing on the bridge to account for the smell, but, leaning over the low wall, I observed on the bank, almost level with the water, four or five persons, one of whom seemed to be a woman, gathered round a fire on which something was cooking, maybe fish. Involuntarily my feet moved along the Quai des Orfèvres until I found steps to go down. I had walked along this part of the bank before and knew that the *clochards* are fond of lying or sitting by the wall of the quay or under an arch. I walked idly past the group whom I had suspected of cooking and found that they were merely burning large green leaves. I continued my walk to the arch of the bridge and then turned to find my way up to the quay again, thinking of all I had heard about the *clochards*. Though they look wretched and poor, they are full of independence and dignity. They seldom accept money from anybody without doing some service for it; they preserve their liberty and earn their bread chiefly by gathering rags and scavenging; they hold aloof from gossiping strangers; and the Paris police leave them alone. I feel that they deserve respect rather than pity.

I came up the Quai des Orfèvres near the Boulevard du

Palais. Someone stopped to tell me that along this quay there used to be the famous goldsmith's shop of Boehmer and Bosange and many vendors of diamond necklaces. The goldsmiths were jewellers to Marie-Antoinette 160 years ago. There are no shops now. Passing the Palais de Justice, I stopped to examine the

impressive wrought-iron gate, partly gilded. At that moment a number of people, including several youngsters, came out of a passage on the left of the central courtyard and many more entered the same passage. I followed them. A uniformed guide stood at the entrance and admitted us like a herd of cows to a milking shed.

In view of the excellent taste of the French in building and town-planning, I could not but find odd the position of the Sainte Chapelle. There was no proper entrance to this important shrine from any main road or from any bigger edifice. The guide told us that it was built in 1246 by St Louis to house the Crown of Thorns and other holy relics acquired by him. But why did later architects, when commissioned to build and rebuild the Palais de Justice, not try to incorporate the Sainte Chapelle in their designs or give it proper breathing space? It seems to have been ignored completely in their ground plan; the lines of its walls do not even run exactly parallel with those of the courtyard in which it stands. Were it not for its beautiful gilded spire, which soars gracefully into the sky, this pearl might be overlooked among so many fish-eyes, as an old Chinese saying, "*Yü-mu-hun-chu*", puts it.

We did not stay long in the lower chapel, which was used by the servants of the royal household. In the upper chapel we saw the place where the king and his family sat for divine service. The guide drew our attention to the very narrow strips of highly-coloured stained glass, indicating which sections dated from the thirteenth century and which were later additions, matching the old. They all looked equally old to me. What difference do 200 or 300 years make to such antiquity? The whole set of windows comprises 1,134 scenes. If I could have stood close to the lower panes, I might have been able to make out some of them, but as most of them were a yard or two above our heads, there was little hope of distinguishing them, let alone those close to the ceiling. It brought home to me the argument of modern architects that well-placed patterns of coloured glass can give a very good effect without minutely painted scenes. The detailed picture of a religious faith is there, of course, for all time, and perhaps it does not matter that the casual visitor can grasp little of it. The stained glass of the Sainte Chapelle, impressive and magnificent as it is, yet failed to inspire in me any feeling of awe such as I have experienced in many a cathedral. This may have been the fault of the too-elegant stone pillars and over-refined arches of the nave, which are so wonderfully, and indeed miraculously, constructed that at first I thought they were of wood, like those in many Buddhist temples in China, especially as all are painted dark red or blue, with additional decorations in gold leaf. The walls are painted and decorated similarly. When I realised that this was stone-work, my admiration for the artistry and craftsmanship displayed in the Sainte-Chapelle increased. Yet all its richness and over-refinement reacted on me outwardly; it did not give me inner satisfaction. There was a chilly air about it. It was a toy-jewel, like the Taj Mahal in India, but the latter covers a much wider area and its beauty is unique.

I was glad when the guide took us out to the porch of the upper chapel. The panel on the lintel, a scene of the Last Judgement and the Resurrection, with many naked sinners being ushered into Hell, was very fine, and interested me. The carvings on the panels of the walls represented the creation of the world. According to the guide, the panels were carved because few people in the thirteenth century could read and this was a means of teaching them the creation story. The guide then drew a small boy of six to the front and pointed out to him in turn the panels representing the creation of Heaven, earth, sun, moon, stars, until he came to man. Then, with a deprecatory cough, he said that the panel showing the creation of woman came seven stages later. This amused everyone. Presently came the panel showing Adam and Eve in a manner which can only be described as unusual. The guide stopped talking suddenly, shrugged his shoulders and closed his eyes. Explanation was unnecessary. He acted his commentary. The previous amusement became a roar of merriment.

I felt I had seen enough. Slipping out into the open air, I made my way to the Tour de l'Horloge. Mentally I compared the guides in the three big Western cities I know. Those in London incline to boastful reminiscence of the Boer War or other personal war experiences, for they are generally retired servicemen. Those in New York are generally young girls the smartness of whose appearance seems intended to compensate for the mechanical manner in which they recite words learned by heart. Those in Paris act a part!

Near the Tour de l'Horloge a board hangs on a door with the words *Secours aux Noyés et Asphyxiés*, 'help for the drowning and suffocating'. Evidently there is need on occasion for such help, but how do the victims reach it? I walked on to the Pont au Change to look from the Tour de l'Horloge at the three other towers, the Tour de César, the Tour d'Argent and the Tour de Bonbec. It is one of the most impressive sights in Paris. A few people were entering the Conciergerie, and I soon left the bridge to follow them. We were first taken to see the servants' hall and kitchens of the old palace of the kings of France, which in 1360 ceased to be the royal residence. Then we saw the old prison room, and some rooms now used for housing soldiers; a few with historic significance have been left as prison cells. The guide mentioned many names and events, but most of the people in the group he was conducting, judging by their faces, knew as little about French history as I did and paid no heed—until he came to the name of Marie-Antoinette. Then a squarish lady pushed me aside unceremoniously and stepped nearer to the guide to be sure of hearing what he said. The death of this Queen put life into the party.

The cell occupied by Marie-Antoinette from September 11th till her execution on October 16th, 1793, was converted by Louis XVIII into a chapel to her memory. She lived during that time, however, in only half the space now covered by the chapel: a partition divided the cell, the other half of which was occupied by two guards who were set to watch her day and night. No matter how vigilant the authorities thought they had

to be, it was harsh to keep a woman prisoner under the constant watch of two men! The Queen must have longed for death or to go mad. But in the letter which she wrote to her sister-in-law Elizabeth on the eve of her death (which I saw in the Archives Nationales) her handwriting is clear and firm, showing perfect self-control.

I did not stay long in the Conciergerie, partly because I could not follow the guide, who had so much to say, and partly because the air was oppressive. A middle-aged couple from America followed me out. They turned right for the Pont au Change and I moved slowly leftwards along the Quai de l'Horloge.

I leaned on the low wall of the quay near the Rue de Harley for a moment. A few fishermen sat silently on the bank below

Marvellous Clouds from the Pont Neuf

with their rods projecting in front of them, and some *clochards* lay under the trees near an arch of the bridge. I wondered if there had been much change round this part of the Seine since Marie-Antoinette's days. The condemned Queen is said to have sat on a small chair facing the door most of the time. If there had been a little window through which she could have seen the Seine, might she not have been comforted a little?

As I was about to move along the quay, the white marble steps and animal sculptures of the main entrance of the Palais de Justice caught my eye. I turned into the rue de Harley to look at them. Nobody was about except two policemen on guard. One of them approached me as I stood in front of the building looking over the Place Dauphine to a gap between two dense rows of trees, beyond which the white pedestal with the statue of Henri IV could be vaguely seen. He asked if I was sketching and remarked, "*C'est une belle vue.*" I agreed. Paris policemen have a taste for art. There was absolute quietness. The houses lining the triangle-like Place Dauphine behind the trees seemed to be ideal dwellings.

Presently I walked through the gap at the apex of the triangle and came out again on the Pont Neuf. Crossing the central part of the bridge, I leant against the pedestal of Henri IV's statue to look back over the way I had come. This side was fine, too. All I had read about the old days of the Pont Neuf rose again in my mind. I visualised Henri IV crossing the new bridge in state. There was enough space for a grand procession. The incessant noise and endless activity on the bridge was in full view. I could see that much-talked-of 'Grand Thomas', dressed in a scarlet suit with peacock feathers adorning his three-cornered hat, standing by his stall (as he did in 1715) and trying to sell his infallible quack medicine called 'Solar Balm'. He is said to have dominated the new bridge for about twenty years. Such a character could easily have been found in a country market in China a few years ago.

At length I stretched myself and walked round the sides of the pedestal to study the bas-reliefs. One panel showed Henri IV commanding food to be distributed to the inhabitants of Paris during the siege. Another showed him entering Paris as a conqueror and giving orders to the Prévost of Paris to carry to the inhabitants an offer of peace. They were fine work, but could easily be overlooked, like all monuments in a big city.

Monuments and statues cause a stir when they are erected, but soon lose their interest and too often become pieces of the pavement—when they are not positive eyesores.

This statue of Henri IV, which I liked, I later learned was not the original one, erected by his widow, Marie de Médicis. That was melted down during the Revolution when copper was needed for the manufacture of cannon. Napoleon wished to replace it by an obelisk of Cherbourg granite with the inscription, L'EMPEREUR NAPOLEON AU PEUPLE FRANCAIS, but this did not materialise. The present statue was cast by order of Louis XVIII out of the metal from several unwanted statues (including one of Napoleon) and was paid for by public subscription. So Henri IV came back to the Pont Neuf. It is a wonder that this statue escaped a fate similar to its predecessor's, for the German Occupation Force melted down many Paris statues during the Second World War. They claimed to be removing only *bad* statues. But suppose the war had lasted longer?

I was interested to read the following story about this statue by Ralph Nevill in his book, *Paris of Today*:

Alluding to that King's famous promise as to *"la poule au pot"*—that everyone should have a chicken in his cooking-pot—an admirer of Louis XVI on the latter's accession hung a placard round the statue's neck, on which in large characters was written *"Resurexit"* (he has come to life again). The next day this had been replaced by another inscription which ran:

> *"Resurrexit: j'approuve fort le mot;*
> *Mais pour y croire, il faut la poule au pot."*

> (*Resurrexit*, much I like the word,
> But to believe it a fowl's required.)

The next day this had been altered to:

> *"Enfin, la poule au pot sera donc bientôt mise*
> *Car depuis deux cents ans qu'on nous l'avait promise*
> *On n'a cessé de la plumer."*

(Since for two hundred years the promised bird's been plucked, 'Tis time, we may assume, 'twill soon be cooked.)

While the Second World War was at its height, I read in an English newspaper that some Parisians or the German Occupation Force had started to eat monkeys from the Vincennes Zoo. I wondered if any witty Frenchman had put a placard on the

statue of Henri IV to say that now everyone should have a
monkey in his cooking-pot!

Some steps descend behind the statue. At the foot a pair of
gates in a thick granite wall give on to a small garden on a

Two Sung-vase gates

tongue of land. The gates are shaped like an ancient Chinese
porcelain vase. It was a common practice in China to build in
gardens a moon gate, a willow-leaf gate, an ancient vase gate,
and so on, and I was pleased to find that the French did likewise. Yet I was surprised that a French vase should have the
same shape as one of our Sung vases of the tenth century.

I stepped back close to the wall under the statue and looked
at the glint of the sunshine on the big tree trunk in the centre of
the garden and the fresh lawn and sandy paths. Two sparrows
flew down to peck. A little boy in a bright red jumper ran away
from his mother's grasp. All this was for me the coloured
decoration painted on the vase, turning it into a Chien-lung
vase of much later date.

After passing through the right-hand gate, I had a stroll
outside the enclosure of the little garden. Reaching the tip of
the tongue of land, I felt I was standing in the stem of a boat
watching the water rushing by swiftly on both sides. A big
willow tree dressed in long green tassels and a smaller cherry
tree covered with pink blossom were growing between me and

the end of the little garden. I thought I had found ideal solitude.
But a moment later a young couple, possibly art students from
the Collège des Beaux Arts, came along. They were very much
at their ease. They sat down on the edge of the bank and the

young woman immediately threw off her shoes, while her
companion took off his coat and shirt. This infected me, and I
too felt hot in the noon sun of early April.

I moved round to the other side and entered through a small
gate to find a seat. The sun seemed to have cast a spell on the
garden. Not even the children playing in the sand pile made a
noise. I sat down. My head was full of my sight-seeing and my
legs were heavy. I closed my eyes, but opened them again when
a gardener popped out of his bower to sweep the footpath.

Again I was wakened from a doze by a shrill cry from a child: "*Un bateau . . . un bateau . . . un bateau. . . .*" He ran to the railings. A few other children followed him, shouting too. A small steamboat with a Seine barge in tow was passing between us and the Quai du Louvre. I was happy to see these children so innocently excited. Their carefree manner

and their unrestricted chatter added further pleasure to my day.

After a little rest, all that I had seen began to sort itself in my head. There is a common saying that 'history repeats itself', but would anyone in France today think of building another Sainte Chapelle? Could another Marie-Antoinette suffer imprisonment in the Conciergerie? Could any of the young children who were shouting "*Un bateau*" a moment ago be enticed into soldiering? I began to feel disillusioned. History is clad in fashion. A fashion alters the look of man, but each boy and girl who grows up from the tender age of those in this garden undergoes a similar process to his or her forefathers. Fashions do not repeat themselves, but take hints from the past. In the same way history cannot repeat itself exactly, but is seldom far different from the old. Nothing is really new. Yet it is called new in its own time, like the Pont Neuf, which is now the oldest bridge in Paris.

The little garden I was sitting in is called the 'Square du Vert Galant'. I remembered a French friend telling me that it was named after Henri IV, whose people gave him this nickname. *Vert* implies 'full of warmth and passion' and *galant* 'a perfect lover'. But besides being very fond of the fair sex, Henri IV was also full of chivalry and courage. He escaped seventeen out of eighteen attempts on his life. The eighteenth attempt took place in 1610 in the rue de la Ferronerie, only a little way from the north end of the Pont Neuf, and he died at his assassin's hand.

Henri was wise as well as brave. Returning incognito from a hunting expedition, he crossed to the Louvre by a ferry situated in those sixteenth-century days along the present-day Quai Voltaire. He asked the ferryman's opinion about a peace treaty which the Government had just concluded. "To tell you the truth," the ferryman replied, "I don't see much advantage in it. What I do know is that everything is terribly taxed—even this wretched little boat is no exception." "Couldn't the King put matters right?" suggested Henri IV. *"Le Roi!* Oh, he's not a bad fellow, but he has a mistress who bleeds him and demands luxurious dresses and expensive jewels for which we have to pay. We do not mind paying, but she is not faithful to him. They say she has many lovers." The gallant Henri IV listened philosophically and laughed with the ferryman. Next morning, the ferryman was brought in front of him and his favourite, the Duchesse de Beaufort. Told to repeat his words, the poor man had no alternative. Each word pricked the ears of the lady like a needle and made her white with anger. She demanded that the man should be hanged. But Henri IV knew a better sequel. Smilingly he turned to the Duchess: "Don't be so wild! We must improve these poor fellows' lot and they will sing a different tune." The ferryman went away thankfully with his head still on his shoulders and a purse full of money in his pocket. And the royal favourite learnt her lesson. Henri IV did not let his passion outstrip his wisdom.

I don't know if any other country has had a king like Henri IV or if anyone else could balance power and passion so finely. There was a Chinese Emperor Hsuan-Tsung of the T'ang Dynasty, about the eighth century A.D., who was a good ruler, gallant and clever, and so interested in painting and music that he made T'ang a golden age of China. But in his declining days he became infatuated by a great beauty, Yang Kwei-Fei, herself talented in music and the dance, and was soon blind to everything but her charms. He did not go out incognito to talk to a

ferryman; instead, he adopted his favourite's lover as a foster-son and made him a marshal. In due course this marshal led his troops to court and demanded the throne. The Emperor fled with his favourite to the mountainous west country, but all his imperial army revolted, demanding Yang Kwei-Fei's death before they would attempt to escort him back to his throne in the capital. The Emperor first raged and then fell into despair. After days of weeping, he handed his beloved a long piece of pure white silk and all the imperial troops witnessed her tying it round her neck to end her days. This most tragic scene has been described in verse and prose and plays ever since the beginning of the ninth century.

A Parisian couple, about forty years of age, now squeezed on to my bench. Both looked well fed. The man had his coat off and seemed to be settling himself for an afternoon nap, but although his eyes were shut at first, he murmured and chuckled in reply to the woman's steady flow of conversation. Soon, however, he was snoring. This did not please his companion, who appeared to like comments to punctuate her talk. She woke him up and annoyed him. He began to talk incessantly too, like the water rolling through the arch of the Pont Neuf.

Her voice joined the hissing in the trees. After straining my ears for a moment, I managed to make out one or two of the man's words: "*Je rêve. . . . Je rêve . . .*" in a rather coarse and angry tone. Being given to dreaming myself, this made me smile. Presently my bench-sharers became really querulous, and I thought it time to get something to eat. On my way out of the garden I remembered an old Chinese story about a man who dreamed in his sleep that he went to a theatrical show with a number of friends. The play was about to begin, it seemed to him, when he was wakened by his wife. He uttered some oaths. "Well, well, don't curse me," retorted the wife. "Hurry up and get to sleep again; the first act is not yet over."

As I sat down to my meal, I thought the following lines from the Persian poet Hafiz, translated by Louisa Stuart Costello, could sum up my day:

> The world to me has been a home;
>   Wherever knowledge could be sought,
> Through differing climes I loved to roam,
>   And every shade of feeling caught
> From minds whose varied fruits supply
>   The food of my philosophy.

XIX

Wingless Herons

An old fisherman with a fishing rod
By the cliffs or in the bay
Comes and goes in his lonely boat, unconstrained.
Seagulls are dotted on the shore and the light waves fade
      In the distance.
The whispering of the bulrushes makes the sunny day seem cool.
I sing loudly as the sunset indicates the late hour.
Of a sudden a golden shadow trembles in the waves:
Lifting my head, I see the moon rising over the eastern hills.

THAT is a rough translation of a song, popular among Chinese
men of letters, written by the eighteenth-century poet, calligrapher and painter, Cheng Pan-Ch'iao. I claim, as I have said,
no knowledge of music, but I had a great liking for this song
and learned to sing it in my day. At that time I was absorbed in
the study of modern science. After the First World War, China
began to realise her position in the modern world, and it was
an urgent task for her young people to acquire scientific
knowledge; such, indeed, is still the position today. But my
mind had been early moulded by tradition. My grandmother
had ruled our family of forty members for nearly fifty years
without ever attempting to make any changes in our family
habits. My father was an artist who specialised in flower and
bird paintings. My brother was a poet to whom we had given
the nickname of 'Madman', since he did not care to occupy
himself with anything but poetry. Whenever I came home from
college in the vacations, no one appeared to take any interest
in what I studied, nor could I bring myself to say a word about
it to any of them, though I managed to get a reasonably good
result each term. Nor was it only in my family that I found no
link with my studies; once outside the college walls the connection seemed to snap. As I wandered about the city streets
or the countryside, it was the old way of living that met my eyes
and captured my imagination. An old fisherman in his lonely
boat coming and going on the river, unconstrained, as the

poem tells, was quite a characteristic sight in my boyhood. That simple way of living still prevailed; it had been tested and admired. The carefree feeling and philosophy expressed in the song had not ceased to hold man's imagination, and I for one found myself still under its spell.

I pondered the old man's feeling towards fishing. What made him become a fisherman? Why did he like fishing? Did he really feel carefree? Could he live on his catch? What kind of fish did he fish for? Such simple questions came far more readily to my mind than the scientific problems I was set at college.

All my experience of fishermen in China was connected with the countryside, with cliffs or a bay. It is possible that in London there are people who fish along the Thames, but I have never seen them. Until I came to Paris it did not occur to me that I was ever likely to see people fishing right in the busiest part of a capital city. But in Paris it was not a case of an odd fisherman or two, but of many fishermen; nor did they fish only on Saturdays and Sundays, but all day and every day. The sight filled me with wonder. In England fishing with rod and line is regarded as a sport or hobby, and one does not expect to practise it every day. Yet many Parisians seemed able to fish with the regularity with which others go to work. Often I wanted to question them, but it was difficult to start, so I just watched. Rarely a day passed without my seeing at least one fisherman, for I was living very close to the left bank of the Seine. Sometimes they seemed to demand my attention whether I was in the mood to watch them or not. In the early morning and at dusk I would see them standing by the river bank, veiled by the thin mist, very much like herons waiting patiently for their prey. The more distant they were the more striking was the resemblance to those birds of contemplation. I have often waited to watch a heron dive to catch a fish and fly away with it. It is a pleasing sight and I love to paint it. In the same way I watched the human-herons along the Seine, but they never took to flight, for they were wingless.

Being wingless, they afforded me better opportunities to study their movements, their poise and ways of handling the rod, adjusting the line and attending to the hook, than did the winged herons. I sketched them from every possible angle. There is a spot below the Quai de la Tournelle where a

number of round wooden boards are fixed on the lower quay.
I saw many a fisherman practising casting his line to hit these
boards. They sat, they squatted, they stood, and they even lay
or crawled on the quayside while taking aim.

Along the Quai de la Gare, which is built with a long steep
slope down to the water's edge with no footpath or level strip

at the brink, fishermen have devised a most ingenious method
of making themselves comfortable. From the top of this quay it
is difficult to make the line reach the deep part of the river, so
the fishermen tie a block of wood to the end of a thick rope, the
other end of which is fastened securely to an iron bar at the top
of the quay. The improvised seat is then lowered down the
slope to the water's edge. Some use a shorter rope and sit on
the block of wood fishing unconcernedly.

The fishermen hereabouts seemed more friendly to one
another than elsewhere. Although it is quite possible to tie the
rope firmly to the iron bar and lower oneself down the slope, the
more common way seems to be to sit on the piece of wood and
get a friend to do the lowering. But whichever way of reaching
the water's edge was employed, the device was interesting and
ingenious. I should have liked to see how the reascent was
accomplished, but I could never stay long enough. At week-
ends sometimes the fishermen brought their families with
them and would talk loudly around me as I squatted on the
bar. Once I saw a fisherman climb very cautiously down the
rope to hand a thermos flask of hot coffee to a friend. He wore
a scared expression as he propelled himself downwards, but
he had a good laugh when he returned safely to the quay again.

I wondered why this awkward stretch of the Seine had become so favourite a fishing ground, the most popular, I should say, after the section by the Pont Neuf, west of the Quai des Grands Augustins, which is the most crowded place of all. One Sunday afternoon I counted forty fishermen between the arch of the bridge and a spot some fifty feet eastward. Some were obliged to stand behind others. Two were on the parapet of the lower quay. Parisian fishing tackle shops sell a gadget with which a rod can be stood upright on the ground behind its owner!

A young French friend of mine, Monsieur Jean-Francois Bouisset, told me that there was an anglers' association in Paris called the 'Union des Pêcheurs de Paris'. With an angling licence, one can fish wherever one likes along the embankment from sunrise to sunset. He added laughingly: "*Un marchand d'articles de pêche qui organise des concours m'a dit que toutes les professions etaient représentées au bord de la Seine depuis le Président de la République jusqu'au balayeur de la rue.*" And he sent me a photograph of a typical Seine fisherman with the remark: "I don't think this one is the *Président de la République. . . .*"

Why the fishermen like to huddle together on the quays of Paris is beyond me. There is a very long stretch of the Seine between Paris and the source of the river and another long stretch between Paris and the sea, and the city itself is small, at least as compared with London. The fishermen could easily take themselves a little way up- or down-river where they would enjoy peaceful surroundings and perhaps better catches. Sometimes I overheard sceptics say that they had never seen a fisherman in Paris catch a fish. Others remarked that fish were caught, but that they were so small they had to be thrown back. Still others questioned if there were any fish left after so many hundreds of fishermen had fished month after month, year after year. A legend often circulated is that there is only one fish in the Seine and that of solid gold, and that this accounts for the perseverance of the fishermen. One cynic remarked to me that if there is still one fish in the Paris reaches of the Seine, it must be a real 'hustler', for none of the fishermen along the quays has managed to catch it!

However, I proved in time that a few small fish are actually caught by the wingless ones. One morning, I decided to visit a friend in the Avenue de New York. As I crossed the Pont

d'Iéna *il tombait des cordes*! So I hastily took shelter in the end
arch under the Passerelle Debilly. Then I noticed an elderly
fisherman standing nearby. He must have been fishing the
whole morning; indeed, his appearance suggested that he had
been there from time immemorial. His unshaven face, bushy

white moustache and shabby clothes made a striking contrast
to the neat, clean lines of the bridge's stonework. The immense
steel structure of the Eiffel Tower appeared softened by the
strings of rain. I began to smile at the wonderful effect rain
can produce. Just at that moment the fisherman, who was
perfectly unconcerned by the rain, wound up his line and a
small fish not more than five inches long came wriggling out of
the water. While unhooking the fish the old man noticed me,
and thinking I was smiling at his good fortune, at once began
to talk to me. He talked and laughed, laughed and talked, and
finally grasped my shoulder to help him keep his balance while
he went on chuckling and talking. I had no chance to interrupt,
but I could not be so unfeeling as not to display pleasure at his
triumph. I ejaculated some words in English, and then, as this
was not fast enough, dropped into Chinese, in which I could
speak as fast as he. I had no idea what he had been telling me,
nor could he understand me, but he needed someone to heed
him, and I was happy to do so. I like travelling in silence, but
days and weeks without being able to utter more than a few
words can be trying.

Another morning I was watching the flowing water from the
parapet of the Pont au Change. Suddenly a loud cry came from
a stout fisherman near the Tour de l'Horloge: *"Il ne m'aime
pas!"* He had just wound up his line and a small fish had got
away as the hook came out of the water. I saw the tiny creature
drop. His remark caused a roar of laughter along the quay, in
which he joined.

The fact that there are so many fishermen on her quays

shows, I felt, that Paris is not—or not only—a great business
centre, but a city of ease, a city of life. This is where Paris
differs from London and any other metropolis I know. And the
fishermen themselves are unique, for one would never find a
visitor from another country among them. Their style of dress,
their gestures and their manner of talking gave me many happy
moments.

I have said a good deal about the wingless herons perched
on the river banks and very little about the finny inhabitants
of the water, for these were rarely revealed to me. The Seine
has carried much mud from its source, and has been carrying
it for a long time. According to the ancient Chinese philosophy,
every one of Nature's millions of creatures, including man, has
a part to play in the eternal rhythm of life. If the finny inhabitants of the Seine were non-existent, the wingless ones on
the banks would be meaningless. But what are the feelings of
the former towards the latter? The Seine is said to be very
deep, particularly in the Paris area, but if there were no wingless herons watching for them, surely the finny ones would rise
to the surface from time to time out of boredom?

My friend Alan White once drew my attention to a poem in
three parts by Leigh Hunt entitled 'The Fish, the Man and the
Spirit'. In the first part man apostrophised the fish:

> O scaly, slippery, wet, swift, staring wights,
>   What is't ye do? what life lead? eh, dull goggles?
> How do ye vary your vile days and nights?
>   How pass your Sundays? . . .

To which the fish retorts:

> Thou that on dry land horribly dost go
>   With a split body and most ridiculous pace,
>   Prong after prong, disgracer of all grace,
> Long-useless-finned, haired, upright, unwet, slow!

Then the fish is turned into a man and learns what it is to be
human; after which he becomes a spirit and expresses his views
on both men and fish:

> Man's life is warm, glad, sad, 'twixt loves and graves,
>   Boundless in hope, honoured with pangs austere,
> Heaven-gazing; and his angel-wings he craves:
>   The fish is swift, small-needing, vague yet clear,
> A cold, sweet, silver life, wrapped in round waves,
>   Quickened with touches of transporting fear.

I like this poem for the way it places men and fishes on a level in nature. Viewed simply as creatures, both are ridiculous, each having in the mysterious course of evolution developed grotesquely stylish ways of performing their functions. Man, it is true, has his spiritual aspirations, while the fish seems quickened only with transporting fear. But spiritual aspirations turn easily into material ambitions; and the small needs of the fish have their compensations in its cold, sweet, silver life, wrapped in round waves.

XX

Twigs and Petals

THE English have always claimed to be great lovers of
Nature, and they are very proud of their trees, especially the
huge, ancient trees of their parklands and varied woodlands.
When I came to England I too learned to appreciate this aspect
of the English countryside, and I am happy to recall that I
contributed a bamboo painting to the first International
Exhibition of the Men of the Trees, held in London in 1934,
under the inspiration of the society's founder, Richard St
Barbe Baker.

But despite this justifiable English pride, I could not help
observing that there are far fewer trees in London than in Paris.
I love the London squares with their many shapely old trees,
and have never grown tired of looking at them at all seasons
of the year. Nevertheless, away from the Squares, one could
walk for hours in London, through street after street, without
seeing a single tree. Paris, on the other hand, is full of graceful
avenues and tree-bordered streets; besides, her many parks and
gardens and the quiet charm of the Seine is greatly enhanced
by the tall, elegant trees, mostly acacias, along its banks. Then,

the pavement cafés, it is generally con-
ceded, add gaiety to the boulevards—
those characteristic street-forms of Paris
—but it is the trees that give them grace.
My lodgings in Paris were within five
minutes' walk of the Jardin du Luxembourg, where it was that I first became
really acquainted with the trees of Paris.
Whenever I was not sight-seeing in some
other part of the city, I would roam here
alone among the leafless trees. During the winter months this
noted playground of the Latin quarter did not seem to live up to
its reputation, for at times it could be described as deserted. It is
surrounded by busy thoroughfares, and many people take

short-cuts through the gardens to their places of business in the morning and back home in the evening. They could not have a pleasanter walk, and should be eternally grateful to Marie de Médicis, Queen of Henri IV, who built the Luxembourg. But long, long ago, the site of the gardens was called L'Enfer (Hell). In the tenth century there lived here a certain King Robert, who repudiated his first wife and married his cousin, Berthe de Bourgogne, and was excommunicated by the Pope for so doing. In those days the region was reputed to be the theatre of infernal practices, where witches held their sabbath, demons assembled by night for their assizes, and villains and vagabonds made it their home. . . . When I thought of all this I felt glad to have been born in a healthier age.

Towards noon, retired black-coated members of the *bourgeosie* would make their appearance, and mothers and nursemaids would come, either wheeling prams or playing ball with their young charges; but the wintry air deterred them from staying long. The fountain in front of the Palace did not play, and in the pond, to which in summer little boys would run down the white steps of the terraces to sail their boats, there was no water. Even the puppet theatre seemed to be closed. Occasionally I would catch sight of a pair of lovers on a bench, with heads close together, gazing dreamily into the distance; the mist-clad twigs and boughs, which framed them, clearly yet obscurely symbolised to me their entangled romance. There was something indescribably touching about the scene.

There are countless busts of poets and painters in the quiet alleys, and I thought they looked their best when the trees were leafless, for then the twigs and boughs provided additional ornament, instead of overpowering or obscuring the figures with their foliage. This sculpture gave me endless pleasure, particularly the statues of Chopin, Watteau and Delacroix. Paris is perhaps the only capital city in the world that gives artists their due of honour. Even the rather dingy statues of the Queens of France, standing in a semicircle before the Palace, looked whiter and more pleasing against the background of winter trees.

Among the monuments I noticed, with happy recognition, a small replica of the colossal Statue of Liberty that stands on Bedloe's Island in New York Bay, and this reminded me that there is another such miniature on one end of the Allée des

Cygnes, a strip of land jutting into the Seine. Francine took me for a walk there one evening, and when we reached the tip, where, on one side of the Pont de Grenelle, the statue stands, she told me about a friend of her mother's, an unconstrained lady from Texas who, on being taken sightseeing here, flew up the steps of the statue and with outstretched arms flung herself on the pedestal, exclaiming loudly, "Oh, my statue! This is my statue! My Liberty! . . ." This sudden emotion and the lady's piercing cry alarmed Francine's mother. What was more remarkable was that one of two French workmen who were eating their lunch by the parapet of the bridge was so astounded that he let fall from his mouth a good-sized sausage.

Later that day we went to have dinner with Francine's uncle, Monsieur André Leredde. Monsieur Leredde went to Peking as a soldier in the far-off Boxer Rebellion days and has many Chinese curios and art treasures in his house. Over dinner the story of the Liberty statue came up again and Francine's mother, Madame Barriere, re-enacted the scene most comically. I remarked that the Texan lady would not have been able to embrace the statue in New York Bay, for it is colossal, and added that I had climbed up to the head of it for a bird's-eye view of New York. This led our host to relate that his father had been connected with the casting of the New York statue. The work was done in Paris, and when it was completed Monsieur Leredde's father took him, then only a small boy of five, inside the head, where a celebration was held before the statue was transported to New York. It must have been a very quaint occasion. But somehow that small replica of Liberty in the Jardin du Luxembourg never looked to me quite at home.

The Luxembourg Gardens lured me not only because they were conveniently near my lodgings, but because they have a less formal and more friendly atmosphere than most of the parks of Paris. I could wander there freely without attracting attention, and contemplate the grace of the wintry boughs and the non-sensuous beauty of the interlacing twigs. Sometimes the trees etched themselves boldly on the silver-grey sky; sometimes the feeble winter sun cast a faint shadow of them on to the walls of palace or terrace; and sometimes they mingled in a mysterious mass of tracery, obscured by the morning or evening mist, a scene which the painter's brush would find it hard to describe. Often, at my approach, a flock of small birds, usually sparrows or starlings, would start up in all directions as if by magic, rousing me from reverie. They would perch on nearby boughs and twigs, generally choosing the highest and most conspicuous projections in order to make me thoroughly aware of their existence, and also to watch me closely and observe what I would do next. I often lingered without considering their perturbation, I am afraid, and enjoyed myself

studying their singularly beautiful poses. Patiently they would wait. As soon as I moved on, they would leave their perches and disappear magically again. To them my movements were clearly a nuisance and a disturbance; to me their flight was a source of simple pleasure.

To contemplate a wintry bough, a bare twig or a darkened trunk is unlike watching and analysing a dead thing; the latter betokens an end, while the former speaks of new beginnings. A wintry tree is full of potential life. Before the appearance of the first tiny shoots the fragile twig is battered by wind, rain, snow and frost, but it struggles on to reach its normal growth and bear fine foliage. To see a tree in its full summer beauty is also to feel some regret for the inevitable fall, but to anticipate the growth of its leaves step by step is like unfolding a long scroll of beautiful, unknown things. This is the source of my love for wintry trees.

The trees along the shores of the Seine seemed to me not only pleasing in themselves, but a great enhancement of the nearby buildings. For instance, from the Quai de l'Hôtel de Ville I marvelled at those leafless trees, tall and elegant, growing along the Quai de Bourbon, which seemed to form a decorative screen for the houses on the Ile St Louis. When they were full of foliage, the houses were quite lost in them. Again, from the little square of St Julien le Pauvre I was fascinated by the wide-spreading boughs of the trees standing behind the second-hand book boxes on the parapets, which looked so disorderly yet added a grace to the severe lines of the twin towers of Notre Dame. Without them, the towers would look over-bearing, out of keeping with the neighbouring buildings. In fact I find the architecture of this renowned church less beautiful than that of some of the other French cathedrals: its lines lack grace and variety, and it is just these qualities which are bestowed on it by the nearby trees, especially in winter. The varied formation of the trunks and boughs beautify and diversify, without obscuring, this great landmark of Paris.

The leafless trees in the Place des Vosges and in the grounds of the Palais Royal absorbed my attention for a different reason. Their twigs and branches were trimmed evenly at the top and the trees seemed to have lost their freedom, though still retaining their life. They reminded me of prisoners, or of a troop of soldiers stripped to the waist for morning exercises and with their hands above their heads. Sometimes I thought of them—especially the very evenly trimmed ones planted in a rectangle at the Palais Royal—as a special kind of stage constructed for a performance by Indian yogis. These Indians are so trained and disciplined that they can walk or lie down at ease on a board stuck full of sharp nails. Whenever I visited those gardens I expected the Palace balconies to fill with gorgeously dressed women and handsome men, and a troop of Indians in colourful turbans to appear suddenly from nowhere and perform somer-saults on the thorn-like platform of the tree-tops. One evening there was a beautiful sunset in Paris and its rays turned every branch and twig in the gardens into red-hot iron bars and nails. Some yogi of the highest skill would come, I felt, to perform very specially in the crimson light.

One of my happiest recollections of winter trees is of a day in the Bois de Boulogne. It was a February morning, cold but dry and bright, when I went for a walk there by myself. At one place I watched some men playing bowls on a strip of dry, sandy ground very unlike the lush greens so characteristic of England. Their style of playing—indeed probably the game itself—was somewhat different from English bowls, but each player addressed himself to the ball with fully Anglo-Saxon

games gravity. At another place I met a teacher in charge of a
large group of schoolchildren who were jumping, skipping and
even wrestling playfully with one another; their chatter and
movement seemed to take on a peculiar importance amid
those countless tall trees whose tops, still veiled in the morning

mist, smiled mysteriously. The trunks and boughs exhibited
a wide variety of shade and shadow, the nearer ones being very
dark, the others progressively lighter as the distance increased.
I moved on, keeping the children a long way ahead of me. As
I walked, the trees seemed to share the sportiveness of the
children, their flickering shadows making them appear to jump
and skip. I was entranced with this new visual experience which
provided so many subjects for my brush. I was making rough
monochrome sketches all the time. Presently I lost sight of the
children, but from the distance the faint outline of a galloping
horse and rider came into view. At that distance the horse
looked no bigger than a large dog and its movements were
unreal like a slow-motion film, the horseman appearing to
charge right *through* the tree trunks. Such were the simple joys
I experienced among the winter trees in the Bois de Boulogne.

Most of the trees in Paris are chestnuts, acacias, elms and
common plane, the last of which is said to like a deep,
moist, loamy soil, of which Paris has plenty. The tree is a sun-
lover and Paris can provide sunshine too. There are more
planes in Paris, particularly on the pavements of the boulevards,
than any other trees. When leafless, the planes have a rather

regular shape with the clusters of boughs and twigs massed
together on one or two straight trunks, or they are trimmed like
that for bordering roads. Chestnut-trees, too, are regular, but
acacias and elms with their interesting boughs and tall, elegant
trunks, which usually branch out into several main stems, are

Riding in the Bois Boulogne

less formal in their shapely twistings, and more refreshing to
the eye. These were chiefly to be found along the quays.

To my mind there should be more willows, especially weeping willows (which are said to have been Napoleon's favourites),
along the Seine. We usually associate willows with rivers and
lakes, but along the length of the Seine in Paris I found only
three. One of them stands on the tip of the Place de Vert
Galant, looking, especially when in full leaf, like a huge
umbrella for an African chieftain. The second is by the Quai
Anatole France, facing the Louvre, and has a very beautiful
rugged shape reminding me of a certain Sung painting. The
third is a very young tree which stretches its arms over the
water from a sandy patch under the Quai de l'Hôtel de Ville.
From its diminutive size it might easily be overlooked, yet I
always noticed it and looked at it affectionately when I passed.
The slender, tasselled branches were never quite black, but
always tinted with a slightly yellowish hue. When winter was
at its depth the golden threads appeared, as if painted by the

hand of spring—the first sketch of the year. Then the little tree
shone among its fellows, shaking off its winter weeds and
donning its spring clothes.

My joy in trees does not cease when winter ends. Trees are
fascinating at all times of the year. From several of the Seine
bridges I gazed with fascination at the groups of trees which
stand along the river in front of the Palais de l'Institut and close
by the Chambre des Députés, changing from deep black to
blueish grey, then to purplish blue, to violet-brown, to brownish
yellow, to yellowish green, to emerald, to grass green, and so on.

My long residence in England has taught me to start looking
for crocuses, "the harbingers of spring", as Wordsworth called
them, near the end of February. But I was deprived of this
pleasure in Paris; it was not until the end of March that I
found some patches of the bulb growing by the pond near the
Eiffel Tower. I was later to learn that this bright little flower,
which in early spring fairly carpets the ground in many English
parks, is much less popular in France. Two young Parisian
friends of mine had not even heard of it.

The first spring flower I met in Paris was the yellow forsythia
—a Chinese plant first introduced into Europe in 1832. I
saw two bushes of it in the Luxembourg Gardens, their bare
branches hung with a mass of golden bells, the gold gleaming
in the fitful winter sunshine against a background of blackish
bushes and tree trunks, an unforgettable sight. In China we
call this flower *Yin chun* or 'Welcoming Spring'. In Paris,
perhaps, it is the forsythia, instead of the crocus, which is
looked upon as the harbinger of spring.

Soon after this I noticed in the Parc Monceau near a hump-
backed bridge that gave it an Oriental effect a small tree with
its few branches dotted with tiny, red-tipped buds. It was
the first almond tree I had seen in Paris. Before I had an
opportunity of returning to see whether the buds had burst, there
seemed to be almond blossom everywhere in Paris—in the
Jardins du Trocadéro, in the Parc du Champs de Mars, by the
Eiffel Tower, along the Quai Branly; and two small trees in
the garden along the Champs Elysées gleamed in the bright
sunshine more splendidly than the rest.

There is a legend current in my birthplace that more than
1,000 years ago there lived near the foot of Lu Mountain a
doctor of supernatural powers called Tung Feng. He treated

people without fee, but stipulated that each patient cured of a
serious illness must plant three almond trees in his (the doctor's)
garden, while those relieved of less severe complaints had to
plant only one. In a few years his garden became an almond
grove famous the whole country over. Each year Tung gathered
the almonds and exchanged them for rice, which he distributed
to the poor. The almond trees of Paris could not have been
planted in this way, but they gave me a happy nostalgia, as if
I were again at home near Lu Mountain.

As Easter approached, Paris changed her blueish-grey
garment for a brighter one. In the little Place de l'Archevêche
by the south wall of Notre-Dame four big cherry trees burst into
bloom as if smiling at the unusual greediness of the pigeons as
they kept snatching at crumbs
thrown by the babies and
toddlers on their afternoon
airings. The smile of the
blossoms was echoed by the
innocently smiling faces of the
youngsters beneath them. It
was a charming spot.

A bird singing on the monument of
Chopin in the Parc Monceau

There were cherry trees,
too, in the Parc du Champ de
Mars near the foot of the Eiffel
Tower. One sunny morning
while I was there trying to
work out a composition for a
painting, with the hilarious
cherry blossom in the foreground and the Eiffel Tower
behind, a bearded showman in rather ragged garments, leading a troup of colourfully-decorated donkeys, came jingling
along between the cherries and me, with several young fellows
in bright red and green waistcoats following behind. They gave
just the dash of new colour to my composition that I wanted.
The combination was a rare one, perhaps only to be met with
in a city of surprises like Paris. It was a happy moment for me.

Magnolias, with their cool colouring and elegant form, do
not vie with the brilliance of cherries and are best kept apart
from them. I saw a number in bloom in the gardens along the
Champs Elysées at the same time that the cherries were at

Donkeys passing by the Eiffel Tower

their best round Notre-Dame. How right the Paris authorities were to separate the magnolias from the cherries. Magnolias need space and suitable surroundings to display their beauty.

These magnolias seemed to be a hybrid variety, perhaps *Magnolia lennei*. The flowers have broad fleshy petals, shaped concavely like spoons and shaded from rose-purple to white. I have written much about this flower in other books, for the magnolia is a distinctively Chinese tree. The Chinese have cultivated it for more than 1,000 years. I have particularly pointed out how our craftsmen drew the inspiration of their designs from Nature and how the potters of the Sung period used the single magnolia petal as the model for their porcelain spoons, with rose-purple glaze outside and white inside. Subsequently this design was extended and developed in vases of various shapes. Magnolia trees always give me a feeling of satisfaction and gratification when I find them in the gardens of Western countries. If only the magnolia's origin were more widely known, it would constitute the best possible typification of China, with its delicacy, its cultured habit, its open, courteous smile and its upright outlook on life. A Chinese may be forgiven for disliking the 'Chinaman' so widely believed to be typical of his race, with hollow chest, long whiskers and cunning smile.

Another variety of magnolia to be seen in Paris is the pure white *Magnolia conspicua*, a shrub somewhat like the Chinese *Yülan* lily tree. I found it growing behind a small bamboo bush near the statue of Alphonse Daudet, and the setting formed a beautiful picture. The blossoms have little scent, whereas the Chinese *Yülan* proper is a highly scented flower. We eat the young white fleshy petals, specially prepared, and consider them a great delicacy.

The Avenue des Champs Elysées, the 'West End' of Paris, where men and women, rather than nature, play the leading part, is appropriately lined with stately formal chestnuts. The somewhat frivolous beauty of cherry blossom would be out of place in such a street. But the chestnuts, with their candle-like flowers in pink and white, like a row of huge chandeliers, transforms the Avenue into a kind of outdoor pavilion for the reception of Paris's International guests. Their sober colouring and uniformity make just the right background for brilliant flashes of colour and varied styles of dresses among the fashionable throng on the pavements below.

o

Chestnut blossom reminds me of England as magnolia reminds me of China. There is a Chinese species of chestnut, a hardier plant than the European species, but I don't remember having seen it blooming in China. In any case it has not been systematically planted in our gardens and parks as it has

Paris in April

in England. I seldom miss seeing the chestnut blossom in Bushey Park, London, where there are innumerable grassy avenues of it. The Bushey chestnuts in full bloom are one of the sights of the year. There are many fine chestnut trees in the roads in my neighbourhood at Oxford. As they reach the fullness of their blossom, the yellow racemes of laburnum also start to open. With this association in my mind I began to look now for laburnums in Paris, but found none. At length, when the cherry blossom had all fallen and been swept away, I came upon one small laburnum with a few yellow tassels dangling over the tall railings by the south wall of Notre-Dame. It looked to me more friendly than many finer specimens I knew before.

One evening in April I strolled from the Chevaux de Marly along the south side of the Champs Elysées towards the Rond-Point. A sweep of brilliant pink spanned the sky as if made by a huge brush. The edges of the stroke merged with the neighbouring clouds, and the colour changed moment by moment; as I approached the Petit Palais the pink turned deep red, then purple, and the whole Avenue des Champs Elysées was tinted— the trees, the houses, the dresses of the moving throng. Even the bronze statue of Clemenceau began to glow, making me think that an orange and black-striped animal was roaming about in the dusk. There were red and white petals of chestnut on the pavements, and it was impossible to believe that they had fallen so soon; some mischievous starlings must have nipped them off. I picked one up: it was redder than *vin rouge*.

I was impelled to sit down under the colourful canopy of a pavement café and order a glass of red wine. While I sipped it I remembered the poem, "Drinking beneath the blossoming trees", by our Yuan poet, Liu Yin, and recited it silently to myself. A translation of it runs like this:

Before the flowers came forth I often made enquiries about them;
When they began to bloom I was in fear of wind and rain.
Since wind and rain have done no harm to the flowers blowing,
Why should we not come and get drunk beneath the blossoming
    trees?
While this year is with us, let us make no plans for the next;
For tomorrow has nothing to do with today.
Look! the vernal breeze, as if admonishing us at the feast,
Lets a petal of blossom drop before our eyes.

眼人春日休來不雨未未
墜一風並作花相至又開
片欲非明花好花恐常
落勸今年下花開開探
紅座日事醉為時時花
當中事明今甚風花開

劉靜修玉樓春

A few days after Easter I went with two friends to an exhibition of azaleas in the Jardin d'Acclimatation. I expected to see something like the annual Chelsea Flower Show in London, but it turned out to be a much smaller affair, with one beautifully arranged hot-house displaying azaleas of every kind and colour. Though most of them were in pots, they were arranged on wooden tiers so that their bases were hidden—the effect was of veritable banks of flowers. We followed the small, winding footpath, admiring the flowers on both sides, one species after another, and finally reached a raised platform, somewhat resembling a small pavilion, with pots of larger azaleas arranged round it. Passing through the middle of the pavilion I noticed a small pond below us containing numerous goldfish gliding silently through the clear reflections of the massed flowers. I told my companions that I had composed the following couplet to describe our visit:

The fish swim *above* hundreds of flowers;
We men walk *inside* a brocade tapestry.

In her public parks and gardens, Paris has as many types of cultivated flowers as London: wallflowers, pansies, geraniums, tulips in abundance; and her flower-stands and florists are more numerous than those of any other city I know. There is a Marché aux Fleurs on the Ile de la Cité and a Quai aux Fleurs on the north side of Notre-Dame; but the picturesque window-boxes that one sees along Whitehall in London I did not see anywhere in Paris; nor did I see many Parisians actually tending their flowers as one sees people doing everywhere in London suburbs. I was often told that the Parisian's sentiment is less bound up with *chez soi*, domesticity, than the Londoner's (there is no French word for 'home'). Parisians love the 'out of doors', and accordingly they have a passion for wild flowers. Whether this is sound logic or not, I certainly saw many flower-sellers at street-corners with baskets piled high with bunches of small wild daffodils. Several Parisian friends went out at week-ends to pick wild daffodils at Chantilly and Fontainebleau. On one occasion I noticed a number of children wearing and making wreaths of wild hyacinths or bluebells, *les clochettes*, while their parents were in raptures of enthusiasm at the blue shimmer of these flowers growing in myriads in the Bois de Boulogne. I was told that these wild bluebells, and also cowslips or *coucous*, were sold every year by hawkers from their picturesque wicker hods in the streets of Paris.

Two days before Easter I went with Joan Hendry to meet her father and Betty Scott from England at the Gare du Nord. While waiting for the train to arrive, we sat down at a pavement café facing the station. Presently a flower-seller came up to my companion and cried: *"Fleurissez-vous, mesdames: voilà le muguet!"* Which was followed by, *"Du muguet! Achetez du muguet! Du bon muguet parfumé."* She was crying lilies of the valley for sale. My companion told me that this was one of the oldest street cries in Paris. I bought two bunches and again learned that there would be a *fête du muguet* on the first of May, when Paris children make presents of bunches of wild lilies of the valley to their elder brothers and sisters, and all the young *midinettes* wear bunches of *muguet* in their bodices. The *muguet des bois* occupies the first place in the Parisian heart. According to herbalists, the petals of the lily of the valley contain a toxic substance which, like digitalis, has a directly stimulating effect upon the heart. It seems to affect Parisians more than Londoners.

Through the introduction of my old friend, Sir William Milner, I went to have lunch with Sir William and Lady Hayter and their daughter Teresa at their home in the Avenue Raymond Poincaré. They had also invited Professor Holland of Trinity College, Cambridge, and his wife, Professor Marjorie Holland, of Girton, and Sir Humphrey Trevelyan from Germany. They had all come to Paris for their Easter holiday. Miss Hayter, sister-in-law of my hostess, was also there from Athens, where she is the representative of the British Council. After lunch, Sir William Hayter, then British Minister in Paris, took me to see the British Embassy on the Faubourg St Honoré. It is an old and imposing building, formerly the Hôtel du duc de Charost. It remained in this Duke's family from 1720 to 1800, afterwards becoming the residence of Pauline Bonaparte, created Princess Borghése, who sold it to the British Government in 1814. The 'Iron Duke' negotiated the purchase. With a broad smile, Sir William pointed out that all these highly-decorated rooms with gilded ceilings and panels in the ornate French style were very suitable for holding receptions and entertaining guests, but not quite so suitable as offices, since they distracted the mind from clerical work. For that reason, a number of rooms in which the daily

work of the Embassy was carried on had had their ceilings and
walls panelled in plain wood. I admired the spaciousness and
tasteful decoration of the room, less ostentatious than some,
in which Sir William himself worked. He explained how much
he enjoyed the advantage of having large windows facing on to
the garden, from which he could indulge his hobby of bird-
watching. He led me out on to the balcony as he said this. In
his conversation Sir William revealed himself to me as a typical
English gentleman of taste, such as I had met from time to
time in England. Smiling and chatting happily, he told me
many details about the Paris parks and gardens, birds, trees
and flowers. He named most of the trees in the spacious
Embassy garden. In his opinion, the design of the Parc des
Buttes Chaumont had a Chinese flavour (at an earlier stage of
his career Sir William spent two years in China as Second
Secretary at the British Embassy at Peking), but he liked best
the gardens of the Château de Bagatelle, which were laid out
in the English style by the Marquess of Hertford (1800–70).
He suggested that if I could stay in Paris till the end of May or
the beginning of June I should be able to enjoy, in the Bagatelle
Gardens, the finest show of roses imaginable. From this our
conversation turned to the great French gardener and flower-
painter, Pierre-Joseph Redouté, whose folio volumes, *Les
Roses*, were the most famous of his works. "Although birds are
more my province," remarked Sir William gently, "there are
many Frenchmen who know flowers best. The French are good
horticulturists."

This was generous praise from an Englishman, for, as I well
know after a long residence in England, every Englishman is
more or less of a gardener and all love flowers and deem other
nations inferior to themselves in this respect. Possibly Sir
William knew what the French writer, Alphonse Karr, wrote
about French horticulturists:

Most cultivators of flowers indulge their taste more from vanity
than love, more to show them than to see them. With very few
exceptions, horticulturists do not love flowers for their own sakes.
Some will plant in the pebble a dahlia (*the white-edged incomparable*),
to insure its being parti-coloured; others will strip all the leaves
from a camellia. In France, flowers have a great deal to do with
politics. On the return of the elder branch of the Bourbons, M.P.
(I don't know what they stood for) guillotined all the imperials in
his garden. Violets, exiled by Louis XVIII, have since been recalled.

M. de Castres, Commandant of the Palace of the Tuileries, banished the carnation. For some years after the revolution of July, lilies disappeared from all the royal gardens. We generally respect all passions and all means of happiness; but we do not believe in the passion of the horticulturist: it is not a real passion.

Though I am not in a position to come to the defence of French horticulturists, I did observe in my few months' stay in Paris that Parisians genuinely care for flowers. The quantity of flowers bought and sold daily seemed to me tremendous; and not only fresh flowers from nurseries, but also artificial ones. On the Boulevard Haussmann a large store sells nothing but varieties of brilliantly coloured artificial flowers.

It was not until Madeleine Chambert took me to see Madame Marguerite Maréchal at work that I realised that the artificial flowers commonly sold in shops were not the best obtainable. Madame Maréchal's workshop lies behind the Avenue de l'Opéra, and there she received us one day. With her white hair and the gentle smile on her calm face, she belied my conception of the typical French elderly lady, with ready wit and excitable gesture; she was so quiet and moved in so calm and dignified a manner. First she showed us a number of brass moulds of flower leaves. She remarked that in view of the present high cost of new moulds she was thankful she still had hundreds of old ones—enough for all her requirements. She must have been a very careful worker; probably all these moulds had been in use for thirty years or more without damage or noticeable wear. In another part of the room a girl assistant put a small piece of green silk into a mould, pressed it, and then showed us the finished leaf perfectly formed with each single vein clearly marked. Madeleine told them that I specialised in flower-painting and showed them my illustration of the ruby-throated hummingbirds and orchids from my book, *The Silent Traveller in New York*. Madame Maréchal smiled and took down from a shelf a box containing a small hummingbird with its three-coloured plumage, perched on the petals of a large purple orchid, as if alive. I was amazed to see such delicate objects produced with such a semblance of reality. They were not arranged like stuffed specimens in a museum case but with genuine artistic taste and fine observation. Many other varieties of artificial flowers—peonies, roses, begonias—were shown to us, all exquisitely made. They were chiefly for use as costume ornament by people attending big receptions, of which an inordinate number seems to be held in Paris, but the market for them was not confined to France. Many boxes of Madame Maréchal's flowers went, for instance, to New York and Washington. Madame Maréchal explained that when she was a girl she loved all flowers so much that when real ones were not in season she tried to make imitation ones. Her mother, too, often made them to please her and this skill seemed to be in her blood. When she grew up she began to observe fresh flowers more keenly, to improve her technique and to experiment with materials; finally, she opened her business some thirty years ago. Since then her work has always been in demand. Though she had helpers to assist her, she always put the final touches herself, and never hurried them. Most of the leaves were cut from silk or linen, and some of the bigger and heavier types of petals were also made of silk or thin velvet. But all the delicate tiny petals were done in birds' feathers. The best feathers were the small, downy ones on the breast of geese, which being soft, delicate and white, could be dyed to any colour desired. The sale of goose-feathers had become a new source of income for Paris *restaurateurs*: girls would go round to the restaurants to buy them. With a sigh Madame Maréchal remarked that a number of materials for her work, including colours and brushes, used to come from the East, mostly China and Japan, and she had not been able to get these for a long time. Her enthusiasm and keen interest in the business she had created left a deep impression on me.

XXI

A New Medium of Art

IN the spring of 1935 a friend of mine who had been in Europe for about a year, mostly spent in Paris, came to see me in London for a few days and brought with him a beautifully printed and lavishly illustrated booklet on the great French liner, *Normandie*, on which he was returning to China. The ship had many attractions, but the one which appealed to me most was the decoration on the walls of the saloon, which consisted of a series of panels in the form of lacquered screens. The booklet described every feature of the ship, including the screens, but it was written in French and I could not read it; nevertheless, I registered a wish to travel back to China on that ship one day. In 1939 the *Normandie* was converted into a troop-ship, and in the course of the war was destroyed by fire in New York Harbour. My hope was destroyed with it. I did not guess then that in 1952 I should meet in Paris the person who had been responsible for the *Normandie's* lacquered screens. He is Monsieur Bernard Dunand.

Madeleine Chambert took me to see Monsieur Dunand one afternoon at his home in the rue Bezont in the Fourteenth Arrondissement. We were shown in by an elderly woman who led us down a long corridor, across a courtyard, and into a lofty hall. Lacquered wood panels of various sizes hung round the walls in carefully spaced pairs. They showed originality and were tastefully arranged against a plain grey back cloth. Some of the designs revealed the influence of Japanese lacquer-work. One big fourfold screen with a design of birds on trees was in the style of the later Tokugawa period. A pair of panels of a really striking originality intrigued me more, however, for, although they were paintings, I could see no sign of brush-strokes nor how the effect had been achieved. They differed from all the other screens, on which the designs had been painted on the surface of the lacquer.

Presently Monsieur Dunand entered the hall and smilingly

apologised for having been detained by a customer. He was in his forties, tall and slim, neatly but unconventionally dressed. He spoke in a clear voice, with enthusiasm and sincerity. He moved round the hall with us, talking about the panels; of the two which had particularly struck me he promised to explain the process later. First he took us into the room where he dried his lacquer-work. Paradoxically, lacquer has to be dried in a moist atmosphere at a temperature of about 70°. The room was full of white steam and a number of panels lay about in rows. From Madeleine's interpretation of Monsieur Dunand, I learned that the process of drying the lacquer usually takes six months. "Very slow," said Monsieur Dunand. "That is what I like about it."

It was evident to me that he employs the old Chinese and Japanese method of lacquering, without artificial varnish. In the south-west of China, chiefly in the provinces of Szechuan and Fukien, a tree is to be found which produces a sap that has a protective quality. This was probably used for lacquering as long as 2,300 years ago. Early Chinese records date the use of this Chi-shu or lacquer tree from the twelfth century B.C. Many Han Dynasty lacquered objects of the first and second centuries B.C. found in recent excavations in Korea and China were in perfect condition. There are some examples in the British Museum showing a highly developed use of the medium. This tree, *Rhus vernicifera*, is indigenous to China, and was introduced into Japan in the sixth century.

On our way to the next work-room, Monsieur Dunand removed a large piece of wood in the floor, disclosing a deep cavity, two or three feet wide, its sides paved with huge stones. He told us that this was a remnant of the water circuit built in Paris by the Romans after their conquest of Gaul. Then we proceeded to a small courtyard which, Monsieur Dunand explained, had once been bigger and had had a large tree growing in it. When the trunk of the tree grew too thick in comparison with the house, Monsieur Dunand's father felt he must do something about it. Not wanting to have the tree cut down, he had a small building erected round the trunk, leaving the long branches to stretch themselves freely above. This concealed the excessive bulk of the tree and gave the garden an effect of size greater than its dimensions. His father had learned this principle of garden-planning in limited space from Japan and China.

We now came to another large room. The rooms had to be large, I suppose, because lacquering is usually done on sizeable wood-panels, screens and pieces of furniture. Two of Monsieur Dunand's colleagues were at work; one was painting the top of a small black table with horses in red, a design reminiscent of Hokusai's wood-prints, and the other a landscape. I could not quite make out how the landscape was going to develop; the painter appeared to be following the manner of Van Gogh in building up the sky and the ground by brush-strokes all in the same colour. Both men were using brushes made in Japan and holding them in the Japanese fashion, slightly slanting—not vertically, as is the Chinese manner. Monsieur Dunand told us that his father, who started the business more than thirty years ago, had previously spent some years in Japan, where he learnt the art of lacquering. Thus, most of his early work had been in the Japanese style, like the examples we had seen in the entrance hall on our arrival. One of his fathers' works was a large folding screen with a typical Japanese subject—a pair of white herons on the branches of an old pine tree. He himself had learnt the lacquering art from his father and had in turn taught his colleagues. But smilingly he added that they had made some experiments and had produced some pieces of lacquer with French blood in them.

We talked about the handling of the Japanese type of brush. I referred to my book, *Chinese Calligraphy*, in which I discuss this matter, and also the execution of beautiful lines and the construction of satisfying forms. My words seemed to interest the young man who was working on the landscape, and to my surprise he began speaking to me in English. He was delighted to talk, and so was I after so much enforced silence. He told me that his mother was English, and "still did not want to learn French", even after nearly thirty years of married life in France. I was very cheered to hear this, for I too had been unable to learn French. On the other hand, I admired his father's enduring love for his wife, despite language obstacles. Presumably he had spent some years in England and had fallen in love with her there. This reminded me of how often young Chinese who go abroad to study for a few years fall in love and marry Western girls. They bring their cherished wives back to their homeland and everything goes very well at first. Gradually, however, the girls either find the Chinese language too difficult to learn or refuse to make the effort. They then become lonely and cut off from their surroundings, and in the end many of these marriages break down.

I learned that this young colleague of Monsieur Dunand had not known anything about lacquer, nor had any idea of working in it, before the outbreak of the Second World War. He met Monsieur Dunand in a German prison camp, and they became friendly. Monsieur Dunand discovered that the young man had been called up immediately on leaving school and had no plans for his future, so he began to interest him in lacquer work and in his own ideas for improving the old methods and developing new techniques. They would sit talking about this at every opportunity. Eventually they returned to Paris, and Monsieur Dunand, on resuming his lacquering business, took him as an assistant. He worked hard and learnt the art. With a smile he added: "Now I am married to Dunand's sister." I returned his smile and shook his hand. A woman generally comes in to make up a man's mind. Lacquering, he told me, occupied his whole mind. So long as his income was enough to keep him and his family his only desire was to achieve something unique in lacquering.

He then explained that the landscape on which he was working was a new development in lacquer resulting from Monsieur Dunand's endless experiments and his own efforts. He was busy with the preliminary stage. It would take several months or even a year to finish the painting, which was to have a number of thin lacquer coatings. The combined effect of the colours through the layers of lacquer was most striking and had to be worked out beforehand. That is to say, the colours he was applying on the wood-panel had been carefully calculated from experiments to achieve a certain effect. He went on to explain in detail how if two colours are combined and are then coated with this or that lacquer, an entirely different colour is produced. For example, a certain dark green somewhat like bottle green, and red, put side by side with some brownish yellow, become under the coatings gold. This behaviour of the colours is quite unlike that of the pigments in oil painting. He had much to say which intrigued me, though he could not, of course, explain the whole process, nor did I press him, for it was, in a way, a professional secret.

While I was deep in the mysteries of colour combinations,

Madeleine was interpreting what I had said about Chinese calligraphy to Monsieur Dunand. Presently the latter came over to me and on hearing what interested me most invited me to follow him into his big work-room which was also his office. He then took down some large books from the top shelf and a great number of small lacquered pieces of wood similar in size but different in colour. These were a record of his many years' experiments. Each piece was registered in the book with its date and the time it had taken to apply the first coating of colour, and the effects of successive applications of different colours. The number of coatings was as varied as that of the colours mixed. He seemed to have worked out his arrangements by the mathematical method of 'combination' and 'multiplication'. He said that he had already done more than 3,000 pieces and was still experimenting. "There is no end to it," he remarked smilingly. Whenever he wanted to achieve a certain colour effect, he just referred to his book and his samples. What an arduous worker he was! I have never known anyone so absorbed in his work as Monsieur Dunand. But real achievement always involves intense application.

The research upon which Monsieur Dunand had recently been working was the achievement of 'transparent lacquer'— that is to say, a lacquer which can be applied on top of another, with the colour or painting underneath remaining visible but imbued with a totally new feeling by subtle changes in the colour scheme not attainable by any of the usual methods. He pointed out a panel on which a pair of mandarin ducks seemed to be swimming happily *inside* the panel rather than on the surface of it. The reds and greens of the birds' plumage, though not particularly bright, looked glossy and lustrous as if the feathers were real. Many more panels of this kind were shown to us; each had its originality. Monsieur Dunand picked out for special notice a landscape painting in transparent lacquer by his brother-in-law. It was like the one upon which he was working when I entered. It was very interesting and totally different from an oil painting.

Monsieur Dunand told me that he had read somewhere the Chinese saying that "One must only help lacquer to be more lacquer". He took this to mean that a lacquer product must not try to imitate oil painting. He repeatedly asked me if I could help him to find out more about the different kinds of

Chinese lacquering, particularly 'transparent' lacquer', if the process was known to us, for he thought Chinese craftsmen in the past had accomplished a great many things about which Westerners have still much to learn. He also urged me to write an article or translate an old essay on the subject for a French paper of which, I believe, he is the editor. I regretted being unable to fulfil either of his requests. But his complete absorrtion in lacquer-work, which is really his life, won my whole-hearted admiration. I feel sure that Monsieur Dunand's and his brother-in-law's achievements have a great contribution to make to the art world.

XXII

Diffusion of Colours

I LIKE the effect of stained glass inside a church and can
endorse every word of Monsieur M. E. Chevreul's comment
in his book, *The Principles of Harmony and Contrast of Colours*:

The stained glass of Gothic churches, by intercepting the white
light which gives too vivid and unsuitable a glare for meditation (as
they only transmit coloured light) have always the most beautiful
effect. If we seek the cause, we shall find it not only in the contrast
of their colours so favourably opposed, but also in the contrast of
their transparency with the opacity of the walls which surround
them and of the lead which binds them together. The impression
produced on the eye, in virtue of this twofold cause, is the more
vivid the more frequently and the longer they are viewed each time.

Again, he writes:

Coloured windows appear to me to produce all the effect of which
they are really capable only in a vast edifice where the differently
coloured rays arrive at the eye of the spectator placed on the floor of
the church, so scattered by the effect of the conical figure of the
rays of light emanating from a single point, that they impinge upon
each other, whence results an harmonious mixture, which is not
found in a small structure lighted by stained windows.

Although Monsieur Chevreul discusses the effect of the diffusion
of colours from a rather technical standpoint, his ideas have
clarified my own impressions. They helped me, for instance, to
understand why I did not feel as much impressed by the stained
glass in the Sainte Chapelle as by that in Notre Dame. The
Sainte Chapelle is not a large edifice and its windows are
narrow and very high, so high that it is difficult to make out
the meaning of the topmost figures. Perhaps those who designed
the windows and their stained glass in the thirteenth century
gave less thought to the effect of light through them than to
their elegance and grace of line, in harmony with the architecture.

In the Chinese Taoist or Buddhist temples there are no

coloured windows; nor in any of the vast edifices where the Chinese honour Confucius, nor in the imperial palaces. Glass is not a Chinese invention and has not been made use of for windows until very recently. It was not until I came to England that I first felt, in Westminster Abbey, the wonderful effect of stained glass. Since then I have entered many big churches and cathedrals simply to experience the effect of the stained glass. Generally speaking, stained-glass windows in churches are the work of specialist artists, but a few of the famous English painters on canvas have also made designs for coloured windows. I like the Burne-Jones windows in Christ Church, Oxford, but somehow I feel the light effect from them is not sufficiently complex and that the result would have been unsatisfactory if the central windows had been designed in the same way. Speaking as a layman, I doubt if the big window designed by Sir Joshua Reynolds for the Chapel of New College, Oxford, can be called successful. The subject-matter is Christian, but the panels look more like paintings for the hall of some mansion than for a shrine of God. The purely diamond-shaped design does not effectively produce the diffusion of colours. Monsieur Chevreul said that "They (stained-glass windows) produce all their effect only when they present the strongest harmonies of contrast, not of colourless, transparent glass with the black produced by the opacity of the walls, iron bars, and strips of lead, but of this black with the intense tones of red, blue, orange, violet, and yellow." The Reynolds window at New College contains these colours but in lighter tones.

I happened to express my curiosity about the technique of stained glass to a French friend, who immediately promised to take me to see Monsieur Max Ingrand, the Vice-Chairman of the Syndicat Général des Cristalleries et Verreries d'Art. Monsieur Ingrand, I was told, is interested in all processes of stained and decorated glass, and specialises in stained-glass windows. Brought up in the shadow of Chartres Cathedral, the windows of which are the most beautiful and famous in the world, Monsieur Ingrand has tried to rediscover the technique of the master stained-glass-makers of the thirteenth century.

The modern French religious painter Monsieur Georges Desvalleres once said: "Before one of Max Ingrand's windows one does not say that it is beautiful; one feels like kneeling. His is really apostolic painting, in its originality of composition,

simplicity of execution and depth of colour. One does not feel
that there is a desire to achieve an effect, but simply to touch
the heart."

On the day of our appointment we were conducted to
Monsieur Ingrand's office. There was plenty of glass about,
including a glass door, a lantern and a number of large mirror
panels similar to those on the walls of the Galérie des Glaces at
Versailles. Monsieur Ingrand soon appeared; he was of medium
height, faultlessly dressed, with his black hair neatly brushed
back. He looked more like a very prosperous businessman in
his early fifties than like the traditional conception of an artist.
He smiled as he talked and showed us many sets of his designs
for stained glass. His latest work was the replacement of the
bomb-damaged windows in a church at Rouen. Smiling at me,
he made a point of explaining that an English ecclesiastical
body had made itself responsible for the cost of these windows.
What interested me most in the designs was that although some
of them were clearly in the spirit of modern painting, yet they
all blended harmoniously with the old windows in the church.

We learned later that Monsieur Ingrand has been entrusted
by the French Government's Historic Buildings Department
with the delicate task of restoring the great number of windows
damaged during the 1939-45 War. He had been working on
many orders for the replacement of windows that had entirely
disappeared.

His way of maintaining harmony between the new and the
old was to match all the colours in the old windows and also
to place the iron bars and the strips of lead identically with
those in the old. The thickness of each line and the proportions
of each figure were also similar to those in the old designs. It
took meticulous calculation as well as a creative imagination
to produce windows which were not mere copies but works of
art inspired with a new spirit. Monsieur Ingrand explained
that he was not content to produce an exact copy of an old
design, but strove always to make something new. Art, he
contended, is in evolution as much as anything else and con-
tributes to the development of civilisation. It would be wrong
if stained-glass, just because it is mostly to be found in churches
—and *old* churches at that—did not develop like all other
forms of art.

Monsieur Ingrand was in a German prison camp for five

P

years, but he showed no sign of resentment or hatred in consequence. During those long years he was able to enjoy the
human relationships in the community life of the camp, and
he now saw the opportunity for better co-operation between
man and man as one of the chief hopes of the future. He was
grateful for the time his captivity gave him for meditation. His
tolerant attitude strengthened my belief that the world is saner
than it used to be.

Presently he suggested showing us round his workshop, which
adjoined his offices. In a very large room more than twenty

people were at work, chiefly
men, but with one or two
women doing the lighter jobs.
First we were shown a big
design evidently enlarged
from the original drawing.
Next we came to the tracing
section, and then to the cutting of the tracing, which
was placed on top of a sheet
of glass in readiness for the
cutting of the glass. We saw
the cut glass being painted
according to the colours of the
design, then the processes of
heating and leading. All the stages in the manufacture of stained
glass were clearly shown to us, and at each stage Monsieur Ingrand
displayed his genial friendship for those who worked under him.
They joked, smiled and laughed together as if there were as
much harmony between them as there was between the parts
of the stained-glass windows they were making. An elderly
workman demonstrated glass-cutting. Monsieur Ingrand told
us that he was over seventy and had been at this work for almost
thirty years. Though it looked easy, in fact it called for years of
experience, for no two pieces of glass should be cut alike, and
they were all cut in crooked lines. Not a fragment of glass
should be wasted, and each piece must be cut to fit precisely
with the adjacent ones. Next he took us to see a middle-aged
man who was cutting a piece of glass to match a design in the
shape of a bird. The small curves on the little creature's back
and its fine claws looked as if they would defy reproduction in

glass, but the cutter moved in the man's hand like a brush or a pencil. Monsieur Ingrand then informed us that this crafts-man was the best and most famous glass-cutter in Paris. He gave the cutter a gentle pat of approbation on the shoulder before we moved away.

We went next into a room where pieces of cut glass of different colours had been placed in a frame against the daylight to test the effect of the diffusion of their colours. This was an import-ant stage, explained Monsieur Ingrand; one needed good and sensitive eyesight to judge which colour was a little weak and which a little too strong. The over-pale bits would have to be re-heated with more colour, and so on. The whole colouring process generally took months, and might even take two or three years. I had never realised that the combination and diffusion of colours called for such detailed tests before a successful stained-glass window could be created.

Monsieur Ingrand maintained that a stained-glass window should be a "glass tapestry" catching the light and reflecting it. It should, as much by virtue of its colours as by its subject-matter, contribute to the stimulation of meditation and spirituality. The soundless symphonies of colour should create an atmosphere for meditation. I wondered if colour alone could achieve that object. If so, modern abstract painting should make the process easier, for the strips of lead would not need to break into the design, passing, for instance, through the face of a figure. But Monsieur Ingrand was sure that the spiritual subject contributed just as much to the total effect as the diffusion of colours.

Finally, Monsieur Ingrand took us to the far end of the workshop, where a different process was going on. Many pieces of coloured glass were lying like débris on the floor. A round metal tray containing innumerable pieces of coloured glass arranged in a design was being heated on a stove. An elderly man was introduced to us as the inventor of the process we were about to watch, and for which he has become famous. On being heated, the glass fragments melt and mingle their colours, and the whole cools to form one sheet of glass. The heating stage is the most important part of the process, and only this workman was sufficiently expert to know how to regulate the temperature. I watched with great interest as the heat on the glass showed a glowing diffusion of colours. Suddenly the elderly man broke the silence to ask me if I were a Japanese; I was delighted that he could speak English. On learning who I was, he talked freely, and apparently knew a good deal about Chinese workmanship. He told me that he often visited museums to see some of the beautiful things made in China. I asked him how long it took to perfect a piece of coloured glass by his process. He said about two weeks, although some more elaborate designs might take longer. I remarked that glass-work was not popular among the Chinese and that we had no stained glass of any sort. He was generous enough to reply that Chinese craftsmen are so skilful that they could learn this craft in less than six months. I was touched by his confidence in my people, and I only hope that Monsieur Ingrand's belief in better human relationships and co-operation will materialise in the future.

XXIII

'Great is the Will to Live'

A strange voice, husky, feeble, almost inaudible, reached my ears as I was pushed aside on the narrow pavement of the rue Mouffetard by an enormous van which could hardly pass. Thinking someone must be in pain, I looked round in case there was something I could do to help. But all the faces around me were jovial, laughing, some even uproarious. The street market was in full swing. There was no sign of pain or sadness.

I stood for a moment waiting for the van to pass, for it was jammed with a small car in the narrowest part of that narrow street. As I waited the strange voice reached me again. It really sounded like groaning—and painful groaning at that: "Ayee—ay-ee—ay-ee . . ." It trailed off faintly. My knowledge of French was scanty and I could not imagine what it meant, nor could I distinguish it properly from the din in the street. As I moved away I heard it for the third time, but though it rang in my ears for a while, I soon forgot it.

The rue Mouffetard was only a short distance from my lodgings; in fact I passed through it nearly every day on my way to other parts of the city, and quite often I visited it again in the evening to buy some fruit or pastries for myself. In the first two weeks after my arrival I answered many queries about my lodgings by mentioning the adjoining street. The information was always received with a mysterious smile. Later I learned that the rue Mouffetard is famed for its significant gatherings of a certain type of Parisian as well as for its week-end markets, particularly its Sunday morning market, which is unique among the markets of Paris.

Being a traveller, I take whatever I find without prejudice, and usually develop a fondness for my surroundings wherever I happen to stay. I liked this narrow, busy thoroughfare: it was the right place for observing the habits of working people, an aspect of a city's life which often escapes the notice of visitors.

Through the windows of some houses on a narrow lane which slopes down to the rue Mouffetard I often watched Degas's women ironing; they had grown much older since that great artist painted them. There are quite a few cosy little cafés along the street, but the one at the corner of the rue Ortolan was my chief haunt. Not that I am a drinker, but it was there that in imagination I saw Paul Cézanne at work on his painting of the card-players. A plump young girl who sold me oranges and bananas now and then smiled and laughed at everyone in her grocery shop, yet she could become very cross with her male colleague; she seemed the reincarnation of a figure from Toulouse-Lautrec's sketch-book. I more often met the type of people who might have come from Daumier's 'Third-class Carriage' than from his 'Second-class Carriage'. In the mornings I occasionally heard some of the old street-cries of Paris, though I could not always make out what was for sale. Once I met a man with a wooden frame hanging on his back on which some sheets of glass of various sizes were fastened with cords. He came along the street shouting at the top of his voice; he must have been a glazier or window-repairer. This was the first time I had ever seen glass being sold that way, and his cry cannot have been one of the old ones. Here was the changeless and ageless Paris.

The rue Mouffetard is a very narrow street compared with the avenues and boulevards, but it must have been regarded as a wide one in the early days of its construction. It is said to be a part of the ancient Roman highway which once joined Paris and Rome. Although the houses on both sides have not stood as long as that, they all wore a look of antiquity with a touch of the poetry of Utrillo's oil paintings, sober and aged. A friend told me that this street suffered terribly at the beginning of the Second Republic. He quoted from a letter written by Renan to his mother on June 24th, 1848: "The insurrection is very fierce in the rue Mouffetard . . . barricaded like fortresses. . . ." Another friend urged me not to be dismayed by its shabby look, for, according to him, in a house in the rue Mouffetard were once found masses of gold pieces hidden in a chimney since 1756; their value was said to be more than a billion francs. This treasure came to light when some house-breakers began to pierce a hole in an old wall in May, 1938. A year after that discovery, it was estimated that eighty-four or more persons

had made claim to be the descendants entitled to the find.
Nobody today knows what happened to the money.

The importance of this narrow street has never diminished.
Here resided a few studious men who wished to remain un-
disturbed by unwanted visitors, among them A. Vestier, the
painter. I was told that several people connected with the art
and theatrical world still lived here. I paid a visit to the small
marionette theatre for children in the rue Mouffetard and found
it entertaining the youngsters better than the true *guignols* in
the Jardin des Tuileries and that of the Luxembourg.

Harold Clunn writes about this street in his book, *The Face
of Paris*: "The inhabitants had no clock which they could
consult other than the rising and setting of the sun, and in
knowledge and culture were three centuries behind their more

Evening paper seller in the rue Mouffetard

refined neighbours. Every private quarrel became a public
dispute, and the angry wife would air her grievance in the
middle of the street, summoning the culprit before the judgement of the populace, while revealing to them the story of her
husband's turpitude. Sometimes these quarrels were settled by
a fight in which one of the combatants would get his face well
scratched, after which they would meet at night-time and make
peace over a bottle of sour wine." This may have been true of
the rue Mouffetard many years ago, but after several months'

stay nearby I found the place very likeable and the people congenial and friendly. Despite my scanty knowledge of French, the proprietor of the little café always welcomed me with a broad smile. His other customers, if they noticed me, would give a friendly nod. Now and then, when returning to my lodgings late at night, I would encounter someone singing in the centre of the street or a small group of people exchanging words hotly at a corner; but the argument always faded away in laughter. The women who took turns in serving in the small pastry shop never failed to impress me by their charming manner, more so, indeed, than their counterparts in other more fashionable quarters of Paris. Shabby surroundings cannot lower the dignity of people, nor can shabby clothes conceal the fine spirit of a man.

The street is at its liveliest during the daytime, particularly round about noon. It is chiefly a market street with a number of groceries, provision-stores, second-hand—perhaps third-hand —furniture shops, and second-hand drapery stores. When its real 'market' days came round, on Friday and Saturday, every possible space on the narrow pavements was taken up by some queerly constructed stall or arrangement of baskets and boxes. Several small adjoining lanes were crammed in the same way. Normally an ordinary car can get by without difficulty, but on market days many big vans bringing provisions and other wares found themselves jammed in the middle of the street. In other parts of Paris I often heard hot words exchanged between drivers in a similar predicament, but never in this street. Always one of them would get down and help, or the bystanders would assist. The cries of the salesmen and the banter of their customers went on all the time, and there seemed to be a happy-go-lucky air pervading the street. The market men and women were a jolly lot and most of the buyers wore a cheerful air.

It was on one of these occasions that I happened to hear again that strange, husky, feeble and almost inaudible voice which I described at the beginning of this chapter. Once more I carefully scrutinised all the faces around me: none of them showed any sign of pain. Suddenly I was brushed aside by a group of excited women who had discovered a bargain in meat, and I found myself being pushed towards a gap between two walls. Now that strange voice broke out again and just

behind my left ear. I quickly turned and found that the cry
was coming from the mouth of an elderly man. He was crying
as hard as he could, but did not appear to be in pain. His hair,
beneath a small worn-out beret, was white and uncombed, his
forehead much wrinkled, his eyes small and sunken, his mouth
covered by a bushy white moustache. He was not tall and wore
an old overcoat which hid his legs. In front of him was a broken
stool on which four bundles of some kind of plant consisting
of three stalks were evenly arranged. He cried again and again
with that same strange voice. I pretended not to notice him,
but I was actually listening carefully. "Ay-e-e! ay-e-e!" came
the groaning cry, but I could not understand it. It puzzled me
greatly. Then I remembered the small French-English dictionary in my pocket and I moved away from him to try and find
a clue. After some searching I discovered that he must have
been calling "*Ail. . . . Ail. . . . Ail. . . .*" The old man was a
garlic-seller. I was happy to have solved the mystery but I felt
some concern over him and his goods. Every one of the green-
grocers in the street had bundles upon bundles of garlic for
sale. The old man's strange cry, so husky and feeble, could
hardly be heard by the noisy throng. For about an hour while
I lingered there, not a soul gave him or his goods a glance.
What could he live on? Yet he looked quite cheerful and not
in the least worried. I moved away eventually, but his cry,
"*Ail. . . . Ail. . . Ail . . .*" seemed to ring in my ears the whole
day long.

From that day on it was impossible for me to go down the
street without glancing at him. Each time I saw him, he was in
exactly the same state with his stand of four bundles of garlic,
each consisting of three stalks. Gradually he seemed to notice
my interest and often met my look with a smile. Once when I
passed very close to him he even murmured a feeble "*Bon jour,
monsieur.*" I tried to exchange a few words with him but his
inaudible tones were beyond me. My friends thought I was
crazy to take such an interest in that ordinary, common garlic-
seller. In time I collected some scraps of information about him.

It appeared that some forty years ago he was an opera singer,
a tenor, who used to perform in the Grand Opera House with
many famous singers. Later he lost his voice after a serious
illness. When he recovered he turned to acting comedy parts
in Molière plays produced at the Odéon theatre not far from

the rue Mouffetard. In those singing and acting days of his, although he never became a leading singer or actor, he was quite well-off and much talked about. But he had a happy, generous nature and spent all he earned, mostly with his friends. In years gone by his friends had helped to support him, but most of them were now dead, and he carried on in his own way. Paris is full of history as well as full of tales, tall or short, reliable or unreliable. I was not sure whether this was the genuine life-story of my friend, but it illustrated an ageless book, written and re-written in one language and another, about the inescapable course of human destiny. Fame brings one glory for a time, and for a time money buys the smiles of others. In the beginning of life we have little of either, and as we near its end both seem insignificant. Yet no one would like to pass through life without them. My mind became rather disturbed after these reflections: I looked through my own life and wished I could do something for the garlic-seller.

I did not see the Mouffetard Sunday market until one Sunday, when a friend called just after I had finished breakfast and suggested we should have a look at it. It took us less than three minutes to reach the place and the market was already in full

swing. The goods for sale were not laid out on any sort of stall, but were heaped on the pavement in an artistic disorder. It began at the part of the street where my acquaintance the old garlic-seller usually stood, and covered the space between the rue St Médard and the rue Lacepède. Goods such as would certainly not be found in any of the big department stores in Paris, such as Le Printemps, La Fayette, and Samaritaine, were on sale. Nevertheless, we rubbed shoulders with prospective buyers one or two of whom were wearing mink or other valuable fur coats and fur gloves. I bent to examine a few rusty nails, pieces of wire an inch or two in length with reddish spots all along, then some paint-brushes with a broken tip or no tip at all, and the like. My friend picked up a shoe from a big pile of shoes of all colours; it had no heel, and the upper gaped from the sole like a frog's mouth. We moved on. Old clothes, even unrecognisable underwear which must have come from the rubbish heap after a family removal, pans without handles, half a sewing box, dusty kitchen utensils and a thousand other items of 'junk' were hopefully displayed. I murmured to my friend: "There is absolutely nothing wasted in Paris!" At the same time I thought, had my grandmother been alive and seen this market she would have been greatly impressed, for her guiding principle in ruling our big family of more than forty members under one roof in China some thirty-five years ago was—to waste nothing!

My mind went back to the old garlic-seller more than once; my friend even remarked that I was quiet and full of thought that morning. I was thinking that perhaps the old man was better off than the people selling their goods in the Mouffetard Sunday Market; for he could at least have Sunday to himself.

It was nearly time for me to leave Paris. For some reason or another I found myself standing near the old garlic-seller again one morning. We exchanged the usual smiles. He could not have had the slightest idea that I had come there on his account. He went his own way. Still "*Ail. . . . Ail. . . . Ail . . .*" sounded at intervals in his husky, feeble and almost inaudible wail. Still four bunches of three stalks of garlic were laid on the still broken stool. Still not one out of the crowds of shoppers and spectators came to have a look at his wares. I stayed for half an hour and not a bunch did he sell. Almost involuntarily I moved a step forward and asked the price of a bunch. Then, to save him trouble with change, I took two bunches, six stalks altogether, for a small banknote of francs. Without giving a thought to what I was going to do with the stuff, I put it in my pocket and took leave of my old acquaintance. "*Ail. . . . Ail. . . .*

Ail . . ." was still ringing in my ears when I lay down in bed that night.

'Great is the will to live!' This name, given to a wild poppy growing in the desert of Arizona, I would like to give to my old acquaintance, the garlic-seller of Paris, too. He grows stubbornly in the desert of human sand on the left bank of the Seine.

XXIV

Feathers and Fur

"Swans? You can see them in the zoo."

This reply, or rebuke, came from a French friend when we were walking along the Allée des Cygnes, between the Pont de Bir-Hareim and the Pont de Grenelle. This is a long strip of land rising from the bed of the river, which is wider at this part. The allée is of uniform width, so that it looks artificial, yet neither verge is paved with stone like the quays. I enjoyed walking in the middle of the river with green grass growing to the water's edge.

I wondered aloud if swans nested here. On the London Embankment swans had for many years past been a customary sight for me, and I saw no reason why they should not be seen on the Seine in Paris too. The Paris quays and river shores are all so continuously paved with stone and brick that they do not provide suitable nesting ground for swans; but here, I thought, along the Allée des Cygnes with its grassy edges, would be ideal for them; the very name of the place implied as much. So when I received the slightly scornful reply I was astonished.

Evidently swans do not visit the Seine as often as they do the Thames—another respect in which Paris differs from London. The only swans I saw during my stay in Paris were a pair in the stream running through the woods at the Château of Chantilly, one in the lake of the Palace of Fontainebleau, another in the lake of the Parc Chaumont, and a pair in each of the two zoos, at the Jardin des Plantes and the Bois de Vincennes. The complete absence of swans from the water-surface or in occasional flight over the Seine leaves the river clear but somewhat bare and lacking in life. A snow-white dot gliding gracefully in the distance, or a pair of swans taking their family out to explore the riverside would add charm to the Seine.

It is not the absence of swans only that makes me find the Seine rather bare and lifeless. Because Paris is farther from the sea than London, its river lacks the screeching noise and swift, flapping movement of gulls. The sky of Paris is quieter than that of London. In London, New York, Dublin, and San Francisco I grew accustomed to the sight of seagulls floating above the heads, almost, of the human sea.

There are ducks on the lakes in the Bois de Boulogne and the Bois de Vincennes, and a few on the lake of the Parc de Butte Chaumont, but these places are not near the centre of Paris. One rainy morning I managed at last to see a duck on the Seine. It was near the Ile St Louis. I had been told that some-one living on the island kept a duck as a pet and took it for a walk every day. I was interested in this new type of pet, but for a long time I failed to catch sight of it. That morning, however, after a tour of the island, when I reached the turning-point along the Quai d'Orleans my attention was held by a man almost enveloped in a large umbrella. I thought at first he was a fisherman, but I presently found that he was as much interested as I in the loud quacking of a lonely duck on the river. I watched the duck swimming further out, then turning round, gliding in a circle, dipping its head into the water as if performing a somersault, splashing water on to its back with its beak, and quacking in greatest ecstasy. It might have been the only happy creature in the world at that moment. Presently the man under the umbrella moved down the slope towards the river's edge, and it was not long before the duck turned and swam towards him quite willingly. It amazed me to see the bird apparently answering its master's call. As the man took it on his arm and stroked it as one would a cat or a dog, I noticed a long string attached to its leg. They went away, passing by me happily, the man murmuring to his pet. This was one of the advantages of living on the Ile St Louis.

Though other birds are lacking, Paris has three of the most common and typical of city birds. The first is the pigeon. The Parisians feed their pigeons in the parks and squares and also along the banks of the Seine, though they do not make a conspicuous sight of it, as do the Londoners in Trafalgar Square. They feed them in the Place de l'Hôtel de Ville, in the Tuileries, and indeed in most places where a public seat invites them to rest for a while. Unlike their brothers and sisters in London, the pigeons of Paris do not congregate in any par-ticular quarter, but are to be seen almost anywhere along the pavements of the boulevards and roads, even in little lanes and passages.

Pigeons are birds with a natural love for trees and the countryside; how they became city-dwellers and acquired the taste for living in cities is beyond me. It is true that there are trees along the boulevards of Paris, but from my observation

the Paris pigeons prefer to walk among men rather than flutter among twigs and branches. I never saw them asleep on trees at night: apparently they prefer to live on stone buildings. I discovered the homes of those who frequent the Cathedral of Notre Dame, for that ancient edifice contains numerous ready-made pigeon-holes in the walls and in the twin towers. I could not count the total number of holes, but I once saw six or seven pigeons waddling out of one of them!

Nowhere did I see more pigeons than just behind the little gate and railings of the small Place de l'Archevêche by the south side of the Cathedral. Several benches are set there under the trees upon which people sit feeding the pigeons in all weathers, for they are sheltered from wind and even rain. As Easter approached all the trees proclaimed themselves to be cherry trees, full of clusters of blossom. One morning as I stood in a corner, a pretty Parisienne in pullover and slacks came, carrying a boy of two or three. They were perhaps sister and brother, or even mother and son. She put the boy down and both began to throw food to the pigeons. Their smiles and laughter under the cherry blossom in the bright sunshine, punctuated by the short flights of the pigeons, made a happy picture.

The Chinese love of pigeons dates back some 2,500 years— long before the building of the Cathedral of Notre Dame. Many ancient relics, such as bronze and jade staff-heads in the form of pigeons, and dating from the third century B.C., have survived to this day. A legend recorded in one of our ancient books tells how at that time the man who was to become the first Emperor of Han Dynasty, Liu Pang, was fighting against his enemy, Hsiang Yü, to secure the throne. He was being closely pursued, but found a hiding-place in a tangled bush.

Hsiang Yü searched the spot, but when a pigeon cooed above the bush, took the presence of the bird as a sign that there was no one in it, and went away. This turned the tide in the struggle for the throne, and Liu Pang became the first Emperor of Han. To commemorate his miraculous escape, he had pigeon-staffs made for presentation to aged people. Every autumn a house-to-house enquiry was conducted throughout the provinces, and those who had attained their seventieth year were given a pigeon-staff and some rice; for those aged eighty the staff-head was made of bronze, and for the few aged ninety of jade.

The pigeon motif of the staff-head portended that the aged persons would have no difficulty in swallowing their food. This strange but pleasant custom has unfortunately long been discontinued. The Chinese not only love the pigeon, but revere it for its many virtues, parental solicitude being one such virtue. The wood-pigeon is believed to hatch out six or seven chicks at a time, and to feed them all with strict impartiality; it is very faithful, for if one parent dies the other never mates again; it is supposed to encourage the virtue of filial piety (I doubt this in the present generation), and it is also credited with steadiness and orderly conduct. I am not myself going to extol the pigeon's virtues, though I am fond of the birds. There were times when I found their multitudinous presence on the pavements of the Paris boulevards and determination to keep pace with me, their heads jerking forwards and backwards on their copper-wired necks, rather irritating. They just would not fly off unless I quickened my steps, which I was always reluctant to do as it seemed impolite.

Another bird common to London and Paris is the house-sparrow. Sparrows are supposed to be the only feathered ones that have attached themselves to man with undaunted spirit, and followed him faithfully wherever he has made his habitation. The sparrow is man's friend, though it seldom gets any real friendship from him; man, rather, ignores sparrows because they are so common and numerous. The Paris sparrows did me a favour by giving me the chance to watch them among the bamboo bushes in the Luxembourg Gardens and near the statue of Alphonse Daudet on the Avenue des Champs Elysées. Sparrows on bamboos are a common sight in China, and Chinese artists are very fond of depicting them thus. It was a delight to me to find it again in Paris. While feeding, the sparrows kept together, darting and hopping among the bushes, fluttering, and chirping, pecking, scolding each other pertly, and even fighting. They seemed to be a quarrelsome lot, but their noisy chattering was fashionable gossip rather than an exchange of hot words. They were especially pleasing when in flight, with the leaves of the bamboos touched by the wind.

It seemed to me that the people who brought bags of bread crumbs to feed the birds seldom had the sparrow in mind. Yet sparrows would be sure to turn up and claim their share of the meal. However, I met an elderly man in the gardens of the Tuileries who fed no other birds but sparrows. At first I thought he was just feeding birds in general and had no definite purpose. I watched him with great interest, for his facial expression coupled with the movement of his shoulders, limbs, hands and feet indicated joy, remorse, anger and satisfaction by turns. Gradually I noticed that he purposely held up his morsel before a number of blackbirds and pigeons before throwing it to some sparrows in the distance. By and by, as if by magic, all the blackbirds and pigeons took themselves off, and he was completely surrounded by sparrows, some of which even flew up to his hands for the bits. He was happy and smiling. Noticing my interest, he began to talk to me like the running water of a rapid. I could only understand the words "*Le moineau. Le moineau.*" But I wished I could have found out why he only fed sparrows. Clearly he was happy in the happiness of the sparrows, and, watching him, I felt happy too.

Regarding the third common bird, the starling, it would be difficult to say whether Paris or London has the greater number of them. The noise they make under the porch of the Church of the Madeleine is hardly greater than that they make in the porch of the National Gallery in London. Nor did I see a larger flock flying over the tree-tops in the Jardin des Plantes than over the dark bushes in Battersea Park. Perhaps they are less obtrusive in Paris owing to the spaciousness of the boulevards, which allows free movement in the air and dampens the effect of their chatter somewhat.

I may have missed many varieties of birds in Paris, since my time could not all be spent in bird-watching. I enjoyed the swallows darting up and down close to the surface of the Seine, and a line of crows or rooks flapping over the river in regular motion as if controlled by someone down below. Sir William Hayter told me that when he was British Minister in Paris he saw from his office window, which faces the garden of the British Embassy on the Faubourg St Honoré, nuthatches, treecreepers, great tits, and once a black-and-white woodpecker, besides, of course, a host of other common birds, such as chaffinches. Lady Hayter also told me that from their flat near the corner of the Avenue Raymond Poincaré and the Avenue Foch they often heard owls at night. Though I never heard one myself, the presence of owls in the city is almost a certainty, since their food consists of rats and mice, and these are no rarity in Paris.

The Bird Market on the Quai de la Mégisserie is so open to the public that I had no difficulty in finding it a few days after my arrival in Paris. I even mingled with the buyers and the salesmen, who held bird-cages in their hands and talked incessantly. There were few varieties of song-birds, nearly all being canaries, and what struck me as curious was that most of the canaries were marked as coming from Yorkshire. An amusing notice under one cage, in which apparently was a very young bird, declared that its song was *guaranteed*. I took this to be a euphemistic way of saying that the bird would sing beautifully later on, but was not doing so just now, and appreciated this example of French wit. I found that more than 400 years ago, a ship partly laden with little green birds captured in the Canary Islands was wrecked near Elba. The birds made their escape, flew to the island and there settled. A number of them were caught by the inhabitants, and on account of their vivacity and the brilliancy of their song, soon became great favourites and rapidly spread over Europe. Their intelligence was tested, and the Germans and the French trained them well. Buffon records in his *Natural History*:

In 1820, a Frenchman exhibited four and twenty Canary Birds in London, many of which he said were from eighteen to twenty-five years of age. Some of these balanced themselves, head downward, on their shoulders, having their legs and tail in the air. One of them, taking a slender stick in its claws, passed its head between its legs, and suffered itself to be turned round, as if in the act of being roasted. Another balanced itself, and was slung backward and forward on a kind of slack rope. A third was dressed in military uniform, having a cap on its head; wearing a sword and pouch, and carrying a firelock in one claw: after some time sitting upright, this bird, at the word of command, freed itself from its dress, and flew away to the cage. A fourth suffered itself to be shot at, and falling down, as if dead, to be put into a little barrow, and wheeled away by one of its comrades; and several of the birds were at the same time placed upon a little firework, and continued there quietly, and without alarm, till it was discharged.

All these seeming impossibilities were accomplished more than a hundred years ago. Now the Paris bird markets sell 'English' canaries.

There are two zoos in Paris; one is a part of the Jardin des Plantes and the other in the Bois de Vincennes. The first lies on the left bank and was within easy walking distance of my lodgings.

I went there a few times, as a rule in the morning, before I strolled to other places. It is a small zoo and has fewer animals than the Regent's Park Zoo of London and the Central Park Zoo of New York. But the structure of the menagerie and cages is fanciful, somewhat resembling the spacious garden of an Eastern sultan, half Oriental, half Occidental, French with a touch of Chinese, as in eighteenth-century 'Chinoiserie'. I think they serve their purpose, for a zoo is a show place and its visitors are chiefly children and ordinary folks. I liked the way this zoo was grouped with other institutions of the kind, such as the Zoological Museum, the Museum of Mineralogy, and the Botanical Gardens. It is convenient for students to make comparative studies. I found many fine statues of animals by famous sculptors dotted among the trees and shrubs; no other zoo I have visited can match that.

The governing idea is akin to Chinese habits. We are taught that man is only one of the millions of creatures in Nature and that he is not superior to others. Paris has many fine statues of kings and queens and also of authors and artists; yet she also gives other animals their due. Apart from those that I found in the Jardin des Plantes, the Luxembourg and the Tuileries, I saw the lion in the centre of the Place Denfert-Rochereau, a rhinoceros and an elephant on the way to St Cloud, and two groups of deer in the Parc de Sceaux.

The big zoo in the Bois de Vincennes is on the border of
Paris and is reached by Metro at the Porte Dorée. I went there
first with a young friend on a windy, wintry afternoon. Despite
the cold, we went up the monkey rock by a lift for a blow.
Later I made a careful round of the Zoo by myself on a sunny
morning. Strangely enough, I was struck by the queer arrangement of the monkey rocks. When I faced them from a distance

against the sun, I found the upper outline resembled certain
mountain peaks in an ancient Chinese painting, possibly by
a Sung master, while their lower parts were hidden in the
dense morning haze. I made a number of sketches. The monkey
rocks have very few monkeys on them, but a lift-shaft has been
cut through so that visitors can go to the top.

Recently my friends John and Helen Tee-Van attended the
International Conference of Zoo Authorities in Paris, for John
is the Director of the Bronx Zoo of New York. They went round
all the zoos in Europe. I asked if they could tell me something
of what they saw. They wrote:

The Zoo at Vincennes we found one of the best in Europe and the
upkeep was particularly fine. . . . They have very elaborate and
well-planned methods, too, of shifting their animals from inside
to outside cages and exhibition places. Another thing that impressed
us was that in the lion and tiger house they had three studios for the
use of artists. These look out through barred windows, invisible to
the public, on to the outdoor enclosures for the animals. Their
service buildings and research laboratories are also very up-to-date
and well equipped. The general plan of the Zoo impressed us, too,
with its large irregularly shaped enclosures, separated by moats
and low walls, so that one could see many different kinds of animals
at one time. . . .

Helen is an artist of animals and has contributed drawings to illustrate the American edition of the *Encyclopædia Britannica*. The French, like the Chinese, only more so, seem always to have an eye alert for a pattern or decorative design.

I am interested in all animals and have been a Fellow of the London Zoological Society and a member of the New York one for many years. Once I start to write about animals, I find it difficult to stop. However, what concerns me now is the

common type of the furred family that we meet in Paris daily. I did not find kittens for sale anywhere in the city, though I met many cats on my strolls. Paris suffered terribly not only during the Revolution but also, later, from the Commune insurrection of 1871. It is said that it was on the left bank of the Seine that Fouquier-Tinville, that tigerish public accuser of the Commune, selected his most distinguished and noble victims. Each devastated house contained, as a rule, a cat, which thenceforward became an outcast and a wanderer, the servants having in many cases shared the fate of their masters and mistresses. The descendants of those outcasts remain wanderers in Paris today. How much truth there is in this story I cannot say, but Paris certainly abounds in stray cats.

On many occasions men with their cats on their shoulders caught my eye in the Luxembourg Gardens. It was on one of these occasions that I started a hot discussion among a small party of friends. On seeing a ginger cat perched on the shoulder of a burly, white-haired man with a face as red as a tomato, I remarked that the group would make a good subject for a painting—full of colour. A London member of our little party involuntarily murmured, "What a queer way to give the cat an airing! The creature should be able to look after herself." He did not realise that we had a hot-blooded, temperamental, and mischievous Parisian student in our midst. Before he could get his last word out, the young Parisian, dancing with excitement, began a diatribe something like the following: "The English have always made out that they were the only animal-lovers in the world, but they don't know how to love animals. This old

The Monkey Rock in the Vincennes Zoo

man exhibits real love for his friend the cat, not like the
English, who just leave their cats dozing on the hearth before
the fire day and night, while they get on with their own work—
sewing, knitting, writing letters, reading. . . . That isn't love;
that's indifference, and selfishness too. Or they leave their cats
curled up in a newly cleaned armchair and invite their guests
to sit on the fender or a foot-stool. That's not love either; that's
over-indulgence. The English force cats to drink milk, milk,
and more milk, and they give the poor creatures boiled beef
and mashed potato, calling it Christian food. But the Bible
never mentions cats. . . ." This was going too far. Our London
friend was as astonished as I. Though he was himself no great
lover of pets, his indomitable English spirit forbade him to
keep silent. He raised his voice, too. The argument soon ceased

to concern itself with cats and dogs at all. He declared that the
French idea of love was vulgar and superficial, whereas love
should spring from the innermost part of one's heart; it was
always there, but it needed some invisible motive to make it
burst out; it could not be forced by any external means. It
springs from within the human being, not from outside. What
was the use of showing love outwardly? To express or show
'love' by outward behaviour was only to do so for others to see.
That was not love. . . .

The hot discussion might have led to a duel if we had been
living fifty years back. Eventually my opinion was sought and
I tried to make peace by resorting to our ancient Chinese
philosophy. According to Taoism, I told them, man and cat
are born with similar functional status in the rhythm of life.

Everyone of us has his own place and part to play, and in fulfilling it we remain in harmony with that rhythm of life. Man's love for man is the same as cat's love for cat; nor will man's love for a cat differ from a cat's love for a man. If the feeling of one side goes to excess, it upsets the balance of the rhythm of life and invites trouble. . . . . They all thought I was talking in riddles and laughingly told me to 'shut up'. One of them even shook his head at me as if to say what an inscrutable Oriental I was. But I felt that my disquisition had relieved the tension by making the party laugh.

Whether or no the French have a special love for cats, they certainly have a predilection for poodles. My friend Brian Vesey-Fitzgerald, an expert broadcaster on animals and a contributor of articles on pets to a London weekly, has some interesting remarks on French poodles:

First of all [he writes] they are certainly not French in origin. 'French' poodle is a misnomer. It was only the fancy clipping that started in France. That was just prior to the Revolution. Nobody knows who did it first—but it seems likely that it was a Court fashion.

There is some evidence that the poodle started in Egypt. There are bas-reliefs of clipped dogs that look a bit poodlish dating from the first century A.D. I am myself inclined to think that this dog, like the Portuguese water-dog, which is a relation of the poodle, is of the retriroco tribe. Other suggestions for origin are: Portugal, Russia, Germany, Italy and Turkey. I think Portugal the most likely myself—and I think it was wine-merchants who brought the dog from Portugal to Holland and thus to Germany. Martin de Vos —in his painting of Tobit and his dog—shows what is undoubtedly a clipped poodle (De Vos, 1531-1603). Albrecht Dürer (1471-1528) also shows a clipped dog that might be a poodle. And Jan Steen's picture (1618 approx.) of a dancing dog is certainly that of a clipped poodle. The clipping is not, of course, the same as the modern French clipping—except for the bobble on the tail.

There are six recognised varieties [of the poodles]—great, medium, miniature, corded, sheep and monkey. Those we see in England are mostly either mediums, miniatures or cordeds. But there is much interbreeding and you get all sorts of heads and legs.

I remember reading somewhere that when the construction of the Pont Neuf was completed and traders were allowed to have their stands on the sides of the bridge, there were men who pestered dog-owners with offers to clip their poodles in the latest fashion for a very small gratuity. Nowadays, I believe, it is not easy to get poodles clipped, as expert clippers are rare and their charges are consequently high. Once I was watching the antics of some puppies in the window of a big dog shop on the

Avenue des Champs-Elysées when peal after peal of laughter rang out from inside. I stepped in and saw a group of people round a tall stool on which sat a black poodle that a shop assistant in a white overall was clipping like an expert hairdresser. The poodle's head was being firmly pressed down, but his eyes looked sadly and patiently upwards. The clipper was talking volubly. Each sentence he uttered was followed by a roar of laughter. He was plainly enjoying himself; the greater the laughter the more witty his remarks. They seemed to be part of his job. I managed to catch a word here and there: "How would you like to look nice and pretty?" "Wouldn't you like to make yourself smart to go out with a nice fashionable lady? . . ."

In London there are certain young men who have earned the name of 'spivs'; they are ultra-smartly dressed and they stand at the street corners with nothing in particular to do. Sometimes they rove the streets and attract a glance or two. Most of

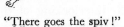

"There goes the spiv!"

the people who visit Paris are smartly dressed; they wander along the boulevards and seem to have nothing particular to do. But they cannot be called 'spivs'. Somehow I feel that the real 'spivs' of Paris are the poodles. They are always on the scene. At any rate, poodles are the 'spivs' of Paris dogs.

XXV

Hand and Head

On my travels I like to be silent and alone, but sometimes it is impossible to be either. In Paris, where I did not know the language and had fewer friends than elsewhere, it seemed likely that I should have little difficulty in being both. But my wish to meet Paris craftsmen and see them at work could not be fulfilled without the help of an interpreter, and that in itself rendered silence impracticable. But on these occasions I was only too glad to find a cicerone among my small acquaintance, and in general I was very fortunate.

The name of a *vannerie* (basket-work) craftswoman had been given me. None of my friends thought this craft of much interest, and I was amused to find them united in opposing my plan as well as my request for the company of one of them. But after much persuasion Fan Chun-P'i promised to go with me, though she was in the midst of a spell of hard work in the Museé Guimet. We set off for the rue Mayet in the Sixth Arrondissement. On our arrival, the *concierge* told us that Madame Chapion lived on the fifth floor. No lift was to be seen. This saddened Fan and made me feel guilty, for I saw that she was really tired and those flights of stairs were formidable. They seemed to take us longer than all the rest of our journey. Madame Chapion welcomed us, but Fan's face remained weary.

The room was small and cosy. We sat at a square table, one side of which was close to the window. There was not much other space. Madame Chapion brought out a number of small articles for us to see. Fan did not seem to find them at all unusual. Presently a tiny flower-basket about four inches in diameter, made in China and looking old, was produced with a stream of words from our hostess in praise of Chinese craftsmanship. She pointed out each interlocking of the bamboo canes with affection. I was touched by her enthusiasm, but it did not cheer Fan. The little basket was bound to be of great interest to Madame Chapion, who had not seen many like it before and who understood the intricate technique required to make it. To us it did not mean so much, for we had played with many similar baskets when we were youngsters some forty years or so before, when they were given to us as toys and torn to pieces in a few days. In the China of those days the cost of these little baskets was almost nothing.

Even Madame Chapion's praise of Chinese handicrafts failed to rouse Fan. The prospect was rather black, for I could not converse in French and Fan's mood was such that she, who could, spoke hardly a word. The atmosphere had to be relieved. I began to tell in Chinese, for Fan to translate, how, recently, great attention had been paid in the United States to the baskets made by the North American Indians because of their technique and designs. The basketry of the Philippines, Hawaii and New Zealand has also received praise. But Chinese basketry may be one of the oldest handicrafts still practised—certainly older than most other handicrafts in China. The *Book of Odes*, written before Confucius, more than 2,500 years ago, mentions it. An interesting use of the basket in ancient China arose out of the convention that men and women should not touch each other's hands. When a man wished to make a present to a woman, she had to receive the gift in a basket. Baskets were used too in the rearing of silk-worms, and in our funeral ceremonies. I began to recite:

> The Chen and Wei
> Run deep and clear;
> That knight and lady,
> Their flower-basket is full.
> The lady says, "Have you looked?"
> The knight says, "Yes, I have finished looking.
> Shall we go and look a little more?"
> Beyond the Wei
> It is very open and pleasant.
> That knight and lady,
> Merrily they sport.
> Then she gives him a peony.

This is an ancient ballad some 3,000 years old. Simply because the use of baskets was so common, the handicraft made constant progress in design and originality. Each province produced a different kind. I found a very good collection of Chinese baskets in the Field Museum of Natural History, Chicago.

Fan interpreted my words to Madame Chapion slowly at first. I watched her closely. I did not think she tried to translate the poem even roughly, but her words began to come more quickly as Madame Chapion's nods showed her interest. Presently they were chattering and laughing gaily together. I marvelled that a lady's tiredness could be chattered away.

The change in Fan's attitude came from a good reason; she had found Madame Chapion not only a skilful craftswoman, but an attractive personality. While they were in conversation, Fan kept me interested by interpreting.

Madame Chapion had not started her career as a *vannière*. Some five years before she had worked in a factory, and one evening after work she went to see a workmate in her home and found her busy tackling another kind of work—basket-making. Her friend complained that she had to finish the basket by a

> 溱與洧，瀏其清矣。
> 士與女，殷其盈矣。
> 女曰觀乎？士曰既且。
> 且往觀乎？洧之外，
> 洵訏且樂。維士與女，
> 伊其將謔，贈之以芍藥。
>
> 詩經

given time and could not find anyone to help her; this was not ordinary basket-making, but needed a skilful hand and intelligence. She had a number of relatives to support, so she had to work in the factory in the daytime and make baskets in the evening. Her type of *vannerie* was in demand, for her father was an expert and had invented a new way of interlacing the thin rattans. He had taught his daughter the art, but she was too hard pressed to have time to think out new designs. Madame Chapion's heart was touched by her friend's hard struggle, and out of friendship she asked if she could help. "Although I have not had much education," said Madame Chapion, "I like to read and to think out solutions to difficult problems. I seem to possess some dexterity in my hands too; each finger moves with automatic skill. For a few months I went to work with my friend at night and learnt all she could teach me." Eventually they decided to form a partnership. Unfortunately, the friend's health broke down from the hard work at night, and she died. Madame Chapion now ran the business single-handed.

Vannerie includes chairs, tables and other furniture made out of the rattans or Malaya *rotang*. Madame Chapion told us that she could have carried on the business in the conventional manner, but she wanted to do something different. She was fond of Nature and used to visit the zoos, and it was there that she found inspiration. She worked out ways of plaiting and interlacing the rattan so as to resemble natural objects. She showed us photographs of work she had displayed at big handicraft exhibitions in France and other countries. Some of her creations were in the form of birds, some of animals and some of human figures, chiefly women. I found them very interesting, for the material did not allow her much freedom, and realism was impossible; yet they were genuinely artistic just because the limitations of the medium made style a necessity. The results were very original, and each seemed the unmistakable product of the hand and head of Madame Chapion and no one else. One photograph showed a young lady seemingly feeding pigeons in the garden of a modern house, all done in basket-work. The effect was charming. I learned that this particular job had been done for an Exhibition of Modern Homes, something like the annual English Ideal Home Exhibition. They must have interested the visitors greatly. Her first success in this kind was a pair of cocks. This established her name as one of the noted craftswomen of France. I sketched a copy  of the cocks from the photograph as being something to be remembered. The cocks brought her much praise; her work began to be used extensively for window-dressing in department stores.

The Manager of one big Paris store ordered a pair of boots in *vannerie*. Madame Chapion made the boots and sent a bill for 10,000 francs. This staggered the Manager, who reminded her that *vannerie* was a cheap line of goods. Madame Chapion replied by demanding the return of her boots, which, she said, were the creation of her imagination as well as of her hands.

Creativeness was worth more than manual skill. This story delighted Fan and me, for we had been brought up to regard all creation—which is to say, work done by hand and head—as something to be valued highly, and money as relatively unimportant. Madame Chapion corrected our false impression that in the West people care more for material gain than for spiritual satisfaction. My long sojourn in England had already brought me into touch with many fine personalities with high ideals; Madame Chapion supplied another excellent example from France. This further strengthened my belief that generalisation often leads to misunderstanding. Personal contact is the best way to promote real understanding between peoples.

Madame Chapion's simplicity and wholeheartedness particularly impressed me. She was neither sophisticated nor hypocritical, despite her success. She said that many people had written about her work, but that she had never bothered to keep Press cuttings. I could not help comparing this with certain Paris craftsmen I had met who took me for a journalist and eagerly produced their Press-cutting books as soon as they had offered me a seat. She said she liked natural behaviour and had not a good word to say for those who tried to twist or exaggerate things. She kept reminding us that both her parents were simple working people, and that her only education had been some elementary instruction in reading and writing. After she became known, she was invited to large social gatherings, but these always embarrassed her, for she could not find words to express what she wished to say. At this, I interrupted her to say that her work would always speak for her.

Fan and Madame Chapion continued to talk. Love of animals became the theme. Madame Chapion kept a cat and a dog and intensely disliked those who were cruel to animals. She went on to say that all people loved peace, and that if only a common language could be devised we could all exchange ideas and work without quarrelling. Everything in her life centred on her work. Having seen specimens of fine Chinese basketry, she was glad to see us just because we were Chinese.

At the end of our visit she brought out some material and showed us how she worked. At times she pointed out this or that method of interlacing the rattan, as if waiting for us to say if we Chinese had a better way. Neither Fan nor I could be of any help. I gave her the title of an illustrated book, *Chinese*

Baskets, published by the Field Museum, Chicago, and suggested that it might give her some ideas.

During one of the meetings of the Conference of Arts and Letters organised by Unesco which I attended in Paris in May, 1947, I made a proposal for an exchange of craftsmen between nations in addition to the exchanges of professors, scholars and students. The suggestion was turned down without discussion, as it was said to be beyond the scope of the particular committee. I had no more to say at the time. But I still think that if professors, scholars and students can do much to promote understanding between peoples, craftsmen can do so too. In fact, the exchange of craftsmen between nations would not only help to promote understanding; it might have far wider repercussions. Professional jealousy might disappear and trade prejudices be broken down. China used to have the reputation of being the only nation that esteemed scholars higher than soldiers and manual workers. But Chinese scholars, some real and some only so in name, often outweighed and lost touch with the rest of China's huge population and unbalanced the whole social system. I hope the world will take China as an example, and not stress only the part to be played by professors, scholars and students, but recognise the importance of craftsmen too.

L'hotel de Beauvais, Paris

XXVI

Between Life and Death

I CAME out of the Guignol show on the Champs Elysées, round the corner from the Avenue de Marigny, at about four o'clock one Saturday towards the end of March. The great street was decorated, as it were, not with flags and bunting, but with leaves. There are more trees along it than along any other avenue in Paris; at any rate, they are more noticeable, particularly from the Rond-Point eastwards to the end of the avenue at the Chevaux de Marly. The warmth in the air was so exhilarating that my body seemed to have no weight.

I had seen all sorts of activity upon this street, by day and by night, but this afternoon the activity was of a different kind. Spring, many think, is the life-giver, but to my mind it is the embellisher. I like the nakedness and truth of winter; but who can resist the *panache* of spring? Most of us dislike swagger, but life quite without ostentation is dry and without style. I thought of all those sitting in the cafés and gazing at the windows of the avenue from the Rond-Point westwards to the Place de l'Etoile: except for the very young, they had experienced their winter days and were now sitting gay and hopeful in the sun.

It was a carefree mood that had brought me to the Guignol show that afternoon. I knew no children in Paris whom I could take there, and I had gone in the expectation of enjoying the rapt expressions and revealing gestures of unknown youngsters. I had also a vague hope of learning some French, as I imagined that the patter, since it was intended for children, would be clear and simple and easy to follow. A friend had introduced me to the Guignol in the Jardin des Tuileries a few days after my arrival in Paris, and in the course of my wanderings I found other shows of the kind—one in the Parc Montsouris and another on the island in Lac Daumesnil in the Bois de Vincennes. I had also patronised the Marionette Theatre in the Luxembourg Gardens. During the Guignol performance the

Spring in the Garden of the Champs Elysées

showman behind the scenes sometimes showed psychological
insight by asking the young audience questions to which, of
course, the player inside the box already knew the answers.
The response always came spontaneously and unanimously.
As far as my progress in French was concerned, I must confess

that it was nil. However, I did learn one thing: why French
men and women kiss each other repeatedly on both cheeks
when they meet or part at Metro stations and bus-stops. The
reason is that they see so many Guignol shows when they are
young that they become infected by the movements of the
Guignol in fighting his enemies. For fear of acquiring the same
habit, I refrained from seeing the infectious Guignol too
frequently.

I was now walking between the trees which line the wide
pavement on the north side of the avenue. This space is a park
in itself, for there is plenty of room for people to move about,
and there are benches to sit on as well as pedlars selling food,
soft drinks and toys. I watched some children dismount from
donkeys, heard the happy scream of a little girl who fell off the
seat of a small cart when the pony unexpectedly started to
move, and shared the laughter of two small boys when their
balloons burst simultaneously. This neighbourhood is one of
the many paradises Paris provides for youngsters. No other
big city that I know cares so much for its young as Paris.

R

Besides the Guignols and children's theatres, there are always special reserves for children in public parks. What is more surprising is that they are always accompanied by their mothers or fathers, if not both. Surely women in modern Paris can find little time for the things which their sisters in other modern cities like to do. Parisian mothers not only dress their children

attractively, but very largely make their own clothes, for which they appear to have a natural aptitude. They are also wonderful cooks. How, then, do they find the time to sit at ease in the parks?

Standing near the Théâtre des Ambassadeurs, I looked in turn towards the Place de la Concorde and the Place de l'Etoile. The road was flecked with gold and silver, reflected from the burnished parts of the continuous stream of cars. It was difficult to believe that such brightness could come from the sun of March.

Presently a cyclist came speeding towards me from the direction of the Place de l'Etoile, moving, it seemed to me, as fast as any car. As he reached the point at which the Avenue de Marigny debouches on the Champs Elysées a huge silver car came rushing at him. With a screech of brakes the car stopped, but not before it had hit the cyclist. The bicycle flew into the air, and the cyclist alighted on the bonnet of the car! A moment later I saw him jump down. I passed my hand over my perspiring face. Then a policeman appeared, notebook in hand, but the cyclist was so shaken that he could not speak. A crowd gathered and I joined it, in case I should be needed as a witness, though two other people were already furnishing voluble accounts of the accident in French. Out of the huge silver car stepped two officials in neat uniform. More policemen arrived. The cyclist still said nothing, but he displayed a scratch on one of his legs; however, though plainly suffering from shock, he was remarkably composed. Eventually an ambulance took him away. The two uniformed officials climbed back into their car and moved off, and the crowd dispersed. But I still stood there.

A moment ago I had been watching so much life: now I had seen something close to death. By a capricious twist of Fate, the cyclist had escaped being killed. Had he reached the corner a fraction of a second later death would have been inevitable. An American poet-friend of mine, John Hall Wheelock, has two striking lines on the subject of life and death:

> Splendid it is to live, but
> Glorious to die.

But what about the stage between life and death? What would the cyclist think of his escape when he recovered from the shock? It is hard to live, even if it is splendid as well; and modern life makes it difficult to die gloriously—the chances of a sudden, ignominious end have so greatly increased. The cyclist's experience cast a shadow over the brightness of the day.

XXVII

No Room in the Inn

FAN CHUN-PI and I met on the Pont d'Arcle. I was leaning on the parapet watching the snow fall. Single flakes
fluttered down reluctantly and, as they touched the water,
vanished.

Fan tapped my shoulder and asked what I was doing. She
was on her way to the Musée Guimet to continue her study of
some Buddhist paintings of the ninth and tenth centuries which
Professor Pelliot had brought back from the Tun-huang caves
of north-west China some forty years before. They are very
important documents of the period, as valuable as the Stein
Collection of Buddhist art in the British Museum. I seldom
have any definite plan for a day's wandering: on this occasion,
in answer to Fan's enquiry, I said that I had it in mind to go
up the towers of Notre Dame. To my surprise, Fan wanted to
join me in the climb. How difficult it is to predict another's
mind; I quite thought she would consider it crazy to attempt
such an ascent in snowy weather.

Finding the door of the tower open, we began our long
climb. The stone steps have long lost their sharp edges through
the constant friction of human soles for centuries, and, being
now wet, they were also slippery. The ascent was not an easy
one, yet Fan preferred to lead the way, being evidently excited
about the adventure. She said that she had never been up
before, though she had been living in Paris on and off for more
than fifteen years.

We presently reached the point where the steps end. A door
lets the daylight in, and we emerged through it. The bridge-
like structure above the big rose window connects the two
towers, and we walked across. I stood between two gargoyles for
a while. On our way back, I saw a bearded young man with
bright red cheeks standing close to the wall not far from the
door and gazing into space, quite oblivious of us. Fan remarked
that he must be a poet. "Perhaps," I assented. "Anyway, just

as mad as I!" My assumption that no one would care to come
up to see the snow falling received another refutation.

Suddenly a stout woman pushed open a door and, bustling
out from the cave-like entrance, shepherded us back into the
tower. Her broad, bent back and almost rough movements

reminded me of the fantastic *Hunchback of Notre-Dame*. I must
admit that the Chinese translation of that admirable novel of
Victor Hugo's, which I read in my college days, did not affect
me much at the time, simply because I had no knowledge of
the religious background of the theme, though the moral in it
is universal. But ever since I saw the film with Charles Laugh-
ton's wonderful portrayal of the hunchback and astonishing
make-up, the story has left a deep impression and caused me to
associate Notre Dame with those unfortunate creatures of the
book. There has never been any lack of unfortunate creatures
in our midst. Has the progress of civilisation done anything to
improve their lot?

We were now standing by a wooden structure inside which
hung an enormous bell. I was trying to visualise how the
hunchback clambered from one beam to another and tried
madly to ring the bell. Just at that moment the woman struck
the bell with a wooden pole for Fan to hear, for she had been
explaining the size, the weight and the history of it in detail.
I could not understand a word and gave up listening.

Up came another visitor, a young fellow with a grinning
face. He wanted to know what the old woman had been
saying. I confessed that I was like a cow grazing beside someone
playing a lute; I could not tell the tune. He turned out to be

a Dutchman who had landed at Paris Airport and found himself with an hour to spare before catching another aeroplane for New York, so he had decided to climb the tower of Notre Dame. "Why?" I asked. "Because this *is* Paris!" he replied. He soon left us and disappeared. It is a common assumption that only Americans make world tours by aeroplane, spending an hour in each city; but this young Netherlander was doing it. Plainly, he would be quite at home in the New World.

Fan made the woman smile with a tip, and we were permitted to go on up. At the top there were no gargoyles like those round the lower platform. We gazed at the panoramic view from each of the four sides. Snow-flakes were still falling as reluctantly as when I saw them on the Pont d'Arcle, but except for those which dropped round my feet, the rest seemed to vanish before reaching the earth. The atmosphere was deliciously calm; there was so much activity in the air, yet a stillness that was almost palpable. The sky was grey, throwing into relief the snow-capped roofs and the rimy trees, like a landscape carved on Chinese ivory plate. The boulevards divided the city like a chess-board. From this height the Seine looked narrow and with its numerous bridges resembled a modern railway track. I found the view so satisfying that I was oblivious of the cold, but Fan was beginning to stamp her feet, and presently she suggested that we return to earth.

After seeing Fan on her way to the Musée Guimet, I strolled round the north side of the Cathedral into the rue Colombe and then into the rue des Ursins, a very narrow road with tall old buildings on one side and a high wall on the other. I found the mixture of architectural styles at the end of the street attractive, some of the houses having a series of bow windows, some having recessed windows, with a shabby looking café down below. Up a few steps I found myself on the Quai aux Fleurs. Three little boys were throwing snowballs at one another and I stopped to watch the game. I remembered a friend's retort to my remark that snowballing was a universal instinct: he declared that African children would certainly not have it. But I don't think he sustained his case; perhaps only Eskimo children are not interested in this sport.

I proceeded to the Pont St Louis. I have become increasingly fond of this bridge and of the Ile St Louis to which it leads. It is perhaps only from there that one can survey the rest of Paris with real detachment. Though the island is so close to the heart of the city, and connected with the Ile de la Cité and the mainland by a number of bridges, it remains isolated. There is hardly any traffic on it and its quays are ideal for loitering. A young French friend told me that the inhabitants of the Ile St Louis regard themselves as islanders and when they want to go shopping in other parts of Paris, they speak of "going abroad".

My association with the Ile St Louis began from a story I heard about the Pont St Louis. It is not a beautiful bridge, but one can walk about on it with complete freedom, since there is no carriageway. When dusk approaches, it is almost deserted. James Joyce, the Irish writer, during the years he lived in Paris, was often seen walking to and fro on the Pont St Louis (or rather upon its predecessor, a very similar structure which collapsed in 1940), flinging his arms in all directions and communing with himself. Some who knew him then dubbed him a madman. In his lifetime he enjoyed notoriety rather than fame, and those who saw him on the bridge might easily have overlooked his antics, for his stature was rather small; or they may just have thought him unremarkable, for Paris is accustomed to eccentrics. And then, nothing can really shock Parisians.

And so that snowy day, standing on the bridge, I tried to picture Joyce walking to and fro, gesticulating, even singing perhaps. He is said to have been a gifted tenor who understood music thoroughly. In the process of literary creation his physical functions, such as hearing, sight and even smell, would be suppressed, while his mental activities were at their height. Inwardly he might have been in agony or ecstasy; outwardly he would have been oblivious of his environment, careless whether others thought him mad. He is known to have struggled ceaselessly for a meagre living. His lodgings were probably cramped, and the Pont St Louis would have been one of the nearest open spaces, easily accessible and yet quiet, for the river dulls noise of traffic.

If I frequented the hideous structure of the Pont St Louis for the sake of its associations with Joyce, it was for other reasons that I liked to stroll round the quays on the adjoining Ile St Louis. Apart from the quietness of the district, which is little bothered by traffic, it contains many handsome old buildings, mostly mansions of the seventeenth century, with artistic and literary associations. One day Francine took me to see her friend, Madame Louise Faure-Favier, a poetess, who lives in one of the few houses at the extreme western tip of the island on the Quai de Bourbon. From the impressive entrance we ascended a wide staircase, floor after floor right to the top. Madame Faure-Favier greeted Francine most affectionately, almost as if she were her grandchild. I was given a seat close to a large window outside which the topmost boughs of the trees grew right up from the quay below and intersected the panes with curious patterns. My chair, Francine told me, was called 'the poet's chair', and here our hostess was accustomed to let her poet-friends sit and gaze at the magnificent view. She herself often sat there too. I felt a little embarrassed at being thus accorded the status of a poet, for although I do sometimes string words together in traditional Chinese metres, I do not think of myself as a poet.

What a view it was! On the left some of the smaller carvings round the roof of Notre Dame were faintly recognisable while the top of the Place de Justice, of the Palais de l'Institut and of the Eiffel Tower rose behind one another in diminishing outline. On the right was the massive Hôtel de Ville, with the tower of St Jacques and the Palais du Louvre in the distance. The evening mists were already falling and had obscured and slightly changed the outline of the buildings. Those in the distance had acquired mystery. The Seine seemed to flow smoothly to where heaven and earth blend. I have seen many other rivers in big cities, but none with so many bridges. From the Eiffel Tower, where an even more extensive view can be got, the appearance of the river is like a rattlesnake with uniform ringed markings, the snake having swallowed the Ile de la Cité and the Ile St Louis, but not yet digested them. From Madame Faure-Favier's window the trees on the north bank, though still leafless, touched with purplish warmth, as though faintly glowing with soft inner fire. Golden specks of street lamps appeared as I watched, enhancing the feeling of there being a delightful miniature world down below. A single small willow tree on the shore below the Quai de l'Hôtel de Ville seemed to share my happiness. Its slender branches turned to gold, like a Chinese girl of an age gone by wearing a long-sleeved gown of yellow silk and swaying her body from side to side in excited

anticipation of some procession about to begin. Momentarily,
it seemed to me that the Seine was a huge ladder ascending to
heaven, placed outside the window especially for me. Involuntarily I stood up and made a movement towards the
window. This was taken as a sign that I wished to take leave,
and my hostess and Francine both rose too. Unable to explain
my complicated thoughts, I remarked jokingly that they had
just prevented a suicide; but the joke appeared to misfire, and
I contented myself with pointing out to Francine the little

willow tree, saying that I had often stood beside it, gazing at
the top row of windows in the houses on the Ile St Louis and
wishing I could see the view from one of them. Now my wish
had come true!

This was only one of many visits which I paid to the tranquil
quays of the Ile St Louis. I enjoyed watching the fishermen on
the Quai de Bourbon and the little fleet of boats, neither
Chinese nor English in shape and mostly painted green and
blue with strips of red, moored to the lower embankment near
the gracefully-arched Pont Marie. They resembled the enormous leaves of some strange waterplant.

One afternoon I was again on the island. I had been round
the quays many a time, but till now I had never walked through

the only street, the rue St. Louis en l'Ile. It is a very straight
and narrow street—quiet, unassuming, even provincial; it
lacks the sophisticated air of some of the old narrow streets and
lanes on the Left Bank. There was hardly any pavement on
either side; people seemed to walk down the middle of the
street and I even saw a group of youngsters playing some sort
of game in the roadway. Incredible as it may seem, there
appeared to be no vehicles at all. There were a few shops, but
very small ones, chiefly for provisions and tobacco. I went into
the church of St Louis and found there many fine wood-
carvings and small statues; they looked old, but were in
beautiful condition. I then looked carefully at the outside of the
Hôtel Lambert, said to have been built by Le Vau in 1640 with
decorations by Le Brun and Lesueur, for I had read long
descriptions of its fine interior. But it was not open to the public.

From there I returned to the riverside and leant on the
parapet not far from the little narrow bridge called Passerelle.
It had already been raining for a while, though not heavily. The
trees sheltered me, but one or two big drops of water made
me uncomfortable when they ran down my neck. The sound of
the raindrops touching the leaves was faintly and pleasantly
audible. The raindrops appeared to jump up from the surface
rather than fall on it.

Now, on the eastern tip of the Ile St Louis, the meaning
and feeling of Jules Supervielles' poem 'La Goutte de Pluie',
which the poet had once recited to me, became clear. I thought
of the centuries-old Chinese phrase, '*Tsan hai yi hsiu*', 'a grain of
rice in the blue sea'. The phrase has been used and interpreted
in many ways. Its chief meaning is the suggestion that man is
relatively but a grain of rice in a wide sea, having no great
importance, but a certain usefulness. It is a traditional Chinese
doctrine that man should subdue his self-importance and play
only his appointed part in the eternal round. I am a grain of
rice in the blue sea, but my brief stay in Paris, particularly this
moment of it by the little Passerelle bridge, became the raindrop
that I saw on the Seine—*un fragile souvenir*—which I would
return to look for some other day.

Looking upwards, my eyes were suddenly bewitched by a
rainbow apparently only a few yards off. I felt I could almost
touch it. The rain had stopped some time ago; the sun had
broken through again, though rather feebly, for it was low in

the west, but the light was bright enough to illuminate the scene through the thin and tinted veil of mist. The mist was something to be thankful for, since it softened the lines of factory chimneys and hid other ugly features, such as the uninteresting roofs of the Halle aux Vins on the Quai St Bernard. Curiously enough, one end of the rainbow seemed to be invisibly connected with those roofs, while the other end faded away beyond the Pont d'Austerlitz.

In ancient China the rainbow symbolised a heavenly dragon stretching its head down to drink. An old Chinese book entitled *Yi Yuan* records that when a certain Hsieh Yuan of the Chinling district saw a rainbow coming to drink in his water tanks and wine barrels, he hastened to open all his other barrels and poured them out for the heavenly visitor. The more he poured, the quicker it drank up everything. When its thirst was satisfied, the rainbow—or dragon—tossed out of its mouth masses of gold pieces and so filled up the barrels again, as if returning a kindness. Mr Hsieh eventually became the richest person in the district. It occurred to me that if the French 'dragon' was behaving in the same way, there would be a good chance of a fight in the Halle aux Vins when the various proprietors met next morning!

Another Chinese interpretation of the rainbow is that it is the bridge of Heaven on which the immortals or angels walk. The following poem by Li Po (A.D. 701-62) exemplifies this:

> From the rocky cliff I gaze at Mount Sung-liao,
> Which appears to be standing in the blue sky.
> How can I get the five-coloured rainbow
> To make a long bridge up to Heaven?
> Immortals, if you love me,
> Beckon to me with your hands!

Such a rough translation cannot convey the force and imagination of the Chinese lines. The beauty of that evening rainbow over the Seine inspired me too to compose a poem, though in a somewhat different mood:

> The rain is tired and the sun reappears;
> In the air hangs a colourful rainbow!
> Is it really the Immortals' idea
> To invite me for a stroll in Heaven?
> Li Po should not feel jealous;
> Today is different from the past.
> I cannot compete with Chuangtze in happy excursions,
> For I am a silent traveller with bad hearing.
> What I love is in the human world
> In the evening light of Paris!

巴 所 行 逍 今 太 邀 豈 懸 雨
黎 戀 者 遙 昔 白 我 真 空 倦
夕 在 啞 邐 各 其 遊 仙 掛 日
照 人 又 跎 不 無 鶩 人 彩 再
中 去 聾 子 同 忌 穹 意 虹 出

I crossed the road and made once more for the centre of the islands. A sudden whim assailed me when I remembered Baudelaire's lines:

> *L'aurore grelattante en robe rose et verte*
> *S'avancait lentement sur la Seine déserte.*

> The glittering dawn, in robe of red and green,
> Moving slowly, on the Seine was seen.

Could I find a top room for the night so that I could watch the dawn break? I managed to make the proprietor of a small hotel understand me, but, alas, there was no room in the inn.

XXVIII

The Catacombs of Paris

WHEN I was first told about 'the Catacombs of Paris',
I thought they sounded romantic, though I had no real idea
what they were. None of my friends had visited them, so they
could tell me nothing. Finally, Joan Hendry and I decided to
go to see them together as an adventure.

We met one afternoon at the Place Denfert-Rochereau and
immediately joined the large crowd waiting outside a wooden

gate. More and more people came. Eventually, long after
2 p.m., the time announced for opening, the gate was unlocked
and we all surged through. Inside I noticed that, in addition to

paying the entrance fee, everyone bought a candle and a piece of wood. So we followed their example.

After walking along the corridor, we came to some narrow spiral stairs, and climbed down step by step, endlessly as it seemed. It gave me a curious sensation—not exactly fearful nor yet cheerful, but rather a sense of excitement, as if we were about to pass through the centre of the earth and emerge in another hemisphere. The small electric lights at each turn of the spiral did not shed their light very far, and at certain corners it was almost pitch dark.

I was surprised at there being no official guide with us. The situation reminded me a little of my visit to the Kent Cavern, near Torquay, but there we had a guide who would suddenly switch off the small lights placed here and there among the rocks, causing all the ladies in the party to scream terribly, for we were far below the level of the beach and unable to see a thing. I also remembered the guide in the Cheddar Caves, whose words never ceased to flow for a single moment.

My companion looked cheerful and expectant, ready for the next move. We were now nearing the mouth of a pitch-dark tunnel. Suddenly we saw for a second, in the far, far distance, a small twinkling light. We remembered the candles in our hands and hurriedly lit them. We two found ourselves the leaders of a long troop, creeping through the tunnel hidden from the light of day. The absolute darkness ahead of us made me feel like a great adventurer and explorer backed by a long retinue of followers. I felt brave and suddenly grown young, too, seeing myself as Tom Sawyer taking his girl with a lighted candle in hand and creeping on and on through the deep caves, along the great Mississipi River. I glanced at my companion, who smiled back at me as if she shared my thoughts.

The tunnel was very long and narrow. There was just room for two to squeeze along abreast without rubbing against the stone walls on either side. The rough, pebbly surface of the ground made the going harder, but we resolutely pressed on.

At last we reached the end of the tunnel, and a black arrow on the wall told us to turn left. On the arrow was written the name of the Paris street beneath which we were walking. We then turned into another long tunnel, similar in every way to the first except that it seemed even longer and darker. When it came at length to an end, yet another arrow indicated to us that we should turn to the right and pass through a third tunnel. After this came yet another. In the first tunnel I heard cheerful remarks and laughter. In the second we walked in dead silence. In the third my ears were disturbed at times by sighs and groans. I myself was on the verge of collapse; all chivalry had drained out of me—except for a last faint impulse that prompted me to say to my companion that I would not mind going back. But that was not possible. There was apparently no method of ventilation in the walls; the air had become damper and closer from our breathing. And this was not the end, perhaps it was little more than the beginning! After another three or four turnings I noticed that we had been walking for nearly half an hour without having any idea of our goal.

Fortunately, something happened to rescue us all from total collapse. Another group of people appeared on the other side of some iron railings which were barring the mouth of a particularly big cave. There seemed to be several young-sters among them, one of whom shouted mockingly at us through the gaps in the railings, immediately cheer-ing us up with his merry laugh. My companion said  he was asking whether we had lost our way. We all felt happier for we knew that we were not far from the end of our journey.

Presently we joined the others in one of a series of cut-out galleries. I raised my candle to look round the cave and read the name "Porte Mahon" inscribed on the wall. I also noticed a number of miniature carvings on the stone inside the cave. Someone remarked that these had been done by an old soldier, once a caretaker here, who for five years had spent his leisure hours in carving out of the stone a plan of Porte Mahon, where he had been a prisoner for some years. What an undertaking! Somewhere near this cave there were said to be some enormous fragments of stone nicely balanced on a point, in which equilibrium they have remained for more than two centuries. I did not linger to look for these interesting boulders, for I had no wish to be left behind there. I fear I lack the explorer's temperament.

The 'Catacombs of Paris' were now close at hand. Here and there the wall stone had been polished and engraved with religious and philosophical reflections on life and death. An altar with a cross came into sight, but vanished again into the darkness as we passed it. Finally, we came to walls lined with human skulls and bones, mostly thigh bones, piled neatly upon one another. Thousands upon thousands of skeletons must have gone to the building of those interminable walls.

The walls were very high, almost reaching the roof of the tunnel, and each was built in the same neat pattern—a row of skulls alternating with a row of thigh bones. In the middle was a design somewhat like the arrangement of a skull and cross bones on the flag of a pirate ship. I felt uncomfortable among all these human remains and tried not to think at all, but simply to follow the crowd as it moved on. My companion had not much to say; nor had I. Suddenly a burst of laughter broke from a small group of youngsters who were holding their burning candles beneath some of the skulls as if to try whether they would burn. I was at once jolted into remembering my nationality. I have been living away from China for many years and have acquired many Western habits, but my early upbringing in ancestor worship has not entirely left me. Worshipping one's ancestors is not a bad practice; there is nothing silly in according one's forbears due respect. To hold a lighted candle under skulls is a bad joke. Who knew whether those very skulls did not belong to the youngsters' own long-deceased ancestors?

It took us almost twenty minutes to reach the end of the walls of bones. We were moving slower than before. Someone remarked that among those thousands of skulls and bones were the remains of Rabelais, Mirabeau, Madame de Pompadour, the Duc d'Orléans, Marat and many other famous people. Our candles had burnt low and now flickered out just as we reached a much bigger circular space, a sort of hall, with a few steps leading up to a door. The door was shut, and the key was missing. We were all prisoners inside; some sat down on the only bench and the rest stood silently waiting. Someone speculated on whether there was a lift on the other side of the door to take us all up to ground-level; the possibility cheered us for a moment.

But there was no lift. We had to climb as many spiral steps as we had descended in the first instance. Eventually we emerged into the street: it was the little Passage Dareau, off the Avenue du Parc Montsouris. The blazing sun dazzled our eyes. My

companion and I were both too much out of breath to speak. My first contact with the fresh air gave me an indescribable sensation of relief. Then we noticed that our shoes and the ends of my trousers were white with lime and dust. A drink at a café tasted good. We then set off to walk in the Parc Montsouris, though our preoccupation with the meaning of all that we had seen in the Catacombs had left us still in a state of bewilderment. To bring our thoughts back to earth, we visited the meteorological observatory; we watched the children riding on rocking horses; we walked down a hill to the lakeside. The nodding heads of the yellow daffodils blown by the willow wind in the twilight helped to clear my mind. I saw my companion on to her bus and found my own way back by Métro.

My friend Monsieur François Secret, a French scholar specialising in French literature, who has spent a number of years teaching in Indo-China and has a charming Indo-Chinese wife whose wonderful cooking I have tasted, later told me many things about the 'Catacombs of Paris'. They were formerly disused quarries, and were converted into a necropolis in 1789, when the remains of about five million persons from several old cemeteries, together with the bodies of many of the victims of the Revolution, were deposited there. The Catacombs cover an area of 150 acres. From those ancient quarries

s

had come much material for building the houses on the south side of the Seine. They were then abandoned and became a source of danger to pedestrians, who could easily fall into them, and also provided hide-outs for undesirable characters. It was Monsieur Le Noir, Lieutenant-General of Police, who originated the idea of converting the disused quarries into catacombs. The immense work of construction to render them fit to receive human remains started in 1777. They were blessed and consecrated on April 7th, 1786, and the entire work was finished in 1790.

I was also told that on the very day when the construction was begun the ground beneath a house in the rue d'Enfer suddenly collapsed and the building was swallowed up into a pit some ninety feet deep. I heard too an amusing story about two students from the Sorbonne who managed to get shut up inside the Catacombs shortly before the last war. Nobody knew when and how they had entered. One theory was that they had been following a crowd through the Catacombs, but had strayed into a different tunnel and so had not come out with the rest. Others thought they might have entered the Catacombs through a secret exit which they had found underneath their lodgings, for there are over seventy different exits from the underground passages. A housewife hearing noises underneath her floors did not suspect that the human remains had come alive, but thought rather of rats. She became alarmed when the noise increased and she was not the only one to hear it; many of her neighbours, whose houses were situated above the underground passages, heard it too. The police were informed. The rumour soon got about that espionage was afoot or even that an invasion had started. A whole regiment of soldiers in addition to a large company of police was assembled to guard the exits while further contingents entered the Catacombs in readiness for battle. After a long while the soldiers and police emerged, followed by two smiling students, who announced that they had had a great fun in exploring the underground passages in complete darkness.

In my younger days a well-known Chinese essay by one of our greatest nature-poets, T'ao Yuan-ming, of the fourth century, caught my imagination. It is called '*T'ao-hua-yuan*', 'Peach-blossom Fountain'. It describes a fisherman who, as he fished, let his boat drift till suddenly he found himself amid a dense grove of peach trees in full bloom. He went ashore and walked through the peach grove; then, wandering into a cave, he eventually came out into a different world, where all the people were dressed in the style of the Ch'in Dynasty (third century B.C.), some 600 or 700 years before. They talked about the events of those days and did not understand the fisherman's conversation. They entertained him hospitably for months, but eventually, in response to his earnest pleading, let him return. As he went back the fisherman marked the roads, but he could never find the peach grove again. Many have followed the fisherman's route, but to this day nobody has found that country again. This essay has turned many Chinese men of letters into seekers after utopias. I took a particular interest in it, for the poet happened to have been born in the town where I myself came into the world. I can recite the essay to this day. I have long given up my search for a utopia, and I hardly think the 'Catacombs of Paris' will lead anyone into an underground utopia as the peach grove led T'ao Yuan-ming's fisherman into another age.

XXIX

Lingering in the Twilight

O N E Sunday early in April Madeleine Chambert, with her younger daughter Nicole and her son Gerard, took me by car to the Palace of Fontainebleau. The rain was falling like a barrier of silver strings, but on we sped. There were few cars on the wide road, along which the great Emperor Napoleon, I was told, used to drive in his gilded carriage with thousands of guards preceding and following him. A glorious pageantry has long passed, to be repeated no more. Perhaps some of the oldest trees on the roadside would have something to tell about what they had witnessed in the past, I thought, but none of them could have heeded us, for we passed them by too quickly. I was oppressed by a sense of *change*.

It was still raining when we reached the main entrance to the palace, but only slightly. We walked straight through the spacious courtyard to the main doorway where the famous horseshoe stairs lie. A good many visitors were already there, gazing round in an absorbed, dreamy way. Probably they were trying, as I was, to visualise how Napoleon reviewed his Guards before marching with them towards Paris to become Emperor. Undoubtedly they were also, like me, trying to imagine where Napoleon stood when he bade farewell to his generals before going into exile.

Through Madeleine's official status, a special guide was assigned to us. He tried to speak slowly for my benefit, but despite this most of his explanations were beyond my understanding. The table on which Napoleon signed his abdication was pointed out to me in the Salon Rouge. The apartments of the Reines Blanches interested me more. The guide said that they were so called because they were reserved for the widows of kings of France, whose custom it was to dress in white. White is the mourning colour in China; I did not know it was also so for the French Royal Family.

It was also in these apartments of the Reines Blanches that

Pope Pius VII was kept prisoner by Napoleon for eighteen months because he would not give his consent to the Emperor's divorce from Josephine. This reminded me of the following passage that I read in an English popular guide-book:

The incidents of this captivity are well worth reading before paying the visit to Fontainebleau, though most of the guides taking parties through the Palace make a point of narrating them, not forgetting the famous interview during which, it is said, the Emperor lost his temper to such an extent as to box the ears of the Pope because he refused to sign away the States of the Church.

Had I not been living outside China for so long, it would have been difficult for me to conceive how an emperor could have been prohibited from doing anything whatever at will, for throughout the whole history of China emperors automatically held absolute power. The people of China have long been under the autocratic control of a single man; even some of our modern rulers, disguised as democratic leaders, have tried to act as if they were emperors. Napoleon, though the most powerful person in Europe at the time, did not have things all his own way!

We did not stay long in any of the rooms, for it was already late in the afternoon when we arrived. At such a pace, which could have been described by the Chinese saying, 'Pao-ma-kuan-hua', 'looking at flowers from a galloping horse', all the rooms looked much the same—coloured, gilded, ornate, impersonal. I found it impossible to think of them as ever having been *lived in*.

The last room we visited was the Galerie des Assiettes, in which were set in oak panels 128 porcelain plaques, each bearing a painted view of one of the palaces of the Kings of France. This unusual set of plaques was made at Sèvres to the order of Louis Philippe. I examined them carefully and searched for some distinctive mark on any of the panels. My friends thought I was interested in the Sèvres porcelain; they could not have realised that I had recalled the following story described in Julius M. Price's book, *My Bohemian Days in Paris*, published in 1913:

. . . I had one of the most curious adventures of my life. It happened in Fontainebleau, where I had gone to spend a week, having obtained permission to sketch in the Palace. . . . One wet afternoon when there were hardly any visitors about I was strolling through one of the rooms when I noticed something peculiar in a panel of the wainscoting. On nearer examination I discovered it was a sort of metal catch or lock, and that the panel itself was a secret door. My curiosity was not unnaturally aroused. I tried it and found that it opened inward, and led into a dark, narrow corridor. The spirit of adventure was strong within me and I did not hesitate. Making sure I was unobserved, I went in and pulled the panel to after me. I then discovered that the passage led to a large private suite of rooms which had evidently not been visited for years, judging from the thick coating of dust and the cobwebs everywhere.

On all sides were magnificent old furniture and faded hangings, which gave an uncanny, ghostly look to the place, which was heightened by the old world odour which pervaded the rooms. . . . Although not large, there seemed no end to the number of rooms which led from one to another, interminably as it seemed—with all manner of unexpected twists and turns; whilst now and again some dark corridor indicated still further surprises.

But I had no time that afternoon to pursue my explorations, as it was getting near dusk, and the time for closing the Palace, so I began to retrace my steps. I forgot to mention that as I came along I had noticed a very beautiful old clock of the eight-day description. I again stopped to admire it, and then passed on. Shortly after I was somewhat surprised to see another clock of precisely the same design; strange, I thought, as I went by it, that there should be two similar. A little farther, to my amazement, I came up to yet another exactly like the two previous ones; then it suddenly dawned on me that I had been walking in a circle, that there was only one clock after all, and that I had lost my way.

I stood aghast. In an instant it flashed through my mind that unless I could find my way back to the secret door the chances of any one coming to my rescue were almost *nil*, for I was in a part of the vast building which was probably almost unknown. So I set about attempting to retrace my footsteps by means of the furniture and other objects that had attracted me as I had come along; but to no purpose, as I soon discovered. I could not remember the way back. All the windows looked out on gardens which were deserted. It was getting dark, and the Palace was now closed, so I could expect no help from outside, unless the attendant had noticed I had not left the building, and was looking for me.

With this hope in my mind, I started walking about rapidly and shouting at the top of my voice, "*Au secours.*" The words echoed and re-echoed through the rooms with ghostly effect, but there was no response. I now began to get seriously alarmed; and had visions of a slow death by starvation. Time was passing, and it would soon be night, so I sat down on a bed to consider my position calmly, as I felt nothing was to be gained by losing my head. How long I sat there I don't remember, as I must have dozed off, I fancy; then I discovered it was now quite dark. Suddenly I heard footsteps on the gravelled walk outside, and the reflection of a light. Rushing to the nearest window I discovered, to my intense relief, that it was a watchman passing with a lantern. I frantically, by lighting a match and tapping vigorously, managed to attract his attention. . . .

I bawled out that I was shut in, and how I'd got where I was, and after a few minutes he understood me. Then, calling out to me to remain where I was, he hurried off. The time now seemed interminable; but at length I heard, to my joy, footsteps resounding through the apartments, and a little group of officials appeared. I was saved. . . .

This story had obsessed me for some time after I read it: how could I help thinking of it now that I was on the very spot? I had not considered what I should do if I found the secret door. Perhaps it was fortunate that I was called away before I could make a discovery.

We had missed out many rooms, including even the Chinese Museum on the west side of the Cour de la Fontaine, for I thought the exhibits there could not be finer than in the Museums of Cernuschi and Guimet. The huge gilded rooms had become a little oppressive, and I was glad when Madeleine expressed our thanks to the guide and led us out on to the terrace at the back of the Palace. The fresh air was most acceptable. The rain had stopped, though the sun had not reappeared. The heavy, lowering clouds had transformed the afternoon into a sort of twilight, neither dull nor bright, yet I felt that there was an enduring quality about it.

Before the terrace was a wide stretch of water with a white fountain in it, slightly to the right, towards the Jardin Anglais. A canal to the east of the palace was pointed out to me, but its shape and course faded mysteriously into the mist left by the rain. The view over the lake was wide, harmonious, and tranquil. Many people, old and young, were bending over the parapets to watch something in the water with peculiar interest, but their chatter and laughter did not seem to disturb the air, but rather enhanced its tranquillity. As we proceeded towards the parapets, a vision of the past suddenly possessed my mind. There must have been many an occasion in the days of the Empire when the French kings and queens came out on to this same terrace with their princes, princesses and nobles, watched the water with similar interest and enthusiasm, and laughed and chattered to one another. I felt that I was actually taking part in one of these royal occasions. The daylight was now so dim that the dresses of the onlookers might well have been of silk, brocade and gold: there were enough sparkles and spots of brilliant colour here and there to sustain the illusion. Suddenly a baby burst out crying and shattered my vision, bringing me back to my own time. But a voice seemed to ring in my ears still saying: "Man is accidental and changeable, but the Palace and the Terrace of Fontainebleau will remain the same."

When we in turn leaned over the parapet, I saw to my surprise and joy countless carp of varying sizes swimming swiftly and snapping at bread-crumbs thrown by our fellow visitors. Nicole pointed out to me a large carp which never missed a catch, despite its size. Gerard moved to and fro pointing and crying, "*Le gros poisson ici!*" and "*Le gros poisson là.*" He had plenty to say to his sister and mother, but his quick, short words in French were unintelligible to my ears. Madeleine smiled and nodded to her happy children. Mothers derive extraordinary satisfaction from such occasions. And I too derived pleasure from her satisfaction.

A swan, a mere white dot in the distance looking like a tiny ornament of carved white jade, detached itself from the fountain and glided towards us. It wanted a share of the crumbs. What a beautiful creature it seemed, with its stately motions, a spot of ideal white lighting up the whole scene. But when it approached the parapet, it hissed angrily on missing a mouthful, and tried to scare the carp away. It had no success, for the carp had the advantage of being able to place its wide mouth close to the surface of the water so as to gobble up the crumbs easily and quickly before the swan could lower its head by curving its long neck. Never before had I seen a lovely creature betray so much clumsiness and ineptitude. The swan does not seem to be gifted by Nature with sharp eyesight, for it cannot catch crumbs in the air as seagulls, for instance, do. The jet-black, bead-like eyes placed almost in the centre of the white face helped to make this swan look fierce, and yet also pathetic because of the constancy with which it missed the food. I must say that this was the first time I had witnessed a quarrel between wings and fins. It seemed rather an improbable situation that a fish and a bird should come to blows over food. They would hardly find an opportunity to fight one another, for the one is deep in the water and the other always above it. Yet here they were. Although the carp was not actually

Carp at Fontainebleau

deprived of its food by the presence of the swan, the latter's arrival and its continued effort undoubtedly disturbed the tranquillity of the scene, for the flapping of the swan's feet in the water was scattering the fishes in all directions. Eventually the swan gave up the struggle and glided away, to look lovely once more.

The carp is a fish with many pleasant associations for a Chinese. It is a frequent motif in Chinese works of art, such as ancient bronze mirrors, carved jade, agate and wood, for it symbolises 'success' or 'plenty'. When a friend presented Confucius with a pair of carp at the time of his son's birth some 2,500 years ago, the sage named the boy after the fish. The carp is also a favourite subject for Chinese to paint. In the Boston Museum of Fine Art there is a masterpiece by an unknown artist of the twelfth century depicting two carp. The thought of painting carp made my hand itch, and I began to make some rough sketches, meditating as I did so upon this remarkable fish.

There are about 1,500 species of carp in the world, and the well-known Chinese goldfish is one of them. Certain carp have a long life; some of the carp at Fontainebleau are said to have been there for more than 100 years; no doubt those which were still there could not distinguish us who fed them from the kings, queens, princes and princesses of former days. I presume they are 'protected', though if so the protection does not prevent their being caught on special occasions, for when King George VI paid a state visit to France, the French President, Monsieur Auriol, gave a banquet which included a dish of carp from the lake of Fontainebleau.

I should be interested to know if the French have ways of cooking this fish peculiar to their cuisine. The Chinese have many ways that I have not come across in the West. Carp are plentiful in most of the rivers of China, those in the Huang-ho or Yellow River being famous for their gastronomic qualities. Huang-ho carp can be very big and heavy; in my boyhood I saw specimens weighing eighty or ninety pounds and more than five feet long. A month or two before the New Year Festival numbers of these huge carp would be caught and carried considerable distances for sale. My native city, Kiukiang, is on the Yangtse River, a long way from the Huang-ho, yet my family (a very big one, with forty members living at the time) was able to buy several hundred pounds of Huango-ho carp for preserving. In my book, *A Chinese Childhood*, I wrote:

The method of preserving fish was more or less the same [as that of preserving pork]. . . . I remember that at the end of the first stage of preserving the pork my uncle would buy about twenty fish for preserving. All the young girls in the house helped to wash them. Then the men-servants cut each fish [along the spine] into two pieces, salted it, and continued as with the pork. (They were then dried in the sun for days.) The best fish looked reddish pink after being steamed, and, like the pork, had to be not too salt. I was particularly addicted to this preserved fish, which I liked cut into half-inch cubes and cooked with small pieces of pork of the same size which had previously been lightly boiled with Chinese soya sauce; a few leaves of garlic should be added too. My grandmother made this dish herself sometimes and it tasted extremely good. My fondness for this dish earned me the nickname 'Carp-eater' when each New Year came round.

It makes my mouth water to think of that dish, and I have not tasted it for twenty years! The preserved fish was, of course, not solely for use during the New Year Festival; salted carp would form part of our diet for months afterwards. Some families used to preserve enough fish to last the whole year round. There are also many delicious ways of cooking fresh carp; one which I specially like is to stew it in chicken broth with fresh soya-bean curd and young bamboo shoots.

My meditation on the subject of how to cook carp had deprived me of many happy moments in watching my young friends' happiness. The grey and blackish clouds had gathered more of their kinsfolk and so darkened the sky that only the mouths of the carp opening and shutting at the surface of the water were visible. This struck me as an original idea for a painting, and I made a sketch note. We then left the terrace and walked through the alley from La Porte Dorée to our car. On our way I noticed the Primaticcio grotto of the Jardin des Pins, with its giants emerging from a rocky background, though the dim light prevented my seeing them clearly.

The chauffeur received us with a beaming smile: he had had a good idea. He told Madeleine that in 1914, when he was in the Army, he had camped in the Forest of Fontainebleau, and he suggested taking us now to the site of the camp. Gérard and Nicole were excited at the proposal, and I was glad of the chance to see something of the forest. It is, I had heard, one of the most extensive in France, sixty-three miles in circumference and over 42,000 acres in extent. I had also heard of the interesting Gorge of Franchard; of the Pharamond, the oldest tree in the forest; the Weeping Rock; and the Brigands' Cave. It goes without saying that, being an artist, I have read long ago the essays which R. L. Stevenson wrote on the painters of Fontainebleau and also the article on the Fontainebleau Schools by Thackeray. At that moment I did not mind where we went so long as I could wander in the forest for a while. We should not have much time before dusk fell.

We soon left the main road and moved, rather joltingly, along a side track among many tall, rather slender trees— chiefly young pines and birches. The latter were not yet in full leaf, but those young leaves which had already come out, scattered among the tiny twigs on the upper branches, formed patterns against the cloudy sky. Thousands of small yellow *jonquilles*, the wild daffodils of France, gave us a smiling greeting.

On and on we went. I was sitting behind the chauffeur and had only a sidelong view of his face, but I could tell that he was beaming with joy at being back in the forest again, for he kept tilting his head and producing little sounds expressive of pleasure. The various scenes *en route* must have stirred up memories. I gathered that he had not been back here since his regiment left the forest for the Front in 1915.

On reaching a glade between many lofty pines, we alighted and set off on foot along a narrow footpath. Before entering the glade, I turned to look back. A wide, level space stretched away for miles. Three French soldiers sitting under a huge oak in the distance indicated that there must still be an Army camp in this vicinity. The chauffeur knew his way and paid no heed to the appearance of the three men in uniform. He led us away confidently.

The footpath was like any other winding woodland path, and we at last came to the rocky part of the forest. Many big rocks lay around in the attractive disorder of Nature. As I looked about from the top of one large rock, I was astonished to hear a cock crow and some hens cluck in a manner suggestive of fear and pursuit. The next moment I realised that Gérard was imitating a cock on one rock and Madeleine and Nicole hens on another. They were great mimics, I was told, and now their mimicry had for a moment really deceived me, though it had puzzled me to understand how fowls could have found their way here, for there was no farmhouse in the vicinity. My friends had succeeded in making me feel like a chaser of fowls! What fun to have had this lively encounter among all those cold-looking rocks interspersed with a few oaks, beeches and hornbeams under the grey, twilit sky!

We had left a pine grove behind, and now beyond it I could see another, and another, and so on all round the borders of the forest. As far as I could judge in the fading light, the trees, apart from the pine groves, were mostly hornbeam, with a few oaks and beeches. I have read that the hornbeam is indigenous to the south-east and east of England, though it is a native of Europe and Asia Minor. Epping Forest outside London is said to contain a larger number of hornbeam than of any other tree. It is 'the hardest, heaviest, and toughest' of all English woods and thrives in any good loam and is at home on chalky soils. Perhaps for these reasons the hornbeam abounded in the Forest of Fontainebleau as well. The rocks on which we were standing were limestone and the soil beneath nothing but chalk.

The Forest of Fontainebleau has attracted many great artists in the past to live in its heart, and there must be many artists of the present day who have come to live there, too. Its main attractions are its varied scenery and great diversity of trees. I can readily understand those who liked to live near this splendid forest, for I am a great lover of trees myself. The hornbeam is certainly a very handsome tree when full-grown. Its flowers are unisexual, produced on the same tree, and it blossoms profusely in the late spring. It is especially beautiful in summer when laden with pendent fruit clusters, and is also lovely to look at when its foliage turns yellow in autumn. Although it was now neither summer nor autumn, those I could see around us were beautiful in their way, with their almost bare twigs and branches interlacing in intriguing patterns and dotted with tiny young leaves, some against the light and some opaque and dull.

A few minutes later the excited barking of several dogs chasing rabbits rent the air. It took me back in a flash to a day when I was standing on a rock on the Yorkshire moors listening to the approach of some English huntsmen on horseback, followed by a large pack of hounds. Now the barking changed; it was like an excited terrier chasing after badgers and rabbits.

But no! Gérard was at his tricks again! He is such a gay little
fellow of twelve that he cannot help enlivening any company
among whom he finds himself.

Gérard's action set me thinking again. Badgers are not the
sort of creatures we should have expected to find in our wanderings through the woods, but I was surprised that we did not see
a single rabbit. That there were hardly any birds was not really
strange, because although the forest is so big, it has few streams
and very little water of any kind. Birds do come, but they
seldom stay long. But even though the forest is dry there must
be *some* rabbits. Nancy Mitford's story of the beginning of the
rabbit epidemic can hardly account for them all. In one of her
articles under the title '*A la Campagne*' she told how Dr Armand-
Delille had grieved over the damage done by Peter Rabbit to
his young plantation in the Province of Eure et Loire and had
injected him with myxomatosis. Peter soon died of the disease,
but not before he had infected his kinsfolk; even distant relations in Europe and Asia succumbed. This made Armand-
Delille very unpopular, for the wild rabbit, or *garenne*, is a
staple article of diet among the French country people. The
breeders of tame rabbits had to inoculate all their beasts every
six months, and that cost money. The
fur trade became desperately short of
skins. The farmers may have felt happy
about their crops, but French farmers
are also hunters, and as such they were
deprived of *la chasse*. Miss Mitford made
the following interesting comment;

The Americans have very
kindly suggested lending and
leasing some of their rabbits,
which are immune from myxomatosis. But American rabbits
are as large as lions and as
fierce as tigers. In fact, to read
the French papers on the
subject, one would suppose
that skyscrapers were invented
to take the Americans as far away as possible from their rabbits.
These ravaging rodents have been refused with thanks.

Miss Mitford's wit eased her readers' minds about the horror
caused by Dr Armand-Delille's ill-considered act. I have

recently seen American rabbits in the deserts of Arizona, Utah and New Mexico. They are called jack rabbits there and are three or four times Peter's size. I met a number of them when driving through the Death Valley and the Painted Desert. Sometimes I walked in the sage brush and encountered them behind low bushes. They did not hide or run away at my approach. Surely if rabbits could live in so dry a place as a desert, they could certainly find living quarters in the Forest of Fontainebleau.

Now the dusk was giving us warning of approaching night by covering up the twigs and branches of the trees with a grey veil of mist and making them more obscure than ever. We could not linger any longer. On our way back to the car, the chauffeur had a lot to say to Madeleine. He described the forest's variety of aspect, never a moment alike from dawn to dusk or from season to season. He also dwelt especially upon warm summer nights under the moon, and upon the marvellous tints of autumn. I could not follow his words except through Madeleine's occasional interpretations, but I felt the intensity of his mood from the gestures of his shoulders, eyebrows and hands. He was full of nostalgic thoughts, yet he mentioned not a single word about his life as a soldier there. Soldiering is one kind of life; it is necessary, and, whether we like it or not, it is imposed on very many of us for a period in our lifetime. But the love of nature is innate in all of us from the beginning of our life till death. Had it not been for the approach of nightfall, the chauffeur would have liked to linger in this lovely forest as much as we should. His share in our pleasure was an added joy on our trip. Many hired drivers would have been bored, if not annoyed, by our lingering so long at that time of the day.

On leaving the forest, we stopped at a café in Moret for a drink. Moret is a picturesque old town by the Loing River and is well known in the art world, many artists having painted its quaint, old-world houses and streets. We strolled along the main street and looked at the age-battered city gate. The wheel of a water-mill lay broken in the mud on one side of the river; on the other a young woman was fishing from the bank, late though it was. Nothing moved. The reflection in the water of the curiously-shaped houses and the bridge looked like a black-and-white drawing, or, to be exact, a Whistler etching.

A few years ago Madeleine had met an elderly gentleman, a poet and historian, who lived in this ancient corner of the world. She wanted me to meet him now, for she thought he would have many interesting anecdotes to tell about the place. But he was not to be found, nor was his name known to any of the present inhabitants whom we asked. She was astonished, and remarked with a sigh that this old town had seen the passing of so many queer people without undergoing the slightest change itself. We returned to the car and drove on. The twilight still lingered with us until we reached Paris and the blazing neon lights of the Avenue de l'Opéra.

XXX

Un Revenant Étranger

IN the train on the way to Versailles my companion and I
agreed not to go inside the palace, but to confine our attention
to the gardens, for we had both seen the inside before.

Only three months previously two of my friends, Mr Root
and Mr Yung, came to stay in Versailles for a week's holiday,
asked me to lunch and afterwards took me to the palace. It was
a rainy Sunday in January. The heavy, mist-clad tree groups
and the wide expanses around the palace buildings intrigued
me, and I strayed away from the party. But my friend, disliking the rain, called me back and took me indoors. Sunday is
a free day for visitors and the crowd inside was indescribable,
despite the season. We followed a series of guides, sometimes
close by, sometimes at a distance, though their explanations
meant little to me, since I could not catch more than two or
three consecutive French words that I understood. Nor was the
rest of the crowd particularly attentive. While the guide was
carefully relating stories and legends to us, many of them talked
and even giggled, and strayed away. The visitors of today must
be very different from those who visited the palace when it was
first opened to the public after the great Exhibition of 1878.
Then the memories of many royal residents would have been
fresh in minds, and the visitors would have listened to the
guides with much more sympathy and attention. Now we all
seemed rather vague about what happened in the Palace of
Versailles some hundred years or more ago; and the rooms
looked empty and striking only on account of their size and
elaborate decorations.

The tour included the Chapel, the Hercules Room, the
Salon de l'Abondance, the Venus Room, the Diana Room,
the Mars Room, the Mercury Room, the Apollo Room
and then the Galérie des Glaces, the Council Room, the
Bedroom of Louis XIV, the Oeil de Bœuf, the Private
Apartments of Marie Antoinette, the Marble Staircases and

The Pond in Front of the Hameaun at Versailles

many other rooms. My eyes were dazzled by the decorative, gilded ceilings, the gilded walls and furniture, and above all by the spaciousness of the rooms and corridors. I was particularly impressed by the Galérie des Glaces, an enormous hall 240 feet long and thirty feet wide, but the huge mirrors on the walls, put almost side by side, puzzled me. They were intended, I learnt, to *increase* the spaciousness of the hall. But why should the architect, with any amount of ground at his disposal when he planned the palace, have wished to make this hall *appear* larger than it is? Why not simply have designed a bigger hall? But perhaps the creation of this mirrored hall has served as an inspiration to modern architects. I have seen several rooms in big New York hotels in which a similar device has been used. Everything in New York is on a large scale, but its land is limited.

I related all this to my companion in the train. I also described the big, oval-shaped table in the palace, at which the signing took place of the Treaty of Peace between the Allies and Germany on June 28th, 1919. I was only a youngster then. Now I have lived through the Second World War, but where and when will another treaty of peace for all the world be signed? I doubt if there will be any table for the coming generations to see. My companion nodded in approval. But she seemed to hold a different point of view when I began to speak of Marie-Antoinette.

In Paris the name of Marie-Antoinette came to our ears wherever we went. She was the most talked-about woman in the history of Paris. Many people thought her greatly to blame for the upheaval of the Revolution, for she was a stupid woman and disliked the French, though she was their Queen. But I felt it was futile to judge whether her conduct was good or bad, for the causes of Revolution were already deep-rooted before Louis XVI came to the throne. How could the strong tide that was surging in be checked without any remedy to serve as a solid dyke? My companion looked at me incredulously.

Later she laughed when I related the story I read in Sir Osbert Sitwell's book, *Great Morning*. The author once opened a drawer in a cabinet on the stairs at Renishaw and found a small envelope with the following words written on it:

A lock of Marie-Antoinette's hair, cut from her head ten minutes after execution.

T

He was puzzled, thinking how odd it was that so interesting a relic should have been left about, just anywhere, in that manner. Later he recollected that over thirty years before his friend Sir Edwin Lutyens had seized a bit of the stuffing from a newly-broken sofa cover and placed it in an envelope after having twisted round it a bit of ribbon, writing the above words on the outside, and then putting it into the drawer, remarking to Sir Osbert as he did so: 'Nobody's likely to find that for a long time, and by then it will have become real.' Unfortunately, the joke had misfired.

I had not been living up to my name at that moment, but I had to say something, for my companion was an even more silent traveller than I, and I had not talked for days owing to my difficulty in learning French. It was only half-past eleven on a sunny morning of early April. Instead of the rainy mist which had enveloped the surroundings during my previous visit, a haze was being dispersed by the brilliant sun. We entered the palace yard, turned to the left of the statue of Louis XIV, and passed through a gate and a small hall to the Orangerie on the south. My companion knew something about the gardens already, and asked a stout guard to direct us to the Petit Trianon. The man, who had just come up from the garden, looked very hot and was carrying his uniform coat on his arm. He told us the way with a good-natured smile. My companion seemed bent upon seeing the Petit Trianon; I did not know why.

Presently we stood at the head of a flight of stone steps facing the Grand Canal, which stretched away, it seemed, to infinity. The sunny haze fused the distant objects, such as big groups of trees, into identical large blobs of greenish-grey on both sides of the long stretch of the Tapis Vert in the centre. There was an unusual stillness in the air. The movements of human figures in the distance or of small birds in flight were so small as almost to pass detection in the enormous expanse of garden. The stately and symmetrical plan emphasised the masterful mind of man: nature was under his command; trees had been carefully grouped and told to grow straight. The designer of this immense park, with its gardens and fountains and its many fine sculptures in bronze conceived a most wonderful vision.

On descending to the foot of the flight of steps, I moved round the edge of the Fountain of Latona and examined the different attitudes of the bronze frogs which spout water from their mouths towards the main statue of Latona, who was said to have transformed the Lycian peasants into frogs as a punishment for having refused her a drink of water. But why should a goddess, who ought surely to be above vindictiveness, take vengeance on a people indiscriminately? Of what use is it for us to condemn modern tyrants when goddesses have set such a bad example? There are similar legends to that of Latona in China, but the peasants are transformed into other animals than frogs. Perhaps Latona is responsible for the French habit of eating frogs!

We then walked slowly along the Tapis Vert on its north side towards the Grand Canal. The sun had risen higher and was inclining slightly towards the west. It had also dispersed the haze above the trees, leaving them exposed clearly to my eyes, though the distant view beyond the Grand Canal was still thickly veiled. Not even a gentle breeze could be detected. Occasionally I noticed a few leaves turning idly this way and that, as if to say that they did not really want to move, but some birds had disturbed them. The stillness of the atmosphere was intense.

When we reached the Basin of Apollo, a number of people appeared in the distance. As they were far away from us, I could not see them properly, and they soon vanished. We remained as the sole occupants of the gardens. It was nearly one o'clock and other visitors were evidently lunching in town before they came. There was no water spouting from the mouths of Apollo's horses. In fact, there was little water in the basin. A workman was cleaning and repairing it for the summer months. I should have liked to linger round the Grand Canal, and suggested finding a place where we could take lunch. But my companion's mind was made up, and she led us on in search of the Petit Trianon.

Following the directions we had from the stout guard, we set our feet northwards along the Allée de la Reine, a wide road lined with tall trees, mostly poplars. Beneath the trees at one point were some convent schoolgirls picnicking and plainly enjoying their food, while two nuns in black sat a little way off doing the same. The sight made me feel hungry, but my companion's pace showed no sign of slackening. When we had followed this long, straight road for some time, we came to a cross-roads. My attention was immediately drawn to a *décrépit* horse-drawn carriage approaching us down the right fork. In the distance the lonely, ancient-looking carriage moving slowly between tall trees looked like a ghost from the past. There might have been some royal personage in the carriage taking an outing to enjoy the lovely warm day; but as the equipage neared us we found it merely contained an elderly driver taking some visitors in modern dress for a round of the gardens. "It would be fun for us to do the same," I remarked. We had now lost our sense of direction.

Shortly, however, we sighted a row of barrack-like houses which must once have housed soldiers or troops of servants. Nearby, through an opening in a pink-washed wall, we entered the garden of the Grand Trianon. The layout of the garden was similar to that surrounding the palace, though on a smaller scale. My companion became excited, for she thought the Petit Trianon could not be far away. She was right. After a short walk, we came to a stone gate leading into a courtyard in front of a plain, two-storied white building. Here was the Petit Trianon at last. The door was shut, so were the windows, but they were all lit up in the bright sunshine. They looked as if they had not been opened for years. My friend gazed dreamily and smilingly at the whole building and at one of the top windows in particular. She told me that Marie-Antoinette had been very fond of this little house and used to spend days there when she was Queen. Some forty or more years ago two English ladies had actually seen her sewing at that window. I asked how that was possible, but my companion left my curiosity unsatisfied.

We walked round the house and entered the garden. A different landscape now confronted us, for the garden here was not formally arranged with flower-beds and terraces in geometrical patterns, as was that of the Grand Trianon. Tall old trees stood about, not troop-like, but in informal groups, on a small hill, with shorter and younger trees in the foreground. A small, bower-like structure was half-hidden by a thick bush and a lofty tree. A tiny river—hardly more than a stream—wound its way out of sight. No view could have been more different from those well-trimmed, formal gardens in other parts of the palace grounds. It was devoid of grandeur, though it had belonged to kings and queens; it was fresh, surprising and mysterious in a way that touched my imagination. Early April painted different shades of green—yellowish, emerald, and bottle—among the bushes and trees. Two small maples stood out clearly with their young five-pointed leaves pink in the sun, while the grey stones of the half-hidden bower reflected the depth of the scene. I took out my small book to make a note of the colour scheme, and afterwards turned to thank my companion for having brought me to see it. But she was deep in her thoughts, gazing dreamily here and there.

We walked along the footpath by the river. A breeze rustled and shivered in the bushes that flanked us on either side. It was most welcome and we both seemed to become lighter and quicker in our movements.

Having passed two small bridges, we faced a thatched-roofed cottage with open balconies, the whole of which was reflected clearly in the water of the lake that lay before it. Ahead of us our path forked. Childishly, we agreed to part, to follow different paths round the lake, and to meet again outside the cottage. I could feel there was something on my companion's mind, for she took the suggestion happily. No sooner was I on my path than I noticed a strange structure: a tower with an outside spiral staircase. Two girls were trying to ascend it. I thought it fitted ill into the scene, though its whole face was partly concealed by the long yellowish-green tassels of the weeping willows which to some extent blended it with the landscape.

My companion reached the cottage before me and was gazing at it intently and dreamily when I arrived. She raised her right hand now and then as if trying to visualise something. I did not disturb her. The cottage was very well-kept and clean, but something was lacking. A sense of depression filled me. A house in the country is an embellishment of Nature, but it needs human beings to live in it to maintain the rhythm of life in Nature. Then I had a look at the miller's house, which, too, was very neat and shiny. The side-window was open, but there was no sign of life. It was like a doll's house.

However, three white ducks floating and playing on the lake came to the rescue. Their presence suggested life and at once the whole scene became lively. Occasionally one of them dived to find something to eat among the long reeds that bordered the lake. When its beak was above the water again, it gave a hoarse soft "Quack", as if to express satisfaction. The surface of the water in the centre of the lake was flat like a sheet of mirror-glass, despite the tiny ripples caused by the ducks. The spotless sky was reflected in the water but deeper in tone, while the reflection of the yellowish-green tassels of the willows hung upside down beside the reddish-brown trunks of the pines. It was fun to watch the double movement of the ducks, each reflection hanging closely to its object.

Suddenly one of the ducks made a quick dash to the centre and the other two followed. There they turned round in circles, swimming to and fro in a yard or two of water and quacking excitedly. They seemed to be feeling mischievous and to want to break up the mirror-like surface. Perhaps they were just like young children who could not resist sliding on so smooth a surface. I smiled. Then I spotted the reason for their dash to the centre. Right down on the bottom of the water, underneath their reflections, appeared a big patch of fleecy white cloud. They were competing with it to see if their bodies were whiter, and they quacked in triumph as if announcing that they were. Having made a note of their movement together with the willows, the pines, the miller's house and the footpath, I went over to speak to my companion. I found her smiling too, but not for the same reason as I.

On our way back to the Grand Canal we looked round again at the Petit Trianon. My companion waved her right hand to bid it 'goodbye', and automatically I did the same, though I could not tell why. We walked on through a large stretch of grassland between many tall trees. There was much repair work and spring-cleaning in progress for the season of the Grandes Eaux from May to September.

Reaching the shore of the Canal I gazed over the wide expanse of the open space and, expanding my chest, inhaled a long, deep breath. By comparison the air over the small lake where I had watched the ducks seemed rather chilly. At last the shop-sign of a restaurant came in sight on the north bank of the canal, reminding me that I was hungry. I made no hesitation in leading the way in and my companion followed smilingly this time. It was about three o'clock and we had had no lunch. Various dishes disappeared quickly and enjoyably, and the glass of *vin blanc* seemed unusually tasty to me. Before we came, many people had already been sitting at tables along the edge of the restaurant under a huge, umbrella-like canopy with silky tassels. They had the advantage of being able to watch the people rowing on the Grand Canal and others walking by. Visitors must have poured in to see the Palace and its park while we were in the grounds of the Petit Trianon. However, that did not worry me, for what I needed then was a good rest. Nor could it have upset my companion's mind, for she was not only enjoying the rest, but also reconstructing the scenes that we had seen a few minutes before.

Her attitude throughout this visit of ours to Versailles had puzzled me. Now after a good lunch and rest I wanted to know why she had picked on the Petit Trianon as the special object of her visit, and why she was so abstracted and absorbed by all she saw there. She told me that the Petit Trianon was originally built by Louis XV as a present to his mistress, Madame du Barry. It was afterwards given by Louis XVI to Marie-Antoinette, who had the gardens laid out in the English style and added the model of a Swiss village, where she and her courtiers amused themselves by playing at farm life, making butter in the dairy and rearing poultry, the profits from the sale of the produce being distributed among the poor of the neighbourhood. It became known through the testimony of two English visitors that the Petit Trianon was haunted, and that Marie-Antoinette would appear there with her retinue at a certain time of the year. The two English visitors were Miss C. A. E. Moberly and Miss E. F. Jourdain, who described their joint experience of having seen Marie-Antoinette and many of her courtiers on their first visit to Versailles in August, 1901, in a book entitled *An Adventure*. My companion had read the book long ago and was delighted to have seen the Petit Trianon for herself. During our tour of the gardens she had been tracing the scenes described in the book as well as hoping to catch a glimpse of a ghost! Though she had not succeeded in this last, she had thoroughly enjoyed following in the steps of Miss Moberly and Miss Jourdain. I drew a long breath of wonder that I had not thought about Marie-Antoinette during our visit. Perhaps it was all for the best. I thanked my friend for not having told me before what was in her mind; otherwise my feeling about the garden of the Petit Trianon would have been quite different. Afterwards we took a train back to Paris. On parting, I asked my friend if she had seen the three white ducks on the lake in front of Marie-Antoinette's Swiss village, but she had had no eyes for ducks.

Days and months passed after that visit of ours to Versailles. Another friend of mine, Marjorie White, lent me the book, *An Adventure*, to read. Marjorie said that she believed what was described in the book. So did my companion of the trip, Betty Scott. Who could refute it? Both Miss Moberly and Miss Jourdain were highly educated women who held important educational positions in their time. I looked through the book and realised what Betty had hoped to see during our visit to the Petit Trianon. In the yard of the forecourt, which was the Cour d'Honneur, Miss Moberly saw a young man who in the jaunty manner of a footman offered to show them round. On the terrace they saw a lady holding out a paper as though to look at it at arm's length. In the garden kiosk which resembled a small bandstand—the bower I had noticed—had been a man with a most repulsive face, its expression, as described in the book, utterly odious. The footpath we walked along was the one that the two ladies followed, and Betty had chosen the right side of the lake, for Miss Moberly says that nothing would induce her to go to the left, as I had done. The original papers describing their adventure are now in the Bodleian Library at Oxford. The co-authors of the book showed patience and enthusiasm in their years of study to identify the persons who appeared to them. They had no reason to be untruthful.

An Adventure had kept me wondering and pondering. Two French gentlemen went for a walk with the co-authors to check various points, and one of them signed a statement confirming the accuracy of the ladies' account. An appendix to the book relates the similar experience of an American family living in Versailles in the years 1907-8. I feel that if a French person with these experiences could describe the dresses worn by the ghosts in accurate detail, it would be more convincing to readers like me. Why did no French person come forward to tell his or her experience of the place when Miss Moberly and Miss Jourdain published their paper in 1911? It was out of the question for me to have had such an adventure, for I should just have taken the ghosts for real people.

My mind leaps again to Peking Palace, which is rich in ghost stories. If Miss Moberly and Miss Jourdain had paid a visit there and encountered beings from the past, how would they have described the look of them and the dresses they wore? Might we not have read of men with long whiskers, women with bowed heads and walking with quick, tiny steps, as we see in caricatures and on the English stage at the present time? It would have given them great difficulty to identify each character, even more than I have had in trying to recognise the characters mentioned in their book about the Petit Trianon.

I am pretty sure that I cannot live for another fifty years, and I am quite positive that in 100 years time I shall be a ghost, if I have not succeeded in getting to Heaven. There used to be a strong belief in China in my young days that on becoming a ghost one would rove again through all the places one had known in life. As I have visited the Petit Trianon and its gardens during my life, it is possible that at that distant date my ghost may be moved to re-visit them as *un revenant étranger*. For the benefit of anyone who happens to encounter my ghostly self then, here are some identifying details of the Silent Traveller:

> Face flat; nose virtually without a bridge; hair jet black, with a few white threads; eyes slanting only very slightly, and downwards instead of upwards; wearing an English fifty-shilling tailored grey suit; does not walk like an Englishman; was perhaps an idiot, for he gazed at a small maple tree without blinking for a long while and at three white ducks on the lake even longer; strolled along as if he had been an invalid in hospital for years.

I doubt if the identification will cause a sensation. After all, who will have the time, 100 years hence, to bother about identifying this uninteresting and insignificant *revenant étranger*?